Beginning with the question 'Who is a Jew?', this book proceeds to offer a lucid account of Judaism and the Jewish people. Written for Jews and non-Jews alike, be they students or teachers or general interested readers, the book brings out the extraordinary richness and variety of Judaism: its historical depth, and the vigour and at times amazing endurance of its traditions – in the home, in the synagogue, in its literature, in individual and community life.

Nicholas de Lange writes as a Jewish scholar, a knowledgeable insider, explaining the history and details of inherited rituals and customs; of organised religion (be it Orthodox, Conservative, Reform or Liberal); of concepts such as Zionism, Diaspora, Messianism. Half of the world's Jews live in North America and the rest are widely scattered, and the book is sensitive to the global context of Judaism, both historically and in our postmodern age. The philosophy and theology of Judaism are examined, particularly in the wake of the Holocaust, and there are speculations on the future. Dr de Lange does not shirk the difficulties posed by questions of Jewish identity and by some of the irreconcilable differences which exist within Judaism as well as between Judaism and other cultures.

An Introduction to Judaism contains illustrative tables and maps, a full glossary, chronology, bibliography and index, and can be used for reference, to check details and dates, as well as read consecutively or dipped into at leisure. This is a stimulating and comprehensive introduction to a major world culture.

Nicholas de Lange is Reader in Hebrew and Jewish Studies in the University of Cambridge. A distinguished scholar and translator and a rabbi, he is author of the popular *Atlas of the Jewish World* and *Judaism*. His many translations include novels by Israeli writers such as Amos Oz and A. B. Yehoshua. With Cambridge, Dr de Lange has published *Origen and the Jews* and the English translation of Oz's *Under this Blazing Light*.

AN INTRODUCTION TO JUDAISM

NICHOLAS DE LANGE

University of Cambridge

CAMBRIDGE
UNIVERSITY PRESS

PUBLISHED BY THE PRESS SYNDICATE OF THE UNIVERSITY OF CAMBRIDGE
The Pitt Building, Trumpington Street, Cambridge, United Kingdom

CAMBRIDGE UNIVERSITY PRESS
The Edinburgh Building, Cambridge CB2 2RU, UK http://www.cup.cam.ac.uk
40 West 20th Street, New York, NY 10011-4211, USA http://www.cup.org
10 Stamford Road, Oakleigh, Melbourne 3166, Australia

First published 2000

Printed in the United Kingdom at the University Press, Cambridge

Typeset in Monotype Baskerville 11/12½ [SE]

A catalogue record for this book is available from the British Library

Library of Congress cataloguing in publication data

De Lange, N. R. M. (Nicholas Robert Michael), 1944–
An introduction to Judaism / Nicholas de Lange.
p.   cm.
Includes bibliographical references and index.
ISBN 0–521–46073–5 (hb)
1. Judaism.   1. Title.
BM561.D378   2000
296–dc21   99–27938 CIP

ISBN 0 521 46073 5 hardback
ISBN 0 521 46624 5 paperback

For Alexander

Contents

Illustrations

Tables

Preface

This book is intended for students of religion and others who seek an introduction to Judaism. It is, as its title says, an introduction, and nothing more. Some suggestions for further reading are given at the end. I hope I have covered the main points, without becoming too embroiled in details. I make no apology, however, for including a certain number of quotations, from the prayer book and other sources, because Judaism is a text-based religion, and to describe beliefs or rituals without giving texts would be to offer a very faint glimpse.

The focus throughout is on contemporary Judaism. Insofar as I delve into history, I do so through the eyes of the present. There are many books which tell the story of the Jewish people, but what matters for this introduction is the way that the past is perceived today and the ways that it affects contemporary Judaism.

Judaism today is very fragmented, as I have tried to explain in the book, and I have been careful to try to do justice to the different strands, roughly in proportion to their numerical importance. If I have been less than fair to secular Judaism that is because it does not yet seem to be as articulate about itself as the other trends.

The main centres of Judaism today are in the United States and Israel, and I have tried to reflect that importance in the book. However, I have also referred to Judaism in Europe, not only before the Second World War but today as well. Although the heyday of European Judaism lies in the past, it cannot be written off.

I have designed the book so that the chapters can be read in any order, and have deliberately included some repetition and cross-reference to that end. However, I believe there is a certain logic in the order in which the subject is presented, and recommend readers to follow the good advice to 'begin at the beginning'.

I acknowledge that my attempts to avoid sexist language may seem half-hearted. I have aimed at a compromise between accuracy and elegance, and I know I have not always succeeded. It is hard to avoid sexism completely when writing about Judaism, because it pervades the sources. I do hope, though, that when I refer to God as 'he' I do not give the impression that he has a sex or gender, and I sincerely hope I do not use the word 'Jew' to mean 'male Jew'.

Since this is an introduction, I have allowed myself to use a simplified system of transliteration of Hebrew, which aims to give an approximation of the pronunciation, rather than to permit words to be retranscribed directly into the Hebrew alphabet. There are pitfalls: in particular, the letter *h* is used for two Hebrew letters, one of which is a harder sound than English *h*. Those readers who know some Hebrew should have no difficulty in identifying the transliterated words, but for added clarity I have inserted a more exact transcription of each word in the Glossary.

I have incurred many debts while writing this book. I must thank the Weizmann Institute, Rehovot, for offering me shelter while I was researching the Israeli aspects, and the Oxford Centre for Hebrew and Jewish Studies, Yarnton, for similar hospitality during the writing. I derived terrestrial and intellectual nourishment from friends in both places. I am grateful to my students in Cambridge and during a brief stay at the Free University of Berlin for letting me test out my ideas on them, and for trusting me with some of their own. Several friends have offered advice and suggestions, for which I am duly grateful. Finally, my warm thanks to my mother and to my children for not letting me stray too far from reality, and for putting me right on lots of details.

Chronology

c. 1225 BCE	Suggested date for Exodus of Israelites from Egypt
c. 1000 BCE	Kingdom of David and Solomon
c. 950 BCE	First Temple
722 BCE	Sargon of Assyria conquers kingdom of Israel
586 BCE	First Temple destroyed by Babylonians. Babylonian exile. Beginning of eastern Diaspora
c. 520 BCE	Second Temple
333–323 BCE	Conquests of Alexander the Great
167 BCE	Revolt of the Maccabees (Hasmoneans) against Seleucid rule
164 BCE	Hasmoneans capture Jerusalem. Hasmonean dynasty
40–4 BCE	Herod the Great king of Judaea
66–74 CE	Great revolt; sack of Jerusalem by Romans (70 CE)
77–8	Flavius Josephus, *Jewish War*
115–17	Diaspora revolt
132–5	Bar Kokhba revolt
c. 220	Mishnah compiled
313	Emperor Constantine establishes tolerance of Christianity: beginning of Christian dominance
c. 415	Jerusalem Talmud compiled
589	Beginning of the Geonic period; Babylonian Talmud compiled
eighth century	Rise of Karaism
1040–1105	Rashi
1096	Crusaders massacre Jews in Rhineland
1138–1204	Maimonides
c. 1275	*Zohar* compiled
1488	First printed Hebrew Bible
1492	Unbaptised Jews expelled from Spain

1534–72	Isaac Luria
1567	*Shulhan Arukh* published
1626–76	Shabbetai Tsvi
1654	Jews arrive in New Amsterdam
1698–1760	Baal Shem Tov, founder of Hasidism
1720–97	Elijah of Vilna (the 'Vilna Gaon')
1729–86	Moses Mendelssohn
1730	First public synagogue in New York
1791	Russian Pale of Settlement, Jews of France emancipated
1817	First Reformed congregation in Hamburg
1873	Union of American Hebrew Congregations
from 1881	Pogroms in Russia; rise of antisemitism; migrations
1882–1903	First *aliyah* (Zionist immigration to Israel)
1885	Codification of Reform Judaism (Pittsburgh Platform)
1886	Jewish Theological Seminary of America
1894–9	'Dreyfus Affair' in France
1897	First Zionist Congress; founding of the Bund (Jewish Workers' Union)
1917	Emancipation in Russia following the Revolution; Balfour Declaration
1920–48	Palestine under British Mandate
1925	Founding of Hebrew University of Jerusalem
1933–45	Nazi persecution; the Holocaust
1934	Birobidzhan proclaimed 'Jewish Autonomous Oblast'
1936	World Jewish Congress
1948	State of Israel founded
1967	Six Day War
1973	Yom Kippur War

Map of the Jewish world in 1930 (a)

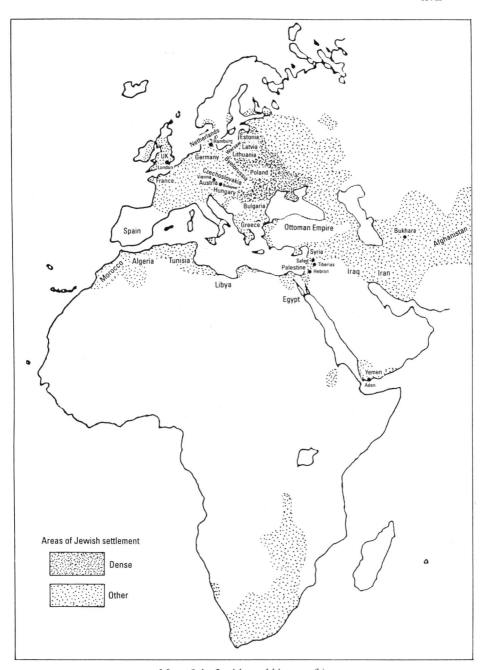

Map of the Jewish world in 1930 (b)

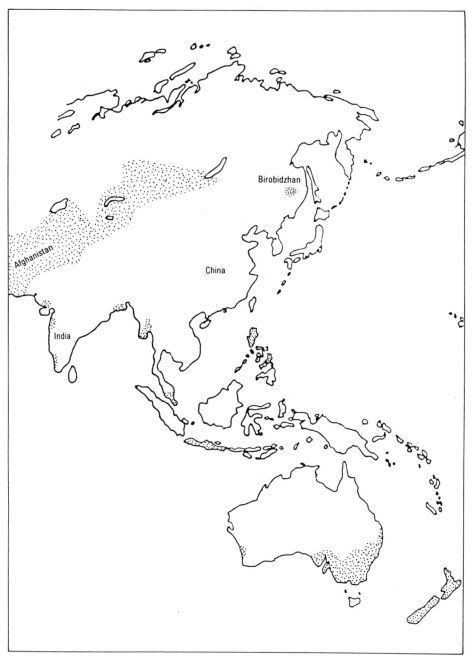

Map of the Jewish world in 1930 (c)

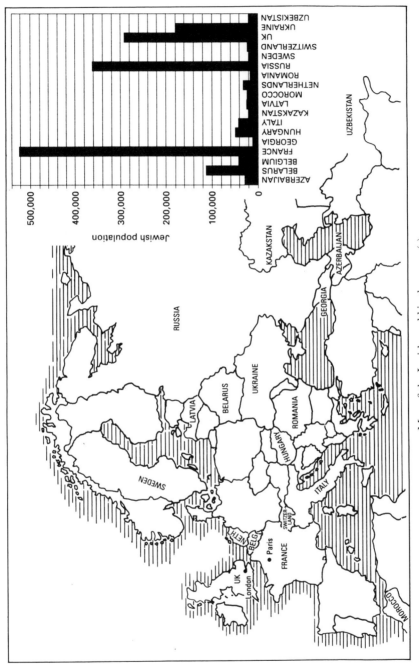

Map of the Jewish world in the 1990s (a)

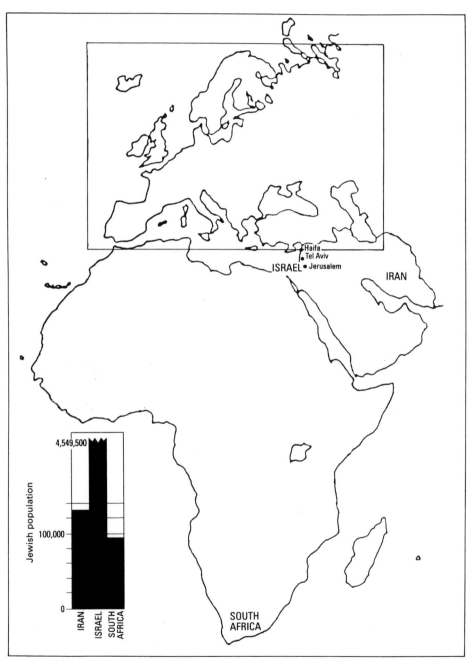

Map of the Jewish world in the 1990s (b)

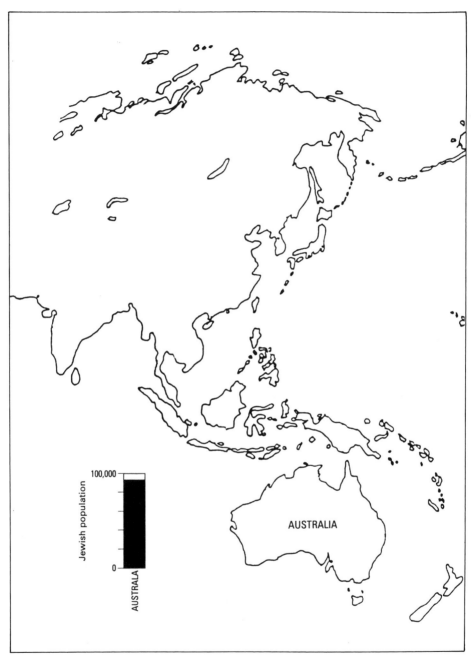

Map of the Jewish world in the 1990s (c)

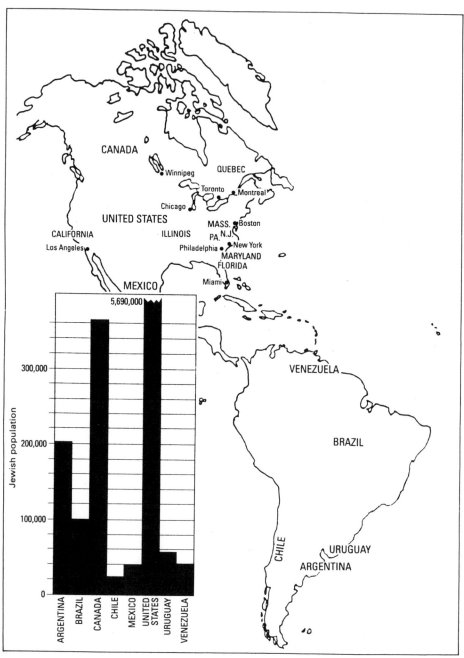

Map of the Jewish world in the 1990s (d)

CHAPTER ONE

The Jews in the world

WHO ARE THE JEWS?

The Jews are a scattered people. They live in many different countries, and with one exception they are a numerically insignificant minority in all of them. They belong to many different ethnic and linguistic groupings, and many different cultural backgrounds. Even within a single country these differences divide the Jewish communities from one another. So what is it that binds them all together, and allows us to speak in general terms about 'the Jews'?

One superficially attractive but actually misleading answer is that they are united by a common religion. There *is* a Jewish religion, and for very many Jews it is the focus of their lives and a strong cement binding them to other Jews. But it would be unrealistic to maintain that it is the Jewish religion that unites the Jewish people. In fact the Jewish religion divides the Jewish people today, perhaps almost as much as it divides Jews from non-Jews. And even the most pious Jews would probably admit that it is not their religion that defines them as Jews. They practise the Jewish religion because they are Jews, not the other way around.

What is it then that makes a Jew a Jew? In today's world, although there are many 'Jews by choice', the overwhelming majority of Jews are born into Jewish families. Most Jews would answer the question 'why are you a Jew?' by saying 'because I was born a Jew'.

This basic fact has important implications. It is sometimes said that 'Judaism is not a proselytising religion', meaning that Jews do not actively seek to make converts to Judaism. Yet this formulation is fundamentally misleading. Religious Jews are generally proud of their religion, they are happy to explain it to non-Jews, they welcome and are even flattered by the interest of outsiders. But since in their minds the religion is somehow secondary to Jewish identity, it is not conversion to Judaism that is the issue. In the relatively rare cases where a non-Jew does

opt to become a Jew, this is probably seen more in terms of joining a
people than subscribing to a faith. Indeed, as we shall see, even within
the Jewish religion belief itself occupies a somewhat secondary role.

Secondly, since the Jew's sense of being a Jew springs primarily from
birth rather than from personal commitment, links to other Jews tend
also to be based on birth at least as much as on other factors. In other
words, the family tends to play a large part in the consciousness of Jews,
and the sense of family is very broad, encompassing the most distant
cousins.

This feeling also leads Jews to have a very intimate connection with
the past of the Jewish people. This connection is reinforced by established religious maxims: all Jews should consider themselves as if they
personally were led out of Egyptian slavery by Moses, stood before God
at Mount Sinai and received the gift of the Torah. But it is a general,
spontaneous feeling nonetheless, by no means limited to religious Jews,
but shared by many who reject religious belief.

Nahum Goldmann, one of the outstanding Jewish leaders of the
twentieth century in the political rather than the religious sphere, wrote
these words in his memoirs about the Jew of the Lithuanian *shtetl* into
which he was born:

Not only did he live on an intimate family footing with his fellow Jews, who were
much more to him than members of the same race or religion; he experienced
a heartfelt closeness to the past of his people and to his God. When, as a child,
he learned about Moses, he saw him not as a mythical figure but as an important though perhaps somewhat distant uncle. When, as a student at the rabbinical academy, the *yeshiva*, he analysed Rabbi Akiba or Rabbi Judah, he was not
an antiquarian studying history so much as a man engaged in a living discussion with an older, wiser relative.[1]

The whole Jewish past, not the past of a single family or a local Jewish
community, is in a sense part and parcel of the inner experience and
identity of every single Jew. And since Jews everywhere share this sense
of their history, they are all somehow part of the same huge, scattered
family.

Note that the expression 'Jewish race', which is still occasionally
encountered, is no longer appropriate. It came into use in a period when
the definition of 'race' was much looser than it is today, and when one
could speak, for instance, of the 'English race'. Antisemitism, a
European political movement that gained many adherents from the

[1] Nahum Goldmann, *Memories* (London, 1970), p. 6.

early 1880s on, attempted to isolate the Jews from the rest of society by pretending that they were somehow genetically different from other people. In some European countries, traumatised by recent dramatic political and economic upheavals, the antisemites really did succeed in driving a wedge between friends, neighbours, business associates. (English-speaking countries have been largely immune to their efforts.) But this view of Jewish identity was never realistic. There are no racial characteristics that are shared by Jews and that distinguish them from non-Jews, and a moment's reflection will show that it would be extraordinary if there were, because the boundaries of Jewish identity have never been watertight. Throughout the recorded history of Europe individuals have joined or left the Jewish communities, and sometimes whole populations have changed their allegiance. Christianity at its inception spread among Jews, and all the churches have devoted strenuous efforts at different times to converting Jews, sometimes by force. In 1215 the Fourth Lateran Council, wishing to segregate Jews from Christians, ruled that they must wear special badges sewn to their clothing to distinguish them: apparently 800 years ago it was considered that Jews and Christians did not differ outwardly, and when the Nazi Germans in their race laws of 1935 revived the Jewish badge they were implicitly reaffirming the same belief, despite their strident racial mouthings. The Nazi laws define a Jew as someone with at least one Jewish grandparent, and this turned out to be a very unrealistic and haphazard definition in a Germany where Jews and Christians had been intermarrying for generations.

Jewish law has its own definition of Jewish identity: one becomes a Jew either by birth or by choice. In the former case the traditional law defines the child of two Jewish parents or of a Jewish mother alone as a Jew, but today the most liberal movements in Judaism consider the child of a non-Jewish mother to be Jewish if the father is a Jew and the child has been raised as a Jew. A non-Jew can become Jewish by applying to a court (nowadays usually consisting of three rabbis, although traditionally it was not necessary for any of the three to be rabbis), by studying, and by undergoing the rituals of immersion in water and (in the case of males only) circumcision. Some add that there must be a period of time spent within a Jewish family or community, and a commitment to continue to observe the commandments; but there is a contrary view, based on ancient rabbinic opinion, that only minimal study is necessary if the commitment is strong, because the process of learning will be more effective if it is pursued within the community after acceptance.

FACTS AND FIGURES

There are some thirteen million Jews in the world today, according to the most reliable estimates.[2] The Jewish people thus ranks among the smaller scattered peoples, and Judaism has far fewer adherents than any of the other main world religions.

Naturally it is impossible to obtain accurate statistics about the numbers of Jews, because of the lack of agreement over how to define a Jew. As has already been mentioned, definitions range from the very strict and narrow definition of the traditional law, the so called 'halakhic definition', to various much broader and vaguer definitions. Some published statistics are based on people's own definitions of themselves, others are based on synagogue membership, and some are based on pure speculation.

Many countries, including some of those with the largest Jewish populations (notably the USA), do not keep official figures about the number of Jews in the population. In the statistics from Israel, where 'Jewish' is an officially recognised 'nationality', the figures are based on the halakhic definition but are augmented by the non-Jewish members of 'Jewish' families, who sometimes outnumber the Jewish members.

Consequently all these statistics must be treated with reserve.[3] Certain broad facts, however, are indisputable. First, although Jews are scattered among a very large number of countries, the vast majority are concentrated in very few countries. Of the thirteen million Jews in the world 5.69 million (43.6%) are believed to live in the United States and 4.55 million (34.8%) in Israel. No other country approaches anywhere near these figures: the next in rank is France with about half a million Jews.

Again, certain regions of the world are far more strongly represented on a map of Jewish populations than others. Outside Israel, most Jews live in North or South America, Europe, South Africa or Australia. In the rest of Africa and Asia Jews are few and far between, and even within individual countries the Jewish population tends to be concentrated in specific regions or cities.

Another way of looking at the figures is in terms of the ratio of Jews to the total population. Here, on a national basis, Israel is totally exceptional, with Jews constituting just over 80% of the population, whereas elsewhere only three countries (USA, Canada, and, among the smallest communities, Gibraltar) count more than ten Jews per thousand of the

---

[2] *American Jewish Year Book* 1997, p. 517. All the statistics given here are taken from that publication.
[3] See ibid., pp. 515ff.

Table 1.1. *Countries with the largest Jewish populations, 1995*[a]

Rank	Country	Jewish population	% of population of country	% of world Jewish population
1	United States	5,690,000	2.14	43.6
2	Israel	4,549,500	80.97	34.8
3	France	525,000	0.90	4.0
4	Canada	362,000	1.22	2.8
5	Russia	360,000	0.25	2.8
6	United Kingdom	292,000	0.50	2.2
7	Argentina	206,000	0.59	1.6
8	Ukraine	180,000	0.35	1.4
9	Brazil	100,000	0.06	0.8
10	South Africa	95,000	0.22	0.7
11	Australia	92,000	0.50	0.7

Notes:
[a] Source: *American Jewish Year Book* 1997, p. 543.

population, and elsewhere the Jewish presence is numerically insignificant.

The Jewish population is predominantly urban. This is in line with a general trend in the world, but Jews are more liable to live in towns, and particularly large conurbations, than the general population and, with the exception of a few countries where deliberate efforts have been made to settle them on the land, they rarely live in villages or isolated settlements. This is not a new phenomenon, although before the Nazi genocide it was common to see Jews living in villages or on rural estates and even farming the land in eastern Europe. Today the overwhelming majority of Jews live in large urban areas, and indeed more than half of world Jewry lives in ten large metropolitan areas in the United States, Israel and France.

Well over half the Jews in the world live in English-speaking countries, and while it would be an exaggeration to say that all Jews speak or understand English it is probably true that English is the most important means of communication among Jews, and the largest number of books and periodicals aimed at a Jewish readership are in English. Hebrew is also an important language for Jews, both because it is the main official language of Israel and because it is used either exclusively or side by side with the local vernacular as a liturgical language in synagogues around the world. As the language of the ancient scriptures, Hebrew is uniquely

Table 1.2. *Metropolitan areas with the largest Jewish populations, 1995*[a]

Rank	Metropolitan area	Jewish population
1	New York	1,917,000
2	Tel Aviv	1,878,000
3	Los Angeles	585,000
4	Jerusalem	470,000
5	Haifa	432,000
6	Miami	382,000
7	Philadelphia	314,000
8	Paris	310,000
9	Chicago	261,000
10	Boston	228,000

Note:
[a] Source: *American Jewish Year Book* 1997, p. 544.

associated with the Jews: although non-Jews sometimes study it, they have only rarely used it as a medium of self-expression or communication. Russian is also spoken or understood by a large minority of Jews. In the past many Jews have spoken other languages, such as Arabic, Spanish, German, Yiddish and French, and all these languages are still spoken by some Jews today. Going back further in history an important place was once held by Aramaic (a Semitic language closely related to Hebrew) and Greek, but both these languages have very few Jewish speakers today; in fact Aramaic is almost extinct as a spoken language, although it still plays a part in Jewish worship and study.

NATIVES OR IMMIGRANTS?

Paradoxically, although Jews justifiably consider themselves as one of the oldest of peoples, a majority of Jews today would see themselves as newcomers in the places where they live. Relatively few Jews live where their grandparents or their great-grandparents were born. The story of the Jewish people over the past century or more has been a story of dramatic upheavals and displacements, and the map of the Jewish world has been subject to constant and kaleidoscopic change.[4]

If we look back to the beginning of the nineteenth century we detect a pattern of settlement that in its main outlines had not changed for cen-

[4] See Nicholas de Lange, *Atlas of the Jewish World* (New York/Oxford, 1984).

turies. Most Jews lived either in the Christian countries of Europe or in the Muslim lands centred on the Ottoman Empire and stretching from Morocco in the west to Iran and Bukhara in the east. The Jews constituted a prominent presence in the towns of North Africa, but already an unprecedentedly dense concentration was building up on the territory of what had been (until the recent partitions) Poland. The Jews of North Africa and the Middle East mainly spoke Arabic or a distinctive form of Spanish, whereas in central and eastern Europe the majority spoke a form of German peculiar to the Jews and known locally as Yiddish (meaning 'Jewish'). Outside this main area of Jewish settlement there were some small and fairly isolated outposts, either old ones, such as those in India and China, or new ones, in the Dutch colonies, in the United States and in Canada. Some Christian lands were deliberately closed to Jewish settlement by the policy of their rulers: the most extensive of these were Spain and Portugal and their considerable overseas colonies, and the Russian Empire outside the frontiers of the former Polish kingdom. Russia kept its Jews penned inside those old frontiers, in what came to be known as the Pale of Settlement, which was to have an enormous impact on Jewish history and culture.

Within the Pale of Settlement the Jewish population grew in the course of the nineteenth century by leaps and bounds. In 1800 there were little more than a million Jews in the territories of what had been Poland, of whom three quarters lived under Russian rule; already Jews outnumbered Christians in some places. By 1880 Europe contained some seven million Jews, accounting for about 90% of the Jews in the whole world, and most of them lived in the eastern half of the continent, with about four million in the Pale of Settlement. Warsaw alone counted more Jews than the whole of Britain or France. And although there was a constant emigration westward into central and western Europe, and on to North America and other parts of the New World, the population of the Pale continued to grow dramatically. In the early 1880s, when to economic hardship was added anti-Jewish violence, the trickle of emigration became a flood. Between 1881 and 1914 (when the outbreak of war made travel difficult) some 2.75 million Jews left eastern Europe, more than a third of all the Jews in the region and more than a quarter of all the Jews in the world. Eighty-five percent of them settled in the United States, where they constituted one of the largest immigrant groups. Population movement on this scale was virtually unprecedented in Jewish history, and its consequences were enormous.

These eastern European Jews had a very strong and cohesive culture, the main elements of which originated in the Middle Ages in the Rhineland, from where the Jews known as Ashkenazim began to migrate eastwards from the thirteenth century. Being strictly separated from the Christian population they maintained their own language (Yiddish) and their own distinctive culture over the centuries, and when in modern times they began to migrate westwards again they took their language and culture with them. Although Yiddish is now a dwindling language in terms of numbers of speakers, it can still be heard in many parts of the world, particularly among the older generation, as can the distinctive Ashkenazi pronunciation of Hebrew in the synagogue, although it is rarer than it used to be.

When the Ashkenazim arrived in the cities of western Europe they encountered Sephardim, Jews whose families came from Spain and Portugal. So different were the religious customs and culture of the two groups that they tended to form separate communities, with their own synagogues, and intermarriage between the two was often frowned on. Today the two types of synagogue still exist, but there is generally a more open and friendly relationship. The term 'Sephardi' is properly reserved for Jews of Iberian origin, but in Israel it is applied (rather disdainfully) by Ashkenazim to any non-Ashkenazi Jews. Like the Ashkenazim, Sephardim too migrated in considerable numbers from the Ottoman Empire and Morocco at the end of the last and the beginning of the present century, many of them settling in Spanish-speaking countries of the New World.

In the present century the immigration just described continued, but other movements were added. For example there was massive emigration from Germany, Austria and Czechoslovakia during the period of Nazi ascendancy in the 1930s, and after the Second World War many of the few survivors of the Nazi genocide decided to leave Europe. During the 1950s, as Arab nationalism swept through North Africa, there was an exodus of Jews from the region, and whenever the authorities permitted it Jews also left the Communist countries of central and eastern Europe. After the collapse of Communism this trend became even more pronounced. Meanwhile, for various political reasons, the countries of the Middle East, with the exception of Israel, became almost emptied of Jews, and even in India, where there was no specific political cause, a similar phenomenon was observed. The result of all this movement was to reduce drastically or even obliterate the oldest Jewish communities in the world, and to swell the newer ones. Recently some of the new communities, such as those in southern Africa, have experienced an exodus too.

To take a few examples to illustrate all this movement, between 1930 and 1990 the Jewish population of Canada, Mexico and Sweden doubled, that of Australia and Brazil trebled, while in other countries such as Chile, Uruguay and Venezuela the Jews went from a barely significant to a much more noticeable presence. On the other hand, during the same period important European communities such as Austria, the Baltic republics, Bulgaria, Byelorussia (Belarus), Czechoslovakia, Greece, the Netherlands, Poland and Ukraine were reduced to a miserable shadow of their former selves, and the ancient Jewries of Aden, Afghanistan, Algeria, Egypt, India, Iraq, Libya, Morocco, Syria, Tunisia and Yemen virtually disappeared.

The main countries of immigration, notably the United States and Israel, have welcomed large numbers of Jewish immigrants from many different countries. This inflow has had a marked effect on the character of the Jewish communities within the various countries. In many, Jewish communal and cultural life has been enormously strengthened. However, massive immigration can alter the character of the community, as happened for instance in London with the huge wave of immigration from Russia between 1881 and the early years of the present century, in France with the North African Jews who arrived in the 1950s, or with the Russian Jews who came to Germany in the 1990s.

Israel has absorbed huge numbers of Jewish immigrants since its inauguration in 1948 as a state guaranteeing a refuge to all Jews, against a background of continuing economic and political difficulties. (However, large numbers have emigrated from Israel at the same time, to the great benefit of Hebrew teaching in other countries.) Great efforts have been devoted to teaching the newcomers the Hebrew language and helping them and their children to assimilate to the prevailing culture. At the same time, there is a strong tendency for Jews to maintain and express their distinctive identity, derived from their ethnic background or the country from which they came. It is not so much a melting pot as a fruit salad, particularly so far as the first generation of immigrants is concerned, since their children tend to adapt to a more homogeneous Israeli culture during their period of compulsory military service.

Israel holds a unique place in the affections of Jews around the world, whether or not they consider it to be the holy land or the Jewish homeland in a political sense. Israel itself views itself as different in kind from the rest of the Jewish world, which is called in Hebrew *galut* or *golah*, 'exile'. (In other languages Jews speak of 'Diaspora', from an old Greek term meaning 'dispersion', 'dissemination'.) To go to live in Israel is termed in Hebrew *aliyah*, 'ascent', a term formerly reserved for journeying to the holy city of Jerusalem. Conversely, to emigrate from Israel is termed *yeridah*, 'descent', and is viewed negatively. Emissaries are sent out from Israel to the communities of the Diaspora to inculcate a knowledge and love of Israel and to encourage *aliyah*.

Although Jews tend to feel a strong bond with all other Jews around the world, they are likely to be unaware of the international organisations that bring together, represent, and to some extent protect and sustain Jews in the different countries. There is a multiplicity of such organisations, of which only a few can be mentioned here.

Six Jewish organisations have consultative status with the Economic and Social Council of the United Nations. The World Jewish Congress, founded by Nahum Goldmann, whose name has already been mentioned, first convened in Geneva in 1936. It is a voluntary association of Jewish bodies, communities and organisations from around the world, whose aim is 'to assure the survival, and to foster the unity of the Jewish people'. The International Council of Jewish Women, whose name speaks for itself, was founded in 1912. The International Council on Jewish Social and Welfare Services, the Coordinating Board of Jewish Organisations and the Consultative Council of Jewish Organisations are umbrella bodies representing different national and international agencies. Finally, Agudas Israel World Organisations, founded in 1912, is a traditional Orthodox body having as its aim 'the solution – in the spirit of the Torah – of problems which periodically confront the Jewish people in Eretz Yisroel [the Land of Israel] and the Diaspora'.

Of the other international organisations the most powerful is the World Zionist Organisation, set up by the First Zionist Congress in 1897. The moving spirit in the events leading up to the establishment of the State of Israel in 1948, it continues to work for the strengthening of Israel, encouraging *aliyah*, and promoting a distinctive (not necessarily religious) Jewish culture. The World Union for Progressive Judaism fosters the growth of Reform and Liberal Judaism, while the much more recent World Council of Synagogues does the same for Conservative Judaism, and the World Sephardi Federation deals with the religious, cultural and social welfare of Sephardi congregations. The Maccabi World Union is an amateur sporting association. There are many more specialised associations, as well as organisations serving particular groups of countries, such as the European Union or the British Commonwealth. These multifarious organisations reflect the many and

varied currents within World Jewry, as well as the high value traditionally placed upon communal service.

North America

It is convenient to group the United States and Canada together, despite
their different histories and disparate size. Their six million Jews represent the powerhouse and centre of gravity of the whole Jewish world
(with Israel providing something of a counterweight). They wield an
influence out of proportion to their numbers, both within the Jewish
world and beyond. Numerically not much more than 2% of the population, the Jews are self-conscious and self-confident, have well-endowed
and well-organised institutions, and contain among their number some
influential individuals. They thus have a disproportionate impact politically, religiously, culturally, and in terms of welfare aid and social issues
both on their own countries and on the wider Jewish world.

The experience of Jewish immigrants in the United States, often
arriving from countries of very limited opportunity for Jews if not out-
right discrimination against them, has not set them apart greatly from
other immigrants, and has presented them with enormous opportunities
for self-fulfilment and advancement, even if, inevitably, they have had to
face serious hardships and challenges. Like other immigrant groups, the
Jews have had to adapt to very new circumstances and to the demands
of a cultural and social 'melting pot', which yet offers very distinct possibilities and even pressures to maintain their own distinctive identity
and way of life. Jewish responses to these conflicting pressures have
ranged very widely, from total assimilation and abandonment of Jewish
identity at one extreme, passing through various modes of religious and
social accommodation, to the maintenance of a very traditional and separate existence at the other.

Unlike the European countries from which most Jews came, the
United States accorded religious and other freedoms to its citizens from
its inception. The constitution of 1787 explicitly forbade religious tests
for public office (although some states retained them until much later),
and the Bill of Rights of 1791 guaranteed total freedom of religion. The
numbers of Jews affected by this momentous change were very small at
first, but they rose very quickly in the course of the nineteenth century,
from a few thousand to more than a quarter of a million by 1880. The

Table 1.3. *American states with the largest Jewish populations, 1995[a]*

Rank	State	Jewish population	% of total population
1	New York	1,652,000	9.1
2	California	921,000	2.9
3	Florida	644,000	4.5
4	New Jersey	435,000	5.5
5	Pennsylvania	325,000	2.7
6	Massachusetts	268,000	4.4
7	Illinois	268,000	2.3
8	Maryland	212,000	4.2

Note:
[a] Source: *American Jewish Year Book* 1997.

period of really momentous immigration began after that date, with the outbreak of pogroms in Russia, and by 1900 the Jewish population had already quadrupled to one million; by 1910 it was estimated at over two million, by 1914 at over three million, and in the middle of the 1920s at four million. Whereas the pre-1880 immigrants came mainly from central Europe, the newcomers originated predominantly in eastern Europe, and were mostly very poor. Despite low wages, frequent unemployment and disease they gradually improved their position by hard work and self-help, and they were probably the most dramatically successful of all the immigrant groups of the period.

Today immigration continues on a relatively small scale, mainly from the former Soviet Union and Israel, helping to compensate for the very low birthrate of the native Jewish population. Nearly half the Jews in the US live in the north-east (as compared to less than one fifth of the general population)

The American Jewish community is served by a large variety of organisations with very different aims. One of the most venerable is the American Jewish Committee, set up in 1906, at a time of growing anti-semitism, by members of the Jewish elite, whose concern was spiritual and cultural as well as social and political. In its distinguished history of involvement in campaigns against discrimination and prejudice it has frequently met with opposition from other groups, particularly those of a socialist or Zionist complexion, such as the American Jewish Congress, a politically vocal and partisan organisation with a decidedly Zionist orientation. At the head of the many Zionist organisations is the Zionist Organization of America (founded 1897) and the women's organisation,

Hadassa (founded 1912). The B'nai B'rith, which began life in 1843 as a fraternal order of Masonic type, is now a broadly based organisation, particularly devoted to youth work, student counselling and combating antisemitism. The United Jewish Appeal (founded 1939) channels funds raised in a massive annual campaign into a wide range of deserving causes. Its foremost beneficiary is Israel, which has received enormous funds destined particularly for the absorption of immigrants, but help is given to humanitarian projects in many countries. Two other important organisations which continue the American Jewish tradition of rendering practical assistance to the less fortunate are the Hebrew Immigrant Aid Society (HIAS, founded 1880) and the American Jewish Joint Distribution Committee (JDC, founded 1914). HIAS is a worldwide migration agency, which does invaluable practical work in the resettlement and rehabilitation of refugees, while the JDC works to relieve hardship overseas, in Israel, North Africa, eastern Europe and elsewhere. While both these organisations concentrate their efforts on Jews they also help needy non-Jews.

American Judaism is as dynamic, as varied and as unique as American Jewry. Its variety reflects the different waves of immigration and their experiences of adapting themselves to a free and open society. The few congregations of the Colonial period were Sephardi; then the 'German' immigrations of the nineteenth century brought Ashkenazi religious leaders from central Europe, schooled in the dominant forms of Jewish modernism (whether Orthodox or Reform). By 1880 there were over 200 congregations, and all but a handful were Reform. The huge immigration from Russia brought Jews who, even if they were avowed secularists, were accustomed to the old-style religion of the ghetto. Three hundred new congregations had been founded by 1890, and they were traditionalist in flavour. As the newcomers established themselves and adopted an American way of life they developed their own style of Orthodoxy, and meanwhile immigrants from the old Ottoman lands brought a style of Sephardi religiosity far removed from that of the established American Sephardi synagogues, so they too established congregations of their own. Later refugees from Nazi Europe included adherents of the more evolved forms of European Liberalism, as well as communities of Hasidim with a highly developed folk tradition strongly resistant to new external influences. The most recent waves of immigration, from Israel and the former Soviet Union, stem from highly assimilated societies in which religion has ceased to be a living force for most Jews.

The differences between these various strands of Jewish religion will be discussed in a later chapter. For the present it is important to note that religious pluralism is a real feature of the Jewish community in America, just as it is in the population as a whole. A survey of denominational preferences in 1990 showed that very similar numbers of Jews were attracted to Reform and Conservative Judaism (39% and 40%) respectively, while 6% expressed a preference for Orthodoxy. If those who are not members of a synagogue are omitted, the figures are respectively 35%, 51% and 10%.[5] These three movements have their own separate congregational associations, rabbinical assemblies and rabbinic seminaries. A later offshoot is Reconstructionism, which has its own institutions, and in recent years there has been a proliferation of less formal, 'alternative' Jewish religious groups.

Canada's political history is very different from that of the United States, and Canadian Jews are more likely than those in the US to think of themselves as Jews first and foremost. Anti-Zionism, which has been quite strong at various times in the US, is all but unknown in Canada.

The Jews of Canada were granted full citizen rights in 1832 (well ahead of parallel developments in Britain), but their numbers at first were relatively small. As in the US, it was immigration from Russia after 1880 that laid the real foundations of the large present-day community.[6] Between 1881 and 1921 the Jewish population rose from 2,400 to over 126,000 (out of a total population of nearly nine million). Most of the immigrants settled in Montreal and Toronto, where they tended to concentrate in dense voluntary ghettos, but many travelled across the plains to the growing towns of the west. Winnipeg soon established itself as the third largest community, with 14,5000 Jews by 1921. Some agricultural settlements were also established in Manitoba, Saskatchewan and Alberta. Recent uncertainty about the future of Quebec has led to a noticeable movement of English-speaking Jews from Montreal to Ontario and as far away as Vancouver. A survey in 1991 showed that 21% of the Jews in Montreal were Sephardi, and 70% of these gave French as their mother tongue.

Canadian Judaism conforms more closely to the British than to the American model, in that the large majority of synagogues are Orthodox and only a small minority are Conservative or Reform. The synagogal

---

[5] B. Lazerwitz *et al.*, 'A Study of Jewish Denominational Preferences: Summary Findings', in *American Jewish Year Book* 1997.

[6] See Gerald Tulchinsky, *Taking Root. The Origins of the Canadian Jewish Community* (Toronto, 1992).

associations and rabbinic bodies follow the American pattern, and tend to be associated with their American counterparts.

Like Britain, and unlike the USA, there is a single representative body, the Canadian Jewish Congress (founded 1919), which concerns itself with the welfare of the community and provides a unified voice for Canadian Jewry. A distinctive feature of Canadian Jewry is the strong emphasis on Jewish education. All communities of any size have at least one Jewish day school, and these schools are very successful in attracting pupils.

Israel

Israel is unique in the Jewish world, not only because the large majority of its population is Jewish, but because it defines itself as a 'Jewish State'. This concept is novel and to a large extent experimental. The Declaration of the State (1948) begins by stressing the place that the land of Israel (Eretz Israel) has always occupied in the hearts and minds of the Jewish people:

Eretz Israel was the birthplace of the Jewish people. Here their spiritual, religious and political identity was shaped. Here they first attained to statehood, created cultural values of national and universal significance and gave the world the eternal Book of Books.

After being exiled from their land, the people kept faith with it throughout their dispersion and never ceased to pray and hope for their return to it and for the restoration in it of their political freedom.

The Declaration concludes:

We appeal to the Jewish people throughout the Diaspora to rally round the Jews of Eretz Israel in the tasks of immigration and upbuilding and to stand by them in the great struggle for the realisation of the age-old dream – the redemption of Israel.[7]

In keeping with this grandiose vision, the Law of Return (1950) begins: 'Every Jew shall have the right to come to this country as an *oleh* [immigrant].'

Thus, although Israel is a secular state with no established religion, Judaism has a central and strong place within it, and the Jewish majority have certain rights and privileges which are not shared by others.

---

[7] For the text of the Declaration, the Law of Return and other key documents see Philip S. Alexander, ed., *Textual Sources for the Study of Judaism* (Manchester, 1984), pp. 164ff. These texts can also, at the time of writing, be found on the internet at http://www.israel.org/gov/laws.

The question of freedom of religion in Israel is a complex one, and this is an area in which there are many tensions. In principle Jews are free from any external constraint, and can practise their religion in whatever way they see fit, indeed this is proclaimed as one of the advantages of living in Israel over life in the Diaspora. In reality it has to be said that many Jews, and particularly immigrants from western countries, where non-Orthodox (Conservative, Reform and Liberal) forms of Judaism predominate numerically, feel frustration at being deprived of certain basic religious freedoms, hampered in the free exercise of their religion, and denied access to the official structure of religious life in the religious councils. This is due to the privileged position accorded to Orthodoxy in Israel for political reasons. In the 1996 elections the three religious political parties increased their representation from sixteen to twenty-three seats, and controlled four ministries, including the Ministry of the Interior. The religious parties at once presented a number of demands, insisting on implementation of Orthodox law in such areas as public observance of the Sabbath and forbidden foods, conversion to Judaism (which as we have seen has a bearing on civil rights), homosexuality, public decency and even archaeology. At the same time, the strong place accorded to religion in general in Israeli public life weighs very heavily upon those citizens who are not religious at all: for example, there is no civil marriage or burial. Constant public controversy focuses on all these issues.

Israel must be considered a country of Jewish immigration, in that the overwhelming majority of Jews are from families that have immigrated in the present century, even though, as we have already seen, Israel has also experienced, and continues to experience, considerable Jewish emigration. The original Jewish inhabitants before the first Zionist *aliyah* in the 1880s were mainly pious Jews who lived in the holy cities of Jerusalem, Hebron, Tiberias and Safed, keeping the flickering flame of Judaism alive through the dark centuries of Muslim and Crusading Christian rule. They are known as the 'Old Yishuv [settlement]', to distinguish them from the 'New Yishuv' that followed. Their numbers were very small. Zionist immigration, before and after the Balfour Declaration of 1917 and the granting of the British Mandate by the League of Nations in 1922, completely changed the nature of the Jewish presence in the Land of Israel. The first census held in British Palestine, in 1922, recorded 84,000 Jews, 11% of the total population, whereas in 1995 there were 4,549,500, forming 81% of the total. As with other countries of immigration, successive waves have come from different coun-

tries. In the early part of this century the immigrants were mainly ideo-
logically committed Zionists from Russia who came 'to build the country
and to be built by it'. They instituted the distinctive form of co-opera-
tive agricultural settlements known as kibbutzim. Later they were joined
by Jews from Poland, Germany and other central European countries,
whose culture was rather different. The declaration of the state in 1948
was followed by the arrival of Holocaust survivors from displaced person
(DP) camps in Europe and later, in the 1950s, by massive immigration
from Arab lands. More recently there has been an airlift of Ethiopian
'Falashas', and a vast influx of Jews from the countries of the former
Soviet Union. Naturally all this immigration has given rise to massive
social problems, but what is particularly interesting for the observer is the
way that in the midst of a 'melting pot' groups successfully strive to
retain something of the flavour of the places from which they came,
including distinctive religious traditions.

All recognised religious institutions in Israel fall under the authority
of the Ministry for Religious Affairs. The Jewish religious establishment consists of chief rabbis, state rabbis, religious councils and rabbinic courts. Under a system inherited from the British and ultimately
from the Ottomans, there are two chief rabbis, one Ashkenazi and one
Sephardi. The main cities also have a dual chief rabbinate. The election of the chief rabbis has caused repeated problems, and the dual
chief rabbinate has led to serious and sometimes apparently absurd
conflicts. The district rabbis and other local rabbis with official positions are appointed, with the approval of the chief rabbinate, by local
religious councils, which also pay their stipends. The religious councils,
another heritage from the period of the British Mandate, are
effectively part of the structure of local government. They are
appointed jointly by the Ministry of Religious Affairs, the local authority and the local rabbinate, and are totally under the influence of the
National Religious Party. Each rabbinic court (*Bet Din*) consists of three
judges (*dayyanim*) who are appointed formally by the president of the
state with the approval of both chief rabbis. The positions are well
paid and highly sought after. The Supreme *Bet Din* is headed by the
two national chief rabbis.

The chief rabbis, the *dayyanim* and other officially appointed rabbis
are state functionaries, and their authority derives from the state rather
than from the consent of the Jewish community or their personal powers
of spiritual leadership. A few chief rabbis have commanded widespread
respect, but they constitute the exception. By contrast other holders of

religious appointments have earned public ridicule and have contributed to the very obvious alienation of many young Israelis from religion. In contrast to most diaspora communities, the image of the rabbinate in Israel tends to be a negative one, particularly among secular Jews. This is not merely a matter of anticlerical prejudice. The state rabbis rarely involve themselves in pastoral care or religious instruction, as their diaspora counterparts do, and so are not treated with the respect and affection accorded to some religious figures who are outside the state system. The authority of the chief rabbis is not recognised by the more extreme Orthodox groups or by the non-Orthodox movements.

The Reform and Conservative congregations are not recognised by the Ministry for Religious Affairs and are not entitled to government funds. The growth of non-Orthodox Judaism has been met by fierce opposition from the Orthodox establishment, and at one point it was seriously suggested that Reform and Conservative Judaism should accept the status of non-Jewish religions, so as to qualify for state aid on the same basis as Christianity and Islam. The growth of both movements was slow at first, but they are now well established and increasingly vocal, mainly thanks to immigration from the United States.

At the other extreme, various very traditional groupings have also remained outside the state system. The Jews of the Old Yishuv, both Sephardi and Ashkenazi, mostly held aloof from Zionism, and opposed the creation of the Jewish state. Their ranks were swollen after the Second World War by obsessively traditionalist immigrants from Hungary. They live in voluntary segregation in their own close-knit communities, mainly concentrated in the Mea Shearim quarter of Jerusalem. There they maintain the lifestyle of the old ghetto, with their own schools and yeshivot (Talmudic colleges). Their numbers are small, and they would remain a quaint curiosity were it not for a streak of religious zealotry which has often led to clashes with the secular powers. Ambulances answering emergency calls on the Sabbath have been pelted with stones, buses have been attacked by rioters complaining of obscene advertisements, and there have been violent demonstrations against sporting, social and cultural centres open to both sexes. Some of these outbreaks are spontaneous, but often they are organised by the Eda Haredit, an umbrella organisation of all the traditionalist groups, and they tend to exacerbate the delicate co-existence between the officially sanctioned religious authorities and the secular organisms of the state.

Former Soviet Bloc countries

Eastern Europe was, as we have already seen, an area of dense Jewish population before the First World War. It was also one of the most active theatres of that war, in which European Jews suffered heavy damage both as combatants and as civilian victims. The end of the war brought a new beginning to the Jews of this troubled region. In Russia the Revolution of February 1917 brought citizen rights to the Jews at last, and the removal of the many disabilities from which they had suffered under the autocratic monarchy. In the other countries of central and eastern Europe the postwar peace treaties incorporated specific guarantees of the Jews' rights as a minority. The hope of progress was short-lived, however, as the triumph of Bolshevism in Russia and later of German state antisemitism made their condition much worse than it had been before the war. While the Jews of the Soviet Union had some hope of being spared the extermination policies of the Germans, they suffered terrible privations during and after the Second World War, while in the territories annexed or occupied by the Germans the Jews were butchered with a brutality that still has the power to shock and haunt us today. The imposition of Communist regimes in most of those countries after the war condemned the survivors to further suffering, both material and spiritual, and hardly anything now survives to remind us of the teeming Jewish life and the glorious cultural achievements of the region.

The sudden and unexpected collapse of the Communist regimes in eastern Europe put an end to a system which, while it had been felt as repressive by many Jews, and particularly by their religious leadership, had also generally respected their ethnic integrity and protected them from the worst effects of popular antisemitism. The restoration of freedom of speech made life easier for Jews in some ways, but also gave greater freedom to the Jews' enemies. Emigration, which had proceeded by fits and starts in response to volatile political opportunities, now became a spate. According to the 1979 Soviet census, based on a national definition of Jewish identity and on respondents' own replies to enumerators' questions, there were 1.81 million Jews in the Soviet Union, of whom 700,000 were in the Russian Federation and 634,000 in Ukraine. In 1995 according to the most reliable estimates there were only 360,000 Jews in Russia and 180,000 in Ukraine.

We have already seen the enormous growth of the Jewish population in the Pale of Settlement in the course of the nineteenth and early twentieth centuries. Their inferior status, poverty and overcrowding in the Pale and a lack of opportunities for self-improvement created a feeling of frustration and despair. In the period of reaction following the assassination of Emperor Alexander II in 1881 the government adopted an openly anti-Jewish policy, and there were savage pogroms that drove many Jews to emigrate or to embrace revolutionary movements. The Revolution of February 1917 was welcomed with enthusiasm. The provisional government abolished all legal restrictions on Jews, and Zionist, socialist and religious parties attracted a mass following. The triumph of Bolshevism led, however, to the abolition of existing autonomous Jewish institutions, and Jewish religion, in common with all religions, came under attack. The Jews were treated as a nation, and when internal passports were introduced in 1933 children of Jewish parents were classified as being of Jewish nationality. Unlike other nations, however, the Jews have no territory of their own in Russia, apart from Birobidzhan, an 'Autonomous Jewish Oblast' established in the far east in the 1920s, which even at its height in the middle of the 1930s never achieved more than 23% Jews in its population. This is not the place to document the hardships suffered by Jews as individuals and as a group under successive Soviet governments, but what it is relevant to underline here is the virtually total disappearance of religious and educational resources before the introduction of new freedoms. With the abolition of the old restrictions, and the facilitation of relations with organisations abroad, there has been a striking revival in Jewish religious and cultural life in these countries. New synagogues have been created, including some non-Orthodox ones, and many educational initiatives have been implemented.

The formerly Communist countries of Europe which were within the Soviet ambit have experienced a similar resurgence of Jewish life.

In no other country was the murderous effect of the Nazi German genocide felt in a more dramatic form than in Poland, both because of the numbers involved and because the killing machine, intended to rid the whole world of Jews, was cynically centred by the Germans in this country, where they calculated there was less likely to be humanitarian protest or resistance than in Germany. Before the Second World War there were more than three million Jews in Poland, nearly 10% of the population, and in some places they formed a majority. At the liberation barely 50,000 remained, and several hundred of these were subsequently killed by their Christian neighbours. Emigration and assimilation have since reduced the number of Jews to a few thousand.

About half of Hungary's 450,000 Jews survived the war, and particularly in the capital, Budapest, where the Germans did not have time to implement their policy of deportation and extermination. Even under the Communist regime, and despite the departure of many young Jews when the borders were briefly opened in 1956, Hungary maintained an active Jewish life, with many functioning synagogues and a rabbinic seminary in Budapest that served not only Hungary but all the Soviet Bloc. Exceptionally in a Europe where most religious Jews are nominally Orthodox, in Hungary a form of Conservative Judaism, termed 'Neolog', is dominant. Today there are about 54,000 Jews in Hungary, who constitute a little over half of 1% of the population of the country, a little more than in Britain.

In Romania the losses of Jews in the war were less heavy than in most other countries, leaving aside the territories (such as Bessarabia, the Bukovina and Transylvania) that were added after the First World War. In these latter regions the deportations were catastrophic, but in old Romania, despite some terrible pogroms, the Jews survived more or less intact, and some religious and communal life continued even under the repressive Communist regime. The current Jewish population is around 14,000.

Czechoslovakia before the Second World War was home to some 360,000 Jewish inhabitants. Today there are about 2,200 in the Czech Republic and 3,700 in Slovakia, who constitute an insignificant proportion of the total population. The same is true of the 3,200 Jews of Bulgaria, where most of the Jews survived the war, but emigrated soon afterwards.

The European Union

Soon after the French Revolution, the French National Assembly began to discuss the issue of emancipating the Jews from the medieval segregation and subjection under which they lived. Resistance to emancipation was strong, and a vote at the end of 1789 was lost by a narrow margin. But the passion for freedom was too strong for the question to be shrugged off, and a decree of enfranchisement was eventually passed on 27 September 1791,[8] inaugurating a new era in the history of the Jews.

The policy of segregating the Jews from the Christians, shutting them away in ghettos behind high walls and gates that were locked at night,

---

[8] This decree applied to Ashkenazim. The Sephardim of the south-west had demanded separate treatment, and were granted equality of citizen rights in a decree of 28 January 1790.

forbidding them to meet or marry Christians or to have any authority or
power over them had been evolved gradually in the Christian states over
centuries: some of the rules can be traced back to the earliest Christian
rulers in the fourth century. The legislation was accompanied by what
we would now call a public relations campaign aimed at persuading
ordinary Christians that the Jews were not merely inferior by nature to
Christians, but also subhuman, demonic, wicked beings, whose aim was
to subvert society. As the position of the Jews in society was gradually
made more and more degraded at the behest of the Church, leaders of
Christian opinion tried to persuade the public that this was imposed by
God as a punishment. Some Christian states took such drastic steps as
baptising all the Jews by force (first decreed in Spain in 613) or expelling
them *en masse* (as happened in England in 1290). At the time of the
French Revolution Judaism was still outlawed in Spain, in consequence
of an edict imposing baptism on all those who refused to leave the
country on the completion of the Christian Reconquest in 1492, an
event which has left a permanent scar on the collective Jewish psyche.
Popular superstition had its roots in Christian teaching: a 'cloven hoof
tax' was levied in some French market towns on cattle and Jews, on
account of the old Christian claim that Jews were the children of the
devil. But popular antagonism was boosted by economic causes for
which the policy of exclusion from society was ultimately responsible.
Although in some respects the Christian policy towards the Jews can be
compared to the white South African racial policy of apartheid, in other
respects it was much more severe, and its legacy can still be felt today,
despite a change of attitude by some Christian churches, and, more
importantly, their loss of political power.

Generally speaking, the European states that emerged in the course
of the nineteenth century, even if they formally recognised the Christian
churches and accorded them some residual powers, tried to tame them
and bring them under the control of the state for the benefit of all citizens. Religious minorities, the Jews included, tended to be treated in a
similar way. The rights of citizens as citizens were protected, and given
priority over the powers of the religious authorities. Thus in France
Napoleon I extended to the Jews a model of state regulation devised for
the Protestant minority. Under this system, which still exists, local con-
sistories send representatives to a central consistory which, among other
functions, maintains the chief rabbinate and the rabbinical seminary.

In France the reforms begun under the Revolution and consolidated
under the Empire were perpetuated under the restored Bourbon mon-

archy. Carried to neighbouring countries by Napoleon's armies, they were temporarily reversed in some, but after stormy ups and downs by the end of the nineteenth century the Jewish minorities had been granted equal civil rights in most of the present member states of the European Union.

The process of emancipation, which was not initiated by the Jews but by political reformers as part of a large-scale package of changes, necessitated an uneasy adjustment on the part of the Jews themselves, which will be explored further in the next chapter. Briefly, if emancipation brought immeasurable advantages for Jews as individuals, it brought a severe challenge to the rights and powers of the Jewish communities (*kehillot*), which had previously enjoyed internal autonomy, and to the rabbis, who found their powers curtailed as they were subordinated to the state. Many of the uncertainties and conflicts still felt today in Europe can be traced back to those momentous changes, which brought the Jews out of their long Middle Ages and into the modern world.

A special word needs to be said here about Great Britain, which has a rather distinctive history in terms of Jewish emancipation, as in so many other respects.

The established position of the Church of England placed citizens belonging to other Christian denominations, as well as Jews, under a range of disabilities, including not only a bar on assuming civic office but even on taking a university degree. In practice the most common disabilities were gradually removed in the course of the nineteenth century, although the Jews had to struggle for longer than the Catholics and Protestant dissenters for equal rights.

Britain also differs from the other EU states in being the only one with a significant Jewish population to have been spared the trauma of the Nazi and Fascist racial legislation and deportations. (A few Jews were, however, deported from the Channel Islands, which were occupied by the Germans.) In all the other countries which had Jewish communities of any size, the Jews were segregated from their neighbours, deprived of their citizen rights, and eventually sent off to the German slave labour and extermination camps. Many managed to escape before the borders were closed, and some survived in hiding or in the camps, but the overall effect of the Nazi war on the Jews was to devastate Jewish life in these countries. After the end of the war the few who survived or returned, often broken in body and spirit, and having lost their families, their homes and their belongings, had to confront the neighbours who had failed to support them in their hour of need, and who too often had betrayed them for material advantage, from fear, or from religious motives. Astonishingly, some semblance of organised Jewish life was gradually pieced together, with help from agencies such as the JDC. The current strength of Jewish life in some countries owes much to postwar immigration. The Jewish community in France has benefited greatly from an influx of Jews from newly independent Algeria, Tunisia and Morocco, as well as from Egypt; Germany has received many Jews from the former Soviet Union; and smaller numbers have arrived in Britain, Italy, Belgium and Holland from former colonies, in Sweden from Poland, in Spain from Morocco and South America, and throughout the region from Israel.

The Jewish religion underwent a veritable reformation in the EU countries in the course of the nineteenth century, a process that went hand-in-hand with political emancipation and the reintegration of the Jews into society. The dominant form of Judaism today throughout the Union is modern Orthodoxy, which is constantly challenged by simultaneous pressure from more radical reforming movements and from traditional types of Judaism introduced by immigrants.

Latin America

During the centuries of Spanish and Portuguese rule Judaism was officially banned in the South American colonies, and for much of the time even Christian descendants of Jews were persecuted. Only the territories that came under English, Dutch or French rule allowed the open practice of Judaism, and some Sephardim today can trace their origins to these colonies. With independence from Spain and Portugal the Inquisition was abolished in the Latin colonies and freedom of religion was gradually introduced, although Roman Catholicism has maintained its dominance. The Jews were not specifically emancipated, but rather benefited from legislation framed with Protestant minorities in mind.

Large-scale Jewish immigration began in the 1880s. From 1880 to 1914 130,000 Jews arrived in the region, most of whom settled in Argentina. About 20% were Sephardim from North Africa, the Balkans and the Ottoman Empire; the rest were Ashkenazim from eastern and central Europe. Although most settled in the larger towns, there was a concerted attempt to settle some in agricultural colonies set up by the Jewish Colonization Association. Immigration continued at a rate of some 10,000 a year until 1940, when it was severely restricted, and since the war there has been much less immigration and substantial emigration, either from one country to another within the region or to the USA and Israel. There are now reckoned to be some 380,000 Jews in Latin America as a whole, the largest concentrations being in Argentina (206,000), Brazil (100,000) and Mexico (40,000).

The different groups of Jewish immigrants have developed their own institutions. The religious associations, centred on synagogues, still reflect differences not only between Ashkenazim and Sephardim, but also between Spanish- and Arabic-speaking Sephardim or between Yiddish- and German-speaking Ashkenazim, or even bringing together settlers from one particular region or town of Europe and the Middle East. Beginning in the 1950s the American Conservative Movement has established synagogues in several countries, and there has also been some growth in American Reform Judaism.

This, then, in broad outline, is the shape of the Jewish world today. Of the countries not mentioned, only South Africa and Australia have significant Jewish populations (over 90,000 in each case). Elsewhere the communities are very small, though some are quite lively. The world Jewish population has not recovered from the catastrophe of the Nazi genocide, and it seems to be declining, mainly because of demographic factors, coupled with a strongly felt consensus opposed to making up the losses through campaigning for new adherents.

CHAPTER TWO

The Jewish people and its past

THE JEWISH NATION

What binds the Jews together is not a creed but a history: a strong sense of a common origin, a shared past and a shared destiny. Even if Ashkenazim acknowledge a history set in Poland and Germany while Sephardim together look to a past set in Spain and Portugal, Ashkenazim and Sephardim look beyond to a more ancient shared experience that makes them both part of a single people. Scattered though this people is across the continents of the world, there is still a strong feeling of unity, which has been strengthened by the 'ingathering of exiles' in the State of Israel.

A comparison between Judaism and Christianity on this point highlights the difference. Christianity is a faith, and the story of Christianity is the story of that faith spreading from modest beginnings in the Middle East through the efforts of missionaries to illumine the hearts of many different peoples around the world, and all the Christian believers in the different countries together constitute the great faith community that is the Christian Church. The Jews are a people, and their story tells how, from equally modest beginnings in the Middle East, the people grew, mainly through natural increase, and became spread throughout the world by voluntary or imposed migration. Whether this dispersion is a good or bad thing is a matter of debate, but there is a strong belief that at the end of history the scattered people will be reunited on the soil of their ancestral land, the Land of Israel.

A key moment in the history of the Jewish people is the Roman conquest of the holy city of Jerusalem in the year 70 CE. The Temple was burned to the ground, and tens of thousands of Jews were killed or sold into slavery. The Land of Israel became the Roman province of Judaea, losing the last vestiges of its political autonomy. For Zionists, this was the beginning of centuries of exile that only ended in 1948 with the declaration of the State of Israel.[1] For traditional and Orthodox Jews it was a sign of divine displeasure at the sins of the people, and the following statement was added to the synagogue liturgy at a point where the solemn sacrifices ordained in the Torah are mentioned:

But because of our sins we have been exiled from our land and been removed far away from our country, and are unable to perform our duties in your chosen house, that great and holy House which bore your name, because of the hand that was stretched forth against your sanctuary.[2]

Terrible though the *hurban* (destruction) was, it is not correct to see it as the beginning of the Diaspora. That can be traced back at least as far as the first *hurban* in 586 BCE, when the Temple was destroyed by the Babylonians and many captives were led off to Babylon. Although seventy years later the temple was rebuilt under Persian rule, the later books of the Bible are deeply marked by the experience of exile, and there is no doubt that the memory of the earlier *hurban* shaped (and continues to shape) responses to the second *hurban*. In fact, in the aftermath of the Roman destruction it was probably assumed that there would be a return and rebuilding after a generation or two, just as had happened the first time.

The concept of the nation that prevailed around the time of the destruction of the Temple was rooted in the holy scriptures. Judaism was already a text-based religion, and the caste of the scribes was entrusted with the copying, studying and teaching of the old writings. In addition to the books that make up the Bible of the Jews today, there were various 'external books', and all of them share more or less the same conception of the Jews as a nation chosen by God and set apart from other nations to be his special people.

Because you loved Abraham, you took him aside secretly one night and showed him everything to the end of time, you made an everlasting pact with him and promised you would never abandon his children. You gave him Isaac, and you gave Isaac Jacob and Esau. You made Jacob your heir, but you hated Esau; so Jacob became a great people. You led them out of Egypt and took them to Mount Sinai. You split the sky and shook the earth, you made the world stand still and the depths shudder, you threw the universe into a whirl, and your glory

---

[1] 'Nearly two thousand years have elapsed since, in an evil hour, after an heroic struggle, the glory of our Temple vanished in fire and our kings and chieftains changed their crowns and diadems for the chains of exile.' Manifesto of Bilu, a Zionist pioneering movement, 1882. See P. R. Mendes-Flohr and J. Reinharz, *The Jew in the Modern World* (New York/Oxford, 1980), p. 421.

[2] The opening words of this prayer in Hebrew are *mipnei hataeinu*, and this phrase has become a catch-phrase of Holocaust theology, with the idea that the Holocaust, like the destruction of the Temple, was a punishment for the people's sin.

passed through the four gates of fire, earthquake, storm and ice to give the Torah to Jacob and teachings to the children of Israel.[3]

Whereas the contemporary Jewish historian Josephus interpreted God's promise to Abraham that he would be the ancestor of a great nation who would subdue their enemies as referring to the remote past, and the entry of the Israelite tribes into the land of Canaan,[4] other readers of the scriptures became convinced that the promises referred to a future time. To Abraham's daughter-in-law God had said:

> Two nations (*goyim*) are in your womb
> and two peoples (*leumim*) will divide from your belly;
> One people shall be stronger than the other,
> and the older shall be the servant of the younger. (Genesis 25:23)

Who were these two nations? The older one was Esau, the supposed ancestor of the Romans, and the other one was Jacob, the ancestor of the Jews. The meaning of the prophecy was that in some future time the Jews would rule over the Romans, just as the Romans had ruled over the Greeks.[5]

> And to Jacob God said:
> I am El Shaddai:
> Be fruitful and multiply.
> A nation and an assembly of nations shall come from you
> and kings shall issue from your loins.
> The land I have given to Abraham and Isaac I give to you
> And to your descendants after you I give this land. (Genesis 35:11–12)

Biblical texts like this one are still influential today, particularly when they are made familiar by the daily, weekly or annual rituals. The annual festivals of Pesah (Passover), Shavuot (Pentecost) and Sukkot (Tabernacles) all focus attention on events connected with the Exodus from Egypt, when a 'mixed multitude' was moulded into a people, given a code of law, and eventually acquired its own land. The Passover ritual recites the biblical verse that encapsulates the rapid growth of the people from tiny beginnings: 'My father was an Aramean nomad: when he went down to Egypt and settled there for a while he was few in number, but

---

[3] Apocalypse of Ezra (also known as 2 Esdras or 4 Ezra) 3:14–19, translated by Nicholas de Lange in *Apocrypha: Jewish Literature of the Hellenistic Age* (New York, 1978), p. 135. This work, preserved in some Christian Bibles, disappeared from Jewish tradition, but gives an authentic glimpse of Jewish attitudes in the aftermath of the destruction of the Temple.

[4] E.g. Josephus, *Jewish Antiquities* 1.235.

[5] See the texts cited in N. R. M. de Lange, 'Jewish Attitudes to the Roman Empire', in *Imperialism in the Ancient World*, ed. P. D. A. Garnsey and C. R. Whittaker (Cambridge, 1978), pp. 255–81, esp. pp. 269–71.

there he became a great nation, mighty and numerous' (Deuteronomy 26:5). Similar references to the biblical idea of the nation as interpreted by the rabbis can be found scattered throughout the prayer books of the synagogue.

The concept of the nation described in these prayers was of great use during the long years of subjection to the power of the Roman Empire and its Christian and Muslim successors. It shaped the way that Jews thought of themselves as both a political and a religious entity. They were a single people, set apart from other nations by their special relationship with God. And one day their God would rescue them from subjection to the other nations, and give them real control of their own destiny again. Even in times of persecution Jews could be buoyed up by this confidence. It is astonishing how very few Jews, during fifteen centuries of Christian rule during which every possible kind of inducement or pressure was tried to make them convert to the ruling faith, abandoned the Jewish people.

The Jewish communities during this period of ostensible powerlessness were successful self-governing entities within a wider state, governed by their own officials according to the Jews' own laws. The Roman Empire, down to the early fifth century, recognised the Patriarch of the Jews as a state functionary; one observer described him as 'hardly different from a ruler of the nation'. The Greek word *laos* (people) was used as a title of the local community as well as the people as a whole.[6] The medieval community was inherently similar, with the rabbis administering the Jewish law and settling disputes and lay leaders dealing with finance and internal politics, and occasionally representing the community in dealings with the higher authorities. And provided the peace was kept and taxes were paid, the rulers of the state were content to allow this system to continue.

Curiously, it was precisely when this pressure was removed because the Church had lost most of its political power that Jews began to defect in large numbers, and even embraced Christianity. A new definition of the nation was gaining currency, that made the old concept seem obsolete and repressive. The new-style nation was identified with the state, and all citizens were members. It was an attractive doctrine, but some Jews drew a different conclusion from the premises: if the Greeks could break away from the Ottoman Empire and have their own state, if subject peoples like the Hungarians or the Czechs could struggle for

---

[6] Examples in Margaret H. Williams, *The Jews among the Greeks and Romans* (London, 1998), pp. 30–1.

their national liberation, the Jews too could square the circle by declaring themselves a nation in the modern sense, and fighting, by force if need be, for their own state. This outlook was strongest in eastern Europe, where civic disabilities continued for longest to weigh on the Jews and where they were surrounded by peoples engaged in a struggle for self-determination. Some of the leaders of the movement, such as the rabbis Zvi Hirsch Kalischer (1795–1874) and Judah Alkalai (1798–1878) and even a socialist like Moses Hess (1812–75) (dubbed by Marx 'the Communist rabbi'), were also influenced by the ancient prophecies of the ingathering of the dispersed at the end of days. However, the religious hope for messianic redemption and the return to the land of Israel was gradually replaced by a secular vision of political self-emancipation. Zionism has often been described as a form of 'secularised Messianism', and there is some truth in this formula.

In nineteenth-century eastern Europe various groups sprang up devoted to the promotion of national resettlement of the Jews in their ancestral homeland, and the cultivation of the Hebrew language. These groups were loosely joined together in the Hovevei Zion (Lovers of Zion) movement, originally an outgrowth of the Hebrew Enlightenment (Haskalah), which gained in strength through the political unrest caused by the rise of antisemitism in Russia and outbreaks of violence against Jews (the so-called pogroms). It was one of the leaders of this movement, Nathan Birnbaum (1864–1937), who first coined the term 'Zionism'.[7]

Leon (or Yehudah Leib) Pinsker (1821–91) gave a great boost to the nationalist movement with his pamphlet *Autoemanzipation* ('Self-emancipation', 1882), written under the impact of the first pogroms. Pinsker argued that antisemitism would not be eliminated by progress in society at large towards greater liberalism. The emancipation of the Jews, granted as a boon by others, did not lead to real equality. The Jews, as a nation without a territory of their own, would always remain an oddity, neither fully independent nor fully integrated. After the publication of his pamphlet Pinsker was invited to join the *Hovevei Zion* and to lead the movement, and he accepted, although he did not share their view that Palestine was the only possible place where their vision could be realised.

A leading figure of the *Hovevei Zion* who made a lasting contribution to the Jewish national movement through his writings was Ahad Ha-am

---

[7] Birnbaum, a founder of the first nationalist Jewish students' movement, Kadimah, and the first German-language Jewish nationalist journal, *Selbstemanzipation* (Self-emancipation), eventually turned against political Zionism and became the first secretary-general of the ultra-Orthodox, anti-Zionist movement Agudas Yisroel.

('One of the People', pen-name of Asher Ginsberg, 1858–1927). He is remembered as an advocate of 'cultural' Zionism: critical of attempts to revive a Jewish nation without first reviving its culture, he was insistent on the need for an ethical content in such a revival (including sensitivity to the existence of a large Arab presence in Palestine). Ahad Ha-am saw Zion not as superseding the Diaspora but as enriching it culturally and ethically. While rejecting traditional Jewish religion as archaic, he built on its historical and moral heritage.

The Austrian journalist Theodor Herzl (1860–1904) has come to be seen with good reason as the father of political Zionism, the movement about which Ahad Ha-am expressed such acute criticisms. If Pinsker was motivated by the shock of the first pogroms, in Herzl's case it was the conviction of the French soldier Captain Alfred Dreyfus on a false charge of treason in 1895 that suddenly made him question the whole process of emancipation. He at once set about writing the short text that was to become the foundation document of political Zionism, *Der Judenstaat*, known in English as *The Jewish State*.[8] Herzl summarised the main ideas of the book in the London *Jewish Chronicle*. He wrote:

We are one people – One People. We have honestly striven everywhere to merge ourselves in the social life of surrounding communities, and to preserve the faith of our fathers. It has not been permitted to us . . . We are one people – our enemies have made us one in our despite, as repeatedly happens in history. Distress binds us together, and thus united, we suddenly discover our strength. Yes, we are strong enough to form a state, and a model state.[9]

In an age of nationalism, Herzl argued, the problem of Jewish identity and the related problem of antisemitism demanded a radical political solution: 'Let the sovereignty be granted us over a portion of the globe large enough to satisfy the rightful requirements of a nation; the rest we shall manage for ourselves.'[10] Herzl worked out his plan in considerable detail, and presented it as a document for discussion and implementation. Among the *Hovevei Zion* in Russia, who were already well prepared for such a project, it met with an enthusiastic response, but the response in the west was more guarded. Nevertheless, Herzl felt sufficiently encouraged to convene an international congress to promote his plan. The First Zionist Congress met at Basle in Switzerland in

---

[8] As Steven Beller points out in his book *Herzl* (London, 1991), p. 35n., 'the proper translation should be *The Jews' State*, or, perhaps better, *The State of the Jews.*'

[9] From *The Jewish Chronicle*, 17 January 1896. See Mendes-Flohr and Reinharz, *The Jew in the Modern World*, p. 423.

[10] Theodor Herzl, *The Jewish State*, tr. Sylvie d'Avigdor (London 1896), 4th edn, London, 1946, p. 28.

August 1897. The Congress adopted the Basle programme, committed
to the establishment of a national homeland for the Jews in Palestine,
recognised by international law. The Congress also set up the World
Zionist Organisation, with Herzl as its president. Herzl devoted the
remainder of his short life to building the WZO into an effective institution, and promoting his vision by every means possible. Herzl's efforts,
although they did not meet with great success in his lifetime, contributed
immensely to the Zionist movement, led by eastern European Jews,
which eventually established the State of Israel in 1948.

It is easy now to forget that only a minority even of Jews who favoured
a national solution to the 'Jewish problem' at the end of the nineteenth
century looked to Palestine, the ancestral Land of Israel, as the location
for a Jewish homeland. Pinsker was not alone in keeping an open mind
on this subject. Herzl himself in *Der Judenstaat* wondered whether
Palestine or Argentina should be chosen for the state. The Zionist movement was torn apart by debate over the possibility of establishing a
homeland in Uganda.

The commonest form of Jewish nationalism in eastern Europe was a
cultural nationalism based on the Yiddish language and rooted in the
countries, particularly the Pale of Settlement, where most Jews lived.
The majority of Jews looked to socialism, with its universal vision of
human solidarity, to solve the problem of antisemitism, but even socialist Jews tended to look for some sort of national status. Since there were
so many nationalities in Russia, surely the national identity of the Jews
could be officially recognised. In 1897 the Bund (*Algemeyner Arbeter Bund
in Polyn un Rusland*/General Jewish Workers' Union in Poland and
Russia) was founded. The Bund sought full civil rights for the Jews in
Russia coupled with recognition of their 'national-cultural autonomy',
similar to other national groups. At first the question of securing
national rights for the Jews was hotly debated, but eventually it was
agreed as an aim. At the same time the Bund was resolutely opposed to
the out-and-out nationalism of the Zionists. The Fourth Party
Convention, in May 1901, declared that 'Zionist propaganda inflames
nationalist feelings and hinders the development of class consciousness
among the Jewish proletariat'.[11] Despite the hostility of the Zionists and
of both Jewish and non-Jewish socialists, the Bund attracted a large following, and continued to be active politically in Poland down to the Nazi
occupation.

---

[11] Mendes-Flohr and Reinharz, *The Jew in the Modern World*, p. 341.

The historian Simon Dubnow (1860–1941) was a proponent of 'autonomism', calling for Jewish communal autonomy and minority rights to be recognised not only within a multinational Russian state but throughout the world. This he felt, was the defining characteristic of Jewish life among the nations down the ages, from the time of the Talmudic rabbis in Roman Palestine and Babylonia through the Jewries of medieval Europe to the Councils which had governed the Jewish communities of Poland and Lithuania in the sixteenth and seventeenth centuries. As a convinced secularist he looked to the synagogues of Germany to convert themselves into secular national organisations, and hoped that a similar type of structure would emerge in America, to which large numbers of European Jews were emigrating. Dubnow came to an original conception of Jewish national identity: the Jews, in uniquely maintaining a sense of nationhood while emancipating themselves from attachment to land or territory, represent the highest form of nation ever to have evolved.

Dubnow was murdered by Nazis in Riga in 1941, and his writings are little read now, but his ideas have been remarkably influential, mainly indirectly through his direct influence on the Bundists and the so-called Yiddishists, both of whom gave a high priority to preserving the national and cultural integrity of the Jewish minority. This aim was written into the peace treaties following the First World War, and in a more muted way has formed the basis of the American Jewish compromise with the 'melting pot' idea. Dubnow's vision of a semi-autonomous community was not a viable proposition, but American Jews mostly accept it as axiomatic that it is possible to be a hundred percent American and a hundred percent Jewish. This idea was advanced by leading figures such as Louis Brandeis (1856–1941) and Horace Kallen (1882–1974), the theorist of cultural pluralism. Mordecai Kaplan (1881–1983) also made a significant contribution, with his definition of Judaism as not a religion but a civilisation. These three men were all Zionists (Brandeis was the leader of American Zionism in his day), but they were also all actively concerned for the maintenance of a distinctive Jewish identity within the American 'melting pot'.

ENEMIES OF THE NATION

The idea of the nation, which is such a strong cement binding Jews together and giving them a common sense of purpose and destiny, has many enemies, both within and without. These enemies are of different kinds: some aim to destroy the Jewish people itself, while others aim to replace the idea of the nation by some alternative vision.

Universalism

In the second of these categories the most powerful enemy of the nation is the concept of universalism. This is the outlook that values the human race as a whole above any single one of its components, including the Jewish people. Jewish universalism is no less deeply rooted than nationalism in the sacred literature of the Jews. The fact that the Bible begins with the creation of the world and humanity instead of the beginnings of the people can be used as an illustration of the centrality of universalism in Judaism. An old rabbinic teaching says: 'The fact that [in the Bible] one man was created [rather than separate founders of each nation] teaches us that none of us can say to another: My father was greater than your father.'[12] The Bible is full of reminders to the Jews that their God is the God of all the nations. 'You Israelites, are you not just like the Ethiopians to me, says the Lord? Just as I brought Israel out of Egypt, did I not bring the Philistines out of Caphtor and the Arameans out of Kir?' (Amos 9:7). The biblical book that expresses this universal vision most powerfully is Isaiah. There is only one God for all humankind, and even if they do not recognise him now they will at a future time:

> I am the Lord, there is no other;
> there is no god besides me.
> I will strengthen you, although you have not known me,
> so that men from the rising and the setting sun
> may know that there is none but me. (45:6)

> The nations shall march towards your [Jerusalem's] light
> and their kings to your sunrise (60:3)

The same idea is expressed in the prayers. In the Ashkenazi liturgy the strongly 'nationalist' Aleynu prayer, which ends every service, is immediately followed and, so to speak, neutralised, by a more universal vision. The first prayer says:

It is our duty to praise the Lord of all things, to magnify the Author of creation, who has not made us like the nations of the lands, nor placed us like the families of the world, who has not made their portion like theirs nor our destiny like that of their multitude . . .

---

[12] Mishnah, *Sanhedrin* 4:5.

And the second:

Therefore we hope in you, Lord our God, that we may soon behold your glorious might, when you remove paganism from the earth and idolatry is uprooted, when the world is set to rights under the kingdom of Shaddai and all mankind call on your name, and all the wicked of the earth are turned towards you. All the inhabitants of the world shall realise and know that it is to you that every knee must bend and every tongue swear loyalty . . .

In this vision, God is the Lord of all humankind, even if his rule cannot be said to be established until all people acknowledge him as God. This is a rather different idea from the one found in many sources, that the universal God chose the Jews to be his special people, and gave them the commands contained in the Torah, but that he gave the non-Jews a simplified law code with only seven laws in it. A gentile who obeys all of these 'laws of the sons of Noah' is as 'good' as a Jew who obeys all 613 commands of the Torah.[13]

The eighteenth-century Enlightenment led to deep embarrassment or impatience with Jewish particularism, and at that time the universalistic side of Judaism was seen as a useful counterbalance to it. For the German philosopher Moses Mendelssohn, for example, Judaism has always consisted of three elements, namely general truths, historical truths and commandments. The second and third categories belong to the Jews as a nation, but the general truths are not revealed by God to the Jews alone, but to all rational beings. 'Their effect is as universal as the salutary influence of the sun.'[14]

Mendelssohn and other Enlightenment thinkers insisted that Judaism does not teach that only Jews can be saved. A later German philosopher, Hermann Cohen (1842–1918), quoted with approval Maimonides' statement that the righteous from among the nations have a share in the Coming Age. Cohen agreed with Mendelssohn in seeing no contradiction between Judaism and the universal religion of reason. He believed that humanity, in the modern era of the nation-state, was being drawn ever closer together and developing towards overcoming national differences, and he identified this universal vision with that of the biblical prophets. He did not define the Jews as a 'nation' (a term he reserved for the citizens of a nation-state) but a 'nationality', a purely ethnic group held together by its religion. The Jews had long ago abandoned

---

[13] See the rabbinic passages collected in *A Rabbinic Anthology*, ed. C. G. Montefiore and H. Loewe, reprinted with a Prolegomenon by Raphael Loewe (New York, 1974), pp. 556–65.

[14] See the extract from Mendelssohn's *Jerusalem* (1783) in Mendes-Flohr and Reinharz, *The Jew in the Modern World*, p. 87.

their statehood, thus pointing towards the supra-national future of mankind. As a Jew, Cohen felt at home in the culture of modern Germany, which he felt to be close to the outlook of the prophets.

We may compare the statement of the so-called 'Protest Rabbis' who united in 1897 to oppose the holding of the first Zionist congress on German soil, at Munich, forcing it to be held in Switzerland instead:

> We comprise a separate community solely in respect of religion. With regard to nationality, we feel totally at one with our fellow Germans, and therefore we strive towards the realisation of the spiritual and moral goals of our dear fatherland with an enthusiasm equalling theirs . . .

> Eighteen hundred years ago history made its decision regarding Jewish nationhood through the dissolution of the Jewish state and the destruction of the Temple.[15]

In other words, although the universal vision of the prophets is perfectly compatible with the idea of the national destiny of the Jews (as it was for the prophets themselves), once this national destiny came to be identified in the modern period as a political one, culminating later in the creation of a specifically Jewish nation-state, some universalists came to see the two as standing in opposition to each other. This attitude is often associated with Liberal Judaism, although it is not confined to it. The 'Protest Rabbis' included both Liberal and Orthodox rabbis. The father of German Orthodoxy, Samson Raphael Hirsch (1808–88), was opposed to expressions of Jewish nationalism, and declared that 'the more the Jew is a Jew, the more universalist will his views and aspirations be . . . the more joyfully will he seize every opportunity to give proof of his mission as a Jew, the task of his Judaism, on new and untrodden ground, the more joyfully will he devote himself to all true progress in civilisation and culture.'[16]

Meanwhile in America the Reform rabbis assembled at Pittsburgh in 1885 issued a declaration along similar lines, firmly rejecting the claims of nationalism:

> We recognise in the modern era of universal culture of heart and intellect the approach of the realization of Israel's great Messianic hope for the establishment of the kingdom of truth, justice and peace among all men. We consider ourselves no longer a nation but a religious community, and therefore expect neither a return to Palestine, nor a sacrificial worship under the administration

---

[15] See Mendes-Flohr and Reinharz, *The Jew in the Modern World*, p. 427–8.

[16] *Judaism Eternal: Selected Essays from the Writings of Rabbi S. R. Hirsch*, ed. and tr. I. Grunfeld (London, 1956), vol. 2, p. 236; see Mendes-Flohr and Reinharz, *The Jew in the Modern World*, p. 180.

of the sons of Aaron, nor the restoration of any of the laws concerning the Jewish state.[17]

This is an implicit rejection of Zionism, as well as a rebuttal of any imputation of dual loyalties. Both Reform and Orthodox Judaism were associated for a long time with anti-Zionism, which was very widespread among middle-class Jews in the West. Since the Holocaust this is no longer the case: declared anti-Zionism is relatively rare, and limited to marginal extreme groups – religious traditionalists on the one hand, who judge it to be a secular usurpation of the divine prerogative, and social-ist universalists who object to its particularism.

Universalist opposition to Jewish nationalism took a different form at the same period among Jewish socialists. In its most extreme form, it asserted such a strong faith in the brotherhood of all people that Rosa Luxemburg (1871–1919), for example, could write to a friend: 'I have no separate corner in my heart for the ghetto: I feel at home in the entire world wherever there are clouds and birds and human tears.'[18] Others found it harder to abandon the idea of the nation entirely. Especially in Russia, where anti-Jewish sentiment was strong even among socialists, and where additionally the ignorance of Russian among the Jewish pro-letariat constituted an obstacle to the dissemination of socialism, many Jewish socialists felt that it was essential to combine the maintenance of the idea of Jewish nationality with the pursuit of socialist goals. This apparent paradox was viewed with disfavour by leading socialists. The Bundist compromise between Zionism and socialist universalism was opposed and ridiculed by Lenin, who stated that 'Whoever, directly or indirectly, presents the slogan of a Jewish "national culture" is (whatever his good intentions may be) an enemy of the proletariat, a supporter of the *old* and of the *caste* among the Jews, an accomplice of the rabbis and the bourgeoisie.'[19] Stalin, too, attacked the Bundists' demands for national autonomy, the protection of the Yiddish language and the Jewish Sabbath, and claimed that the Jews could not be a nation since they lacked a territory of their own and were not united economically.[20] During the great purges he strove to eradicate every trace of a distinc-tive Jewish identity, including Yiddish schools, publishing houses and

---

[17] Full text in Michael A. Meyer, *Response to Modernity: A History of the Reform Movement in Judaism* (New York, 1988), p. 388; Mendes-Flohr and Reinharz, *The Jew in the Modern World*, pp. 371–2.
[18] See Mendes-Flohr and Reinharz, *The Jew in the Modern World*, p. 225.
[19] V. I. Lenin, *Critical Remarks on the Jewish Question, 1913*, quoted in Mendes-Flohr and Reinharz, *The Jew in the Modern World*, pp. 344–5.
[20] Joseph Stalin, *Marxism and the National Question*, quoted in Mendes-Flohr and Reinharz, *The Jew in the Modern World*, pp. 346–8.

theatres. Even the memory of this cultural catastrophe has not pre-
vented some socialists of Jewish origin from perpetuating the assault on
Jewish particularism; although this attitude has some Jewish roots, it
cannot seriously be claimed as an expression of Jewish universalism,
which always maintained some sense of the distinctive existence of the
Jewish people.

Assimilation

The attitude just described exemplifies one of the most powerful forces
threatening the Jewish nation: assimilation.

The political emancipation of the Jews, as we have seen, was allied to
their integration within European society. As a small minority, they could
be absorbed and eventually disappear. Clearly this process represents a
danger not only to the idea of a Jewish nation but to the very existence
of the Jews as a separate entity. It quickly became a nightmare that continues to haunt the Jewish leadership, both political and religious, today.
A good deal of the support enjoyed by Zionism in western Jewish communities can be safely described to a feeling that it represents a bulwark
against assimilation, which is often identified with intermarriage, perceived as the first step towards the extinction of the Jewish people.

Although the changing conditions of the modern world have
intensified the question of assimilation, however, the question itself is an
old one. The purpose of a good number of the commands in the Torah
is thought to be to separate and distance the Israelites from the culture
of the other nations among whom they lived. From the revolt of the
Maccabees on there is a polemic against Hellenising, or adopting Greek
customs (for example by neglecting the dietary laws, abandoning
circumcision, and adopting elements of idolatrous worship). So powerful was the memory of this conflict that the term 'Hellenising' is still
sometimes used as a synonym for assimilation.[21]

Those Jews who welcomed the political emancipation while resisting
the threat of annihilation through assimilation were forced to redefine
Jewish identity, and in Western Europe the preferred model was that of
the *religious minority*. 'We admit of no difference but that of worshipping
the Supreme Being': this was the reply of the assembly of Jewish not-
ables convened by Napoleon in 1806 to the question how Jews are
required by their law to behave towards Frenchmen who are not their

---

[21] See further Yaacov Shavit, *Athens in Jerusalem. Classical Antiquity and Hellenism in the Making of the
Modern Secular Jew*, tr. C. Naor and N. Werner (London and Portland, Oregon, 1997).

co-religionists.[22] And indeed, the provisions instituted by Napoleon to regulate the status of the Jews were similar to those regulating the Protestant minority. As a religious minority, the Jews lost any political rights or privileges they might have enjoyed, and received in exchange freedom to practise their religion on the same basis as other citizens. In some countries, such as France, religion was totally severed from the state, and the rights and obligations of Jews became identical to those of all other citizens. When, in March 1994, an election day fell on a Jewish festival, some Jews demanded special arrangements to enable observant Jews to vote, but the state refused to make an exception. The question of excusing Jewish students from attending state schools on the Sabbath is still an issue in France. In other countries, such as Britain, special rights were eventually accorded to the Jews to enable them to participate in the civic and political life of the country. For example, Jews (like other minorities) are exempted from having to take unacceptable oaths or from swearing on a Christian Bible.

The conflict between the concept of the Jewish nation and that of the religious minority came to a head during the early days of Zionism, which in Britain was largely a popular movement sustained by the recent immigrants from Russia, while the more 'anglicised' establishment rejected any hint of dual national loyalties. The two principal institutions representing the latter group, the Board of Deputies and the Anglo-Jewish Association, formed a common front, and on 24 May 1917 *The Times* newspaper published a joint letter from the presidents of the two bodies containing the following statement, which expresses very clearly this anti-national position:

Emancipated Jews in this country regard themselves primarily as a religious community, and they have always based their claims to political equality with their fellow-citizens of other creeds on this assumption and on its corollary – that they have no separate national aspirations in a political sense. They hold Judaism to be a religious system, with which their political status has no concern, and they maintain that, as citizens of the countries in which they live, they are fully and sincerely identified with the national spirit and interests of those countries. [23]

Some six months later the British Government issued the Balfour Declaration, expressing support for the Zionist aim of establishing a

---

[22] For the complete reply see Mendes-Flohr and Reinharz, *The Jew in the Modern World*, pp. 116–21.
[23] Letter to *The Times* from the presidents of the Board of Deputies and the Anglo-Jewish Association, 24 May 1917. Text in Mendes-Flohr and Reinharz, *The Jew in the Modern World*, p. 456.

national home for the Jewish people in Palestine, 'it being clearly understood that nothing shall be done which may prejudice the rights and
political status enjoyed by Jews in any other country'.[24] The Balfour
Declaration recognises the very deep divisions that existed at the time
between Zionists and anti-nationalist Jews in Britain and elsewhere.
Although with the passing of time and the achievement of the Zionists'
aims anti-Zionism as such has become muted in the Jewish establishment in the West, there is still a strong resistance to representing the Jews
as a nation in any way that implies that they are not loyal citizens of the
countries where they live.

Individualism

At the opposite end of the spectrum, an entirely different counterbalance to the strong emphasis on the nation in classical Judaism is found
in the appeal to the individual. The idea of the nation requires that the
needs of the individual should be subordinated to those of society as a
whole. A striking example of this tension is found in the period of political emancipation. It is embodied at its clearest in the celebrated words
of Count Stanislas de Clermont-Tonnerre, a revolutionary and supporter of Jewish emancipation, to the French National Assembly during
the debate on the eligibility of the Jews for citizenship of France on 23
December 1789: 'As a nation, the Jews should be denied everything; as
individuals, they should be granted everything.'[25] In other words, the
benefits of emancipation were only available to Jews as individuals, on
condition they abandoned their claims for special treatment as a nation.
Very many Jews over the following two centuries have succumbed to this
temptation, despite the strenuous efforts of the rabbis and lay leaders of
the community to retain their allegiance.

This extreme example highlights the conflict between nation and
individual in its most acute form, but there is always a certain tension
between the individual's sense of his or her own needs and the state's
requirement of obedience. Plato attempted to harmonise the two by
arguing the true freedom for the individual can only be found within the
framework of the wise laws of the state, and his philosophy has exerted
a strong influence on Judaism. Biblical law was seen by many to be a
harsh burden imposed on the people of Israel (one ancient commenta-
tor goes so far as to speak of God picking up Mount Sinai, which sym-

---

[24] Full text ibid., p. 458.   [25] Ibid., pp. 103–5.

bolises the divine legislation, and trapping the people underneath it), but a clever preacher explained that the text had been misread: the Torah does not say that the word of God was engraved (*harut*) on the tablets of stone, but that freedom (*herut*) was on the tablets of stone (Exodus 32:16). Obedience to the law is real freedom: the law of God, as interpreted by rabbinic tradition, is not constraint but freedom, whereas what most people take for freedom is actually a kind of slavery.[26]

This view has certainly been very strong in rabbinic Judaism, but it had to face a keen challenge in the Middle Ages from the movement called Karaism, which spread from Iraq throughout the Middle East and eventually became strong in eastern Europe. The Karaites rejected rabbinic tradition and urged a return to the direct reading of the Bible (whence their name, which is derived from the verb *kara*, 'read', and related to Hebrew *mikra*, 'scripture'), and they attached importance to communal consensus, but they also insisted on the judgment of the individual.

Another outlet for individualism is found in personal devotion, which is attested in the Bible, particularly in the Book of Psalms, and throughout the history of Judaism. It is particularly prominent in the mystical tradition, in kabbalism and Hasidism.

Dispersion

A different kind of threat is posed to the nation by physical dispersion, which has been a notable characteristic of the Jewish people for most of its history. Being concentrated in a particular place might seem to be necessary for the formation and preservation of a national identity, although a moment's reflection will yield several examples of nations that are widely dispersed. In the case of the Jews wandering and dispersal has come to seem almost an integral part of the people's experience, and it certainly bulks large in the way the Jewish people thinks of itself. How can a nation survive such dispersion?

Close study of the rabbinic literature reveals two different attitudes to dispersion, and there are traces of a dialectic between them. On the one hand, 'the dispersion of the ungodly is a benefit to them and a benefit to the world, but the dispersion of the righteous is a misfortune to them and a misfortune to the world'.[27] On the other hand:

---

[26] Mishnah, *Avot* 6:2. See C. G. Montefiore and H. Loewe, *A Rabbinic Anthology* (reprint New York, 1974), p. 128. More generally on the subject of individualism see Louis Jacobs, *Religion and the Individual. A Jewish Perspective* (Cambridge, 1992).   [27] Mishnah, *Sanhedrin* 8:6.

Rabbi Eleazar said: God scattered Israel among the nations for the sole purpose that they should gain many proselytes. Rabbi Hoshaya said: God did Israel a favour in scattering them among the nations.[28]

The root meaning of 'diaspora' is to scatter seed (the English word 'spore' comes from the same root), so it can be understood in a positive sense: just as a farmer scatters seed to bring in a richer harvest, so God scattered the people so as to win proselytes. This attitude is meant to counter the view that dispersion means exile and punishment, which has been more prevalent, both in the Bible and in subsequent Jewish tradition.

Another motive for the praise of dispersion in the rabbinic literature is the harshness of Roman rule. 'God knew that Israel would be unable to bear the cruelty of Edom [Rome], and so he exiled them to Babylon.' In Babylon there is peace and prosperity, and the Jews are able to devote themselves to the study of Torah. Furthermore, dispersion makes it less likely that the people will be destroyed by persecution: if they disappear in one place they will survive in another.[29]

A positive evaluation of diaspora existence can be found throughout the ages, though it tends to be silenced by the far more numerous texts that protest against exile and look forward in hope and prayer to the end of the dispersion. The anti-Zionism of Liberal and Orthodox Judaism has become more muted since the creation of the State of Israel, but the theologian Ignaz Maybaum, who was a strong supporter of the idea of a sacred Jewish mission to be a 'light to the nations', declared in a sermon delivered in 1956:

> The Zionist dogma of the end of the Diaspora has been thrown onto the dust-heap of history. The State of Israel is not the successor of the Diaspora, but it is part and parcel of it. As a people of the Diaspora we can only exist as a priestly nation, not as a political nation. The state of Israel is a dearly loved but very vulnerable part of the Diaspora.[30]

In modern times the positive attitude to the Diaspora is associated particularly with Simon Dubnow, who refused to see the Diaspora in a negative light, but chose to interpret it instead as a natural and organic development in Jewish history. Even when they ruled the Land of Israel,

---

[28] Babylonian Talmud, *Pesahim* 87b.

[29] See the texts cited in de Lange, 'Jewish Attitudes to the Roman Empire', pp. 276–81.

[30] Ignaz Maybaum, *The Faith of the Jewish Diaspora* (London, 1962), p. 181; cf. his *The Jewish Mission* (London, [1949]), p. 74. See also Nicholas de Lange, 'Ignaz Maybaum and his Attitude to Zionism', in *Tradition, Transition and Transmission, Jubilee Volume in Honor of Dr I. O. Lehmann*, ed. Brian D. Fox (Cincinnati, 1983), pp. 93–107.

he observed, the Jews chose to establish other centres, in Babylonia and Egypt and eventually throughout the Greek world. They led the other nations of the world in moving away from land and state towards a supra-territorial existence in multiethnic communities.

Fragmentation

Fragmentation is a danger which is related to dispersion, but is different from it. The unity of the Jewish people is something of a myth. Many different elements go to make up the people. We have seen that Sephardi and Ashkenazi synagogues exist side by side in some towns, because the two communities do not feel that they have enough in common to worship together, even though they would readily agree that they serve the same God and are divided by no points of belief. But this is only the tip of the iceberg. There are many different groups of Jews, defined by ethnic or geographic origin, by religious denomination or simply by social class. Even in the State of Israel, where enormous resources and efforts have been devoted to forging a unified and homogeneous society, the differences are all too visible. In some ways fragmentation is one of the most acute dangers threatening the nation, particularly in the light of the continuing debate about the definition of Jewish identity. Already there have been painful disagreements about the Jewish status of such groups as the Samaritans, the Karaites and the Ethiopian Jews, but the large questions which remain to be faced in the future concern the disagreements between the Reform and the Orthodox rabbinates about the criteria for Jewish identity (particularly for proselytes and for those with only one Jewish parent), and the mismatch in Israel between the definitions of Jewish identity adopted by the state and the Orthodox rabbinate.

Genocide

One menace remains to be mentioned, and it is the most alarming of all at the present juncture in history: elimination by force, or genocide. A century ago it would have been hard to imagine that violence on such a scale would be tolerated by the civilised world. Theodor Herzl, who was so alert to the dangers of antisemitism that he devoted his life to the campaign for a Jewish homeland, could not conceive that a really large-scale antisemitic attack on the Jews was still possible. Even today it hardly seems credible that a nation, supposedly among the most civilised in

Europe, fell prey to such appalling collective madness. Yet the possibility of genocide has always been present in the Jewish mind. It is mentioned in the Bible, in the beginning of the book of Exodus and again in the book of Esther, and it is found in the rabbinic literature and in the liturgy, most prominently in the Passover Haggadah. Yet always it is tempered by the belief that God intervenes to protect and save his people. It is certainly possible to argue that this happened in the Nazi Holocaust, that though six million were killed twice as many were saved; but that is not an argument that is usually advanced, and the universal attitude to the Holocaust is that it was an actual destruction, not a threat of destruction that was averted. This attitude has very important consequences for Jewish theology, which we shall look at in a future chapter. For the moment we should note that European antisemitism, the Russian pogroms and the Nazi policy of genocide have actually had the effect of greatly strengthening attachment to the Jewish nation, as an ideal and as a reality. Anti-Zionism has been virtually eliminated, and on the personal level totally assimilated Jews have been brought to a realisation of their Jewish identity: the realisation which dawned on Herzl in 1885 still operates a century and more later.[31]

---

[31] 'I am a Jew who was born and raised in a Catholic country; I never had a religious upbringing; my Jewish identity is largely the result of persecution,' writes the Italian historian Carlo Ginzburg in *Occhiacci di Legno* (Rome, 1998).

CHAPTER THREE

Jewish books

Jewish culture is profoundly textual. Literacy has always been highly valued, and the written word enjoys a status that is all the stronger for want of a strong continuous tradition of musical or visual art. The book has been accorded a status little short of magical. At the heart of Jewish worship is the display, reading and exposition of a written text, the Torah. Public education has been accorded a high priority in Jewish society down the ages, and the possession of books has been a feature of Jewish homes even when it was rare in the surrounding culture. Scholarship has been valued as a profession, and those who earn their livelihood by other means have made time in their lives to pursue it, often to a high standard. The scholars have been the custodians and transmitters of Jewish culture throughout the centuries, and they are the true heroes of Jewish history.

Most of what has been said may seem unremarkable in a society shaped by Christianity, which has adopted or imitated the Jewish respect for sacred texts; and indeed it could be argued that all the world's religions possess sacred scriptures of their own that stand at the core of religious belief and practice. But in Jewish life the place of the book is exceptionally elevated. Jews have tended to show an extraordinary respect for books, and there is no hint of the chaining, censorship or even burning of books as practised in the past by other religions. Respect for the book as an object is enjoined in the codes of Jewish practice, and this applies not only to sacred texts but to books of all kinds, which must not be used for inappropriate purposes, or defaced, or even left lying open or fallen on the ground. When a religious book is no longer fit for use it is not thrown out but given burial with due honours in the cemetery. A great rabbi of the fifteenth century banned from attending his lectures a student who had refused to lend another student a book. With the invention of printing Jewish books were among the first books to be printed in large numbers, and in many places Hebrew presses were the first printing presses to be set up. Even today, when the publishing and reading of books is widespread, Jews are prominent among writers, publishers and readers.

In the specific context of Jewish religion, arguments that in other circles might hinge on an appeal to common sense or rational proof are liable to resort to written authority. This tendency can be discerned everywhere, from old texts like the Talmud to current debates on medical ethics or politics. It is therefore necessary to open our study of Jewish religion with an examination of the main written sources and an assessment of their relative authority.

A Jewish home contains books. It is a commandment to study Torah 'when you sit at home and when you walk abroad' (Deuteronomy 6:7). 'The Jewish book is the great instrument which helps to shape our life according to this commandment. The Jewish book belongs to the Jewish home. Without it the Jewish people cannot continue to exist.'[1]

What are the books we would expect to find in a Jewish home? Two books hold pride of place, and are likely to be found in any Jewish home: the Bible and the prayer book. Larger private libraries might well contain the foundation work of rabbinic Judaism, the Talmud, some manuals of *halakhah* (Jewish practice), particularly the *Shulhan Arukh*, and perhaps (although it is less popular nowadays than in the past) that masterwork of Jewish mysticism, the *Zohar*. Apart from these fundamental books, and commentaries on them, we may find works of philosophy or theology, such as Maimonides' *Guide of the Perplexed* or modern books on similar subjects. This chapter will be devoted to an account of each of these types of work in order.

THE BIBLE

Pride of place belongs to the sacred scriptures, the oldest and most highly esteemed of all Jewish books and in a sense the foundation document upon which the whole of Judaism is built and to which it constantly refers.

The term 'Bible' is borrowed from Christian usage, and the Jewish Bible contains substantially the same texts as the Christian 'Old Testament', although they are arranged differently. The existence of this common ground between Jews and Christians has in the past facilitated controversy and disputation, and today happily provides food for

---

[1] Ignaz Maybaum, *The Jewish Home* (London, [1945]), p. 148.

friendly dialogue and shared study. In few other areas is the mutual influence of these two religions more evident. Jews tend to refer to the Bible in Hebrew, the original language, whereas the Christian biblical tradition has been dominated by the Greek and Latin translations. But the Christian Reformation espoused a return to the original text preserved only by the Jews, and in the King James Bible the 'Old Testament' section was translated from the Hebrew, incorporating insights derived from the Jewish tradition of interpretation. Jews, for their part, commonly use Hebrew texts edited and printed by Christians, and have adopted the Christian chapter divisions, while English-speaking Jews have been comfortable reading the King James Version, recognising that it is a faithful and accurate rendering of the original.

The Hebrew text used by Jews, as indeed by Christian scholars, is the so-called Masoretic Text, which was given its present form by Aaron Ben Asher in Israel in the tenth century. He was the last of a series of textual scholars or Masoretes whose work extended over several centuries. The Masoretic text of the Bible consists of a traditional consonantal text, equipped with vowel signs to assist reading, and other signs that aid liturgical cantillation and phrasing, together with an apparatus containing textual variants, conjectural emendations, and notes on the way certain letters are to be written and on the number of letters, words and verses in each section. Most readers pay only scant attention to these last features, but they respect Masoretic advice about certain preferred variants (termed *qeri*) which are used in reading aloud even if a different form (called *ketiv*), sanctified by tradition, is written in the text.

While a fair amount of information about the activity of the Masoretes is available to scholarship through the study of medieval manuscripts, until recent times the previous history of the Bible text mainly had to be studied by means of comparing the Hebrew with the translations that were made in earlier ages. However, the recovery of older Hebrew manuscripts from the Cairo Genizah and the Judaean Desert has made it possible to trace this prehistory in greater detail. While the ancillary signs are the work of the Masoretes, it is now clear that consonantal text they adopted goes right back to the time of the Second Temple, even if we can also see that other forms of the text existed side by side with it.

Originally the sacred books were written on parchment scrolls, and this ancient form of book is still retained for the copies of the Torah used in the synagogue. The scroll of Esther read at Purim, as well as *mezuzot* and *tefillin*, are also handwritten on parchment. In time, however, for other purposes the scroll gave way to the codex, and the manuscript codex was eventually replaced by the printed book. The Hebrew Bible was first printed in its entirety at Soncino, near Mantua in northern Italy, in 1488, and other editions soon followed. In 1516/17 the 'Rabbinic Bible', that is a Hebrew Bible accompanied by an Aramaic translation (Targum) and rabbinic commentaries, was printed in Venice by a Christian printer, Daniel Bomberg. The Bible has been printed in Hebrew many times since, by Jews and Christians, in various editions. However, there is hardly any variation in the text contained in the different editions, because they are all based ultimately on the Masoretic Text. It is also possible to obtain a printed facsimile of the text as it is written in a scroll, without punctuation or vowel points but with ornaments on many of the letters; this is known as a Tikkun Sofrim, and is useful for scribes and for practising the reading in the synagogue. The Bible has been translated into virtually every language under the sun, mainly by Christians but also by Jews. English translations are available, some equipped with commentaries. Particularly popular editions are the Torah edited by the British Chief Rabbi J. H. Hertz in the 1920s and 1930s (the original edition had a very fine and catholic commentary); the American translation published by the Jewish Publication Society and drawing on traditional and critical scholarship; and the 'ArtScroll' edition, with facing Hebrew and English text.[2]

The Christian term 'Bible' has been adopted into English-speaking Jewish usage. In earlier Hebrew sources we find such designations as 'the books' or 'sacred books', reminding us that the Bible is not a single work but a library composed of many individual volumes. We also find the expression 'reading' (*miqra*), a term that points to public reading. The title that figures on modern editions is *Tanakh*, an acronym made up of the initial letters of the three sections, *Torah*, *Neviim* and *Ketuvim*. This abbreviation has been in use since the Middle Ages.

The three sections in question were compiled at successive stages. The oldest section, *Torah* ('guidance' or 'instruction'), is also the one that is considered most sacred and authoritative. According to an old tradition it was written by Moses, and this tradition is widely maintained today among traditionalist Jews, although it is not supported by critical scholarship. The Torah consists of five books, and for this reason the Hebrew

[2] *Pentateuch and Haftorahs. Hebrew Text, English Translation and Commentary*, ed. J. H. Hertz (5 vols., Oxford/London, 1929–36; 1 vol. London, 1938; 2nd edn, 1 vol., London, 1978); *The Holy Scriptures: the New JPS Translation* (Philadelphia, 1985); *Tanach: the Torah, Prophets, Writings* (ArtScroll series), ed. Nosson Scherman (Brooklyn, 1996).

term *humash* (derived from the word for 'five') is used for a book containing it. The Torah tells the early history of the people of Israel, from the beginning of time to the death of Moses, and it also contains a large body of laws and regulations that are the ultimate source of much of the religious practice of Jews to this day. The whole Torah is read in synagogues in the course of a year.

The second section, *Neviim* ('prophets'), contains eight books, two of which are divided into two parts each, while another consists of twelve short works. These eight books tell the story of the people from the entry into the Land of Canaan under Joshua to the Babylonian exile, and contain the teachings of individual prophets. The authority of the prophets is secondary to that of the Torah. Only short selections are read out in synagogues, chosen to accompany the readings from the Torah in synagogues.

The Ketuvim ('scriptures') constitute a miscellaneous compilation of historical, poetic and other works. The largest component is the Book of Psalms (*Tehillim*), itself divided into five books on the model of the Torah. These poems are used in private and public devotion. The five scrolls (Song of Songs, Ruth, Lamentations, *Kohelet* [Ecclesiastes] and Esther) are read publicly on specific annual occasions, and the Book of Job, a profound meditation on the problem of suffering, is also read among Sephardim. The other books in this section are generally less studied and carry less authority than the rest of the scriptures.

The authority of these various books, the most ancient works to have come down to us in the Jewish tradition, is enormous. However, the different books enjoy different kinds and levels of authority, and different sectors of Jewry have different understandings of the claims the books exert on Jews today. At the heart of the matter is a theological question: whether the books are believed to emanate directly, so to speak, from the 'mouth of God'. These are complicated questions, to which we shall return in later chapters. For the present we should take note of the strongest claim, shared to a greater or lesser extent by more or less the whole of the Jewish tradition down to the beginning of the nineteenth century and by all traditionalist and Orthodox authorities today, that the five books of the Torah at least are a direct revelation from God given to Moses and the people of Israel at Mount Sinai. This tenet has been challenged in the past two centuries from a number of angles, historical, philosophical and theological, but despite all the challenges the authority of the Torah has remained very strong, and is invoked even by Jews who reject any supernatural belief. In the modern period the appeal to

Table 3.1. *Books of the Bible*

	English name	Hebrew name	
Torah	Genesis	*Bereshit*	
	Exodus	*Shemot*	
	Leviticus	*Vayikra*	
	Numbers	*Bemidbar*	
	Deuteronomy	*Devarim*	
Neviim	Joshua	*Yehoshua*	
(Former prophets)	Judges	*Shoftim*	
	Samuel	*Shemuel*	(2 books)
	Kings	*Melakhim*	(2 books)
	Isaiah	*Yeshayah*	
	Jeremiah	*Yirmiyah*	
(Latter prophets)	Ezekiel	*Yehezkel*	
	Twelve Prophets	*Tresar*	(Hosea, Joel, Amos, Obadiah, Jonah, Micah, Nahum, Habakkuk, Zephaniah, Haggai, Zechariah, Malachi)
Ketuvim	Psalms	*Tehillim*	
	Proverbs	*Mishlei*	
	Job	*Iyov*	
	Song of Songs	*Shir Ha-shirim*	
	Ruth	*Rut*	
	Lamentations	*Eikha*	
	Ecclesiastes	*Kohelet*	
	Esther	*Ester*	
	Daniel	*Daniel*	
	Ezra	*Ezra*	
	Nehemiah	*Nehemiah*	
	Chronicles	*Divrei Ha-yamim* (2 books)	

the prophets has also become stronger, particularly among Reform and socialist Jews, who admire the loud and confident cry for justice and compassion for the less privileged members of society.

The reading of the biblical books is inseparable from their interpretation, and the Jewish tradition of interpretation is embodied in a large mass of writings going back to antiquity. Leaving aside various works written by Jews in Greek and other languages and only preserved in the Christian Church, which enable us to reconstruct many otherwise lost interpretations, we have a vast literature, mainly written down in Hebrew or Aramaic, of which the earliest layers are found within the biblical books themselves, as later books rewrite or expound material

1. Torah scroll and pointer, Livorno, eighteenth century. A *Sefer torah* (scroll of the Torah), as used for the public reading of the Torah in synagogues. The Hebrew text, without any vowel signs or other additions, is written by hand on parchment in the traditional way. The silver pointer is used to keep the place and to avoid touching the parchment. This scroll is open at the mid-point of the Torah, in Leviticus chapter 8. From *Jewish Customs: the Life Cycle*, photograph I, by Vojislava Radovanović and Milica Mihailović, 1998, The Federation of Jewish Communities of Yugoslavia, Jewish Historical Museum, Belgrade.

2. The Rabbinic Bible (*Mikraot Gedolot*), printed by Daniel Bomberg (1524). The column in large type gives the pointed Masoretic text (here Exodus 22:28–23:8) accompanied by the Aramaic Targum of Onkelos and the annotations of the Masoretes. The right-hand column contains the commentary of Rashi (in which can be seen some deletions by a Christian censor) and in the left-hand column is the commentary of Abraham Ibn Ezra.

from earlier books. The Masoretic notes also embody a large amount of interpretation, and much more interpretation can be found in the pages of the Talmud, to which we shall return below. However, the main classical rabbinic sources for the interpretation of the biblical books are found in the bodies of writings known as Targum, Midrash and Commentary (*perush*), each of which comprises an enormous mass of written materials. Selections from these three categories of writing accompany the Hebrew text in the Rabbinic Bible, which is the foundation of serious biblical study among Jews, and in the annotated texts that are used by congregants in synagogues for following the public reading.

Targum ('translation') is the name given to various translations of biblical books into Aramaic, which was in ancient times the spoken language of a vast area including the major Jewish centres of Babylonia and the Land of Israel. Their origin is thought to be in synagogal practice, when a vernacular translation was given in conjunction with the Hebrew reading to help the public understand the Hebrew words. Some of the Targums adhere very closely to the actual words of the Hebrew and to what might be called their plain meaning, while others import a greater or lesser amount of explanatory material and even mini-sermons, but all of them represent an interpretation of what the Hebrew text means. The best-known Targum is the one attributed to Onkelos (a shadowy figure of whom nothing is known beyond his name, and indeed even that is in doubt). Onkelos became the favourite Targum of the Torah for eastern (Babylonian) Jews, while Jews in the west (Israel and associated areas) used a variety of different translations.

Midrash ('investigation') is the name given collectively to a mass of works compiled mainly in Israel between the third and eleventh centuries, preserving excerpts from sermons and lectures and other comments on the words of scripture. In the sixteenth century the so-called Midrash Rabbah was published, presenting midrashic compilations on each of the five books of the Torah and the five scrolls from the Ketuvim, and these ten books have acquired a kind of canonical status. However, there are many more midrashic texts surviving in whole or in part, and scholars have hardly begun to grapple with the complexities presented by this literature, which is one of the richest departments of the rabbinic tradition. While the midrashic interpretations do not have explicit religious authority, they are read with interest and cited with affection, and they have exerted a strong influence on biblical commentary and preaching.

Biblical commentary in Hebrew arose in the course of the tenth and eleventh centuries, replacing and at first building on the midrashic

tradition and no doubt echoing trends in contemporary Arabic study of
the Qur'an and Greek study of the classics. The work of the Masoretes
fed an interest in the 'plain' meaning of scripture as opposed to the
flights of fancy that are characteristic of Midrash. Of the commentators
whose writings are still widely known and used the earliest is Rashi
(1040–1105), who lived and wrote in Troyes in Champagne, a region with
little previous history of Jewish scholarship. Rashi's work is characterised by brevity and clarity, and he avoids being drawn into technical
arguments. His commentary is thus remarkably accessible to anyone
who can read Hebrew (although he often explains difficult words in
French), and it is often the first port of call for serious Jewish readers in
search of guidance on the meaning of a biblical obscurity. It is printed
alongside the biblical text in rabbinic bibles and drawn on freely in annotated editions, side by side with the commentaries of Abraham Ibn Ezra
(1089–1164) and David Kimhi (c. 1160–1235), who represent the Spanish
tradition characterised by an interest in the study of grammar and a
rationalist philosophical orientation. Many other commentaries survive
from the Middle Ages.

A new era in Jewish Bible commentary was inaugurated by Moses
Mendelssohn, the towering figure of the German Jewish Enlightenment
movement of the eighteenth century. Mendelssohn published in the
1780s his own translation of the Torah into German, accompanied by a
commentary in Hebrew (known as the *Bi'ur*) composed by a group of
scholars under his direction, and combining traditional comments with
the ideas of the Enlightenment. Subsequent Hebrew commentaries
have tended to follow in Mendelssohn's footsteps in combining traditional and modern insights. Meanwhile, with the rise of secular education since the Enlightenment fewer Jews are at home in Hebrew, and so
editions of the Torah and other parts of the Bible used in the synagogue
are generally accompanied by notes drawing on older and more recent
commentaries.

THE PRAYER BOOK

After the Bible the best-known Jewish book is the prayer book. The
Hebrew prayers were first codified in the ninth century, but considerable
variation between different rites continued, and today with the burgeoning of different religious tendencies and synagogal organisations the
diversity of prayer books has become even more marked. Recent prayer
books of the Liberal wing of Judaism tend to incorporate not only

English translations (first introduced in the late eighteenth century) but also additional English materials of a meditative, instructional or explanatory character.

Whereas the earliest manuscript prayer books tended to encompass prayers for every occasion, nowadays a clear distinction is drawn between the *Siddur*, which contains daily and Sabbath prayers, and the *Mahzor*, containing festival prayers, often with separate volumes for the various festivals. Prayer books are provided in synagogues, but are also commonly found in Jewish homes. Most homes also possess the prayer book for the home celebration of Passover, named the Haggadah.

The origins of Jewish liturgy are obscure in the extreme. The earliest influential codifications, both combining *Siddur* and *Mahzor*, are the *Seder Rav Amram*, compiled in Babylonia in the ninth century, and the *Mahzor Vitry*, made in northern France in the eleventh. Many other documentary sources survive from this period, testifying to the diversity of local rites. Over a certain space of time, the Babylonian rite gradually replaced the Palestinian and other rites virtually everywhere (just as the Babylonian Talmud replaced the Palestinian Talmud). The Land of Israel resumed a central role again, however, in the sixteenth century, with the kabbalistic school of Isaac Luria in Safed. Luria's distinctive prayer book, the *Minhag Ari*, was widely diffused, and became particularly popular among the Hasidim. Although the introduction of printing led to the diappearance of many individual rites, there is still great diversity in prayer books, which has increased to some extent in the past century. In Britain an important milestone in the standardisation of worship was the publication in 1890 of the *Authorised Daily Prayer Book of the United Hebrew Congregations of the British Empire*, commonly known as 'Singer's Prayer Book' after its editor, Simeon Singer. Singer's Prayer Book has been issued in a succession of revised editions, and is still very widely used in British Orthodox synagogues and is found in many homes.[3] The prayer books for the festivals in several matching volumes, popularly known as the 'Routledge Mahzor', are also very popular. Some Orthodox Jews, however, prefer to use other editions brought in from abroad, particularly from Israel and the United States. The American 'ArtScroll' editions are becoming increasingly popular; they adopt a more traditional approach to the service, and are equipped with helpful notes and explanations. Meanwhile the Sephardi, Reform and Liberal congregations have issued their own prayer books, as have

[3] The latest edition was published by Cambridge University Press in 1990.

the Conservative, Reform and Reconstructionist movements in America.

The prayer books have to be considered as a main source of religious ideas, which by dint of repetition are ingrained in the minds of worshippers. In the absence of definitive creeds or catechetical education, they constitute the only induction many Jews ever receive in the theological beliefs of their faith. However, this is a largely unconscious process, and prayer books are not usually referred to or cited to settle disputes about matters of doctrine.

THE TALMUD

The foundation text of rabbinic Judaism is the Talmud, by which is normally meant the Babylonian Talmud (named from its place of compilation) or *Talmud Bavli*. There is also a Jerusalem Talmud (*Talmud Yerushalmi*), which was at one time dominant in the Byzantine Empire, but for historical reasons it was eclipsed by its eastern rival, although there has been a revival of interest in it in modern Israel.

The Talmud is a huge work, which occupies many volumes. Consequently it is not found in many Jewish homes. Moreover, it is written in a mixture of Hebrew and Aramaic, in a distinctive and difficult style, and even people who have learned to read biblical Hebrew fluently are unable to read it without extensive further training. It is therefore the domain of rabbis and scholars, and is not really accessible to the wider Jewish public. Nevertheless its authority in traditional rabbinic Judaism is enormous, even outstripping that of the Bible in some respects. This authority has not gone unchallenged. In the Middle Ages the Karaite movement denied the authority of the Talmud, and in the early nineteenth century the reformer Abraham Geiger declared that it was an 'ungainly colossus' that must be toppled. Study of the Talmud does, however, figure on the syllabuses of contemporary Reform rabbinical colleges, even if the laws and regulations which make up a large part of its subject matter, and have a great influence on Orthodox practice, are not considered binding in Reform Judaism.

The Talmud consists of two intertwined text: the Mishnah, a relatively short work composed in Hebrew in Israel in the early phase of rabbinic Judaism (the period of the teachers known as Tannaim), and the Gemara, a much longer work, mainly in Aramaic, presenting the discussions of the later rabbis or Amoraim. Some tractates of the Mishnah, however, have no Gemara. Both the Mishnah and the Talmud as a whole are sometimes referred to as codes of law, but this designation is doubly misleading, since there is a great deal of material in both which is of a non-legal nature, and since unlike a lawcode they frequently report inconsistent or contradictory rulings side by side without deciding between them. In fact the Gemara consists largely of detailed and strenuously argued disagreements on the meaning and validity of both Mishnaic and biblical laws, in which as much attention is paid to the arguments that are eventually overruled as to those that carry the day. For this reason the close study of the Gemara has been regarded as an excellent mental training. Many commentaries have been written on the Talmud in whole or part, of which the most famous is that of Rashi. Three of Rashi's grandsons were among the Tosafists, 'supplementers' of Rashi's work who lived in France and Germany in the twelfth and thirteenth centuries. Their scholia, the Tosafot, are generally printed alongside Rashi's commentary.

Current editions of the Talmud are based on the text published by the Romm publishing house in Vilna in 1880–6, which in turn was based on the first printed edition, printed by Daniel Bomberg in Venice in 1520–3. In these editions the text is accompanied by Rashi's commentary and by the Tosafot. An English translation of the whole Talmud was published by the Soncino publishing house in London in thirty-five volumes in 1935–52 (reprinted in eighteen volumes in 1961), and a bilingual edition with helpful notes is being produced under the direction of the Israeli rabbi Adin Steinsaltz (New York 1989–   ). An excellent English translation of the Mishnah was made by the Anglican scholar Herbert Danby and published in Oxford in 1933.

The tractates of the Talmud

FIRST ORDER: *Zeraim* ('Seeds')
Berakhot ('Benedictions')
Peah ('Gleanings')
Demai ('Produce Not Certainly Tithed')
Kilaim ('Mixtures')
Sheviit ('The Seventh Year')
Terumot ('Heave Offerings')
Maaserot ('Tithes')
Maaser Sheni ('Second Tithe')
Hallah ('Dough Offering')

Orlah ('Fruit of Young Trees')
Bikkurim ('Firstfruits')

SECOND ORDER: *Moed* ('Set Feasts')
Shabbat ('Sabbath')
Erubin ('Fusion of Sabbath Limits')
Pesahim ('Passover')
Shekalim ('Shekel Dues')
Yoma ('Day of Atonement')
Sukkah ('Tabernacles')
Tom Tov or Betsah ('Festival Days')
Rosh ha-Shanah ('New Year')
Taanit ('Fast Days')
Megillah ('Scroll of Esther')
Moed Katan ('Intermediate Days')
Hagigah ('Festal Offering')

THIRD ORDER: *Nashim* ('Women')
Yevamot ('Sisters-in-law')
Ketubot ('Marriage Deeds')
Nedarim ('Vows')
Nazir ('Nazirite Vow')
Sotah ('Suspected Adulteress')
Gittin ('Bills of Divorce')
Kiddushin ('Betrothal')

FOURTH ORDER: *Nezikin* ('Damages')
Bava Kamma ('The First Gate')
Bava Metzia ('The Middle Gate')
Bava Betra ('The Last Gate')
Sanhedrin ('Lawcourts')
Makkot ('Lashes')
Shevuot ('Oaths')
Eduyot ('Testimonies')
Avodah Zarah ('Idolatry')
Avot ('Sayings of the Fathers')
Horayot ('Instructions')

FIFTH ORDER: *Kodashim* ('Holy Things')
Zevahim ('Animal Offerings')

Menahot ('Meal Offerings')
Hullin ('Animals Killed for Food')
Bekhorot ('Firstlings')
Arakhin ('Vows for Valuation')
Temurah ('Substituted Offering')
Keritot ('Extirpation')
Meilah ('Sacrilege')
Tamid ('Daily Whole-offering')
Middot ('Dimensions')
Kinnim ('Bird Offerings')

SIXTH ORDER: *Tohorot* ('Purities')
Kelim ('Vessels')
Oholot ('Tents')
Negaim ('Leprosy-signs')
Parah ('The Red Heifer')
Tohorot ('Purities')
Mikvaot ('Ritual Baths')
Niddah ('Menstrual Impurity')
Makhshirin ('Rendering Susceptible [to ritual impurity]')
Tevul Yom ('He who has Bathed during the Day')
Yadaim ('Hands')
Uktsin ('Stalks')

THE *SHULHAN ARUKH*

Although the Torah and the Talmud are major sources of *halakhah* (Jewish practice), their prescriptions cannot be applied today without recourse to the enormous subsequent tradition that has refined them and adjusted them to changing conditions and perceptions. Much of this tradition is embodied in a succession of codes produced throughout the course of the Middle Ages, and in collections of responsa–authoritative rabbinic replies to questions, usually of a practical nature. The codes facilitated access to the Talmudic sources and resolved contradictions and uncertainties, while the responsa, in applying the old laws to actual situations in ever-changing circumstances, constantly renewed and extended them.

Observant Jews today seeking the answer to a halakhic question are likely to refer to the *Shulhan Arukh* ('Spread Table'), the latest and most widely accepted of the authoritative codes of *halakhah*, or to one of the various abridgments of it that have been made for popular use.

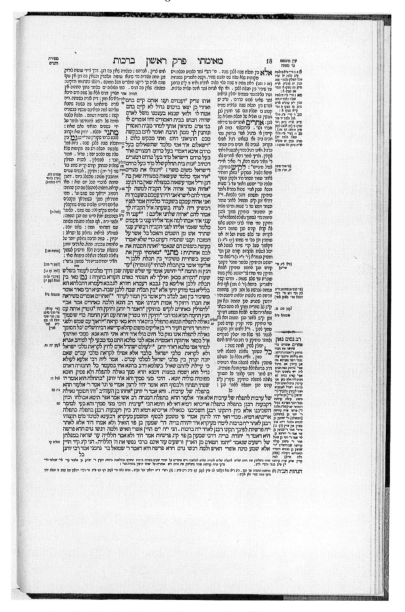

3. A page of the Babylonian Talmud. The text of the Talmud is in larger characters in the middle of the page, surrounded by notes and commentaries. The four letters in larger type near the end of the narrow lines indicate an extract from the Mishnah; the beginning of the Gemara or Talmudic discussion begins four lines later, marked by two larger letters. Source: *Talmud Babli I*, 1886, page 18.

The *Shulhan Arukh*, first published in 1565, was compiled by Joseph Caro (1488–1575), an exile from Spain who settled in Safed, now in northern Israel. It is a digest of Caro's larger work, the *Beit Yosef* ('House of Joseph'), which in turn was based on an earlier compilation, the *Arbaah Turim* ('Four Rows') of Jacob ben Asher (c. 1270–1340). The *Shulhan Arukh* was compiled with the needs of Caro's fellow Sephardim in mind, but an Ashkenazi contemporary, Moses Isserles (c. 1525–72) of Cracow, appended his *Mappah* ('Tablecloth'), providing Ashkenazi rules and customs where these differed. The title *Shulhan Arukh* is nowadays applied to the composite work, which has been deemed acceptable to both main branches of Jewry.

Following the pattern introduced by Jacob ben Asher, Caro divides the laws under four headings. The first section, *Orah Hayyim* ('Path of Life'), deals with the ritual obligations of daily life, including worhsip and prayer and the observance of Sabbath and holy days. *Yoreh Deah* ('Teacher of Knowledge'), the second section, contains ritual and dietary regulations. *Even ha-Ezer* ('Stone of Help') concerns itself with rules of personal status, marriage and divorce. Finally, *Hoshen Mishpat* ('Breastplate of Judgment') covers civil law.

Although it is now more than four hundred years old, and in the intervening period many changes have taken place in Jewish life and many developments have been introduced in *halakhah*, the *Shulhan Arukh* has never been superseded as a basic reference work. Specialised halakhic scholars need to refer of course to the wider halakhic literature, which can fill a whole library, and includes both later treatises and responsa and earlier writings, including Maimonides' great code of Jewish law, the *Mishneh Torah*. There are also innumerable commentaries on the *Shulhan Arukh* itself, beginning almost as soon as it was published. A whole school of commentators existed in Vilna in the seventeenth century, and the commentary by the famous rabbi of Vilna, Elijah ben Solomon, known as the Vilna Gaon (1720–97), relating the laws to their source in the Talmud, helped to spread the influence of the work still further. Indeed, although he was a notorious opponent of the young Hasidic movement, it was probably under the Gaon's influence that the founder of the Habad branch of Hasidism, Shneur Zalman of Lyady (1745–1813), compiled his own reworking of the *Shulhan Arukh*, thus ensuring that his followers would be brought under the discipline of the great halakhic code and respect its authority.

The *Shulhan Arukh* is still viewed with affection and respect by Orthodox Jewish laymen. It is available in abridged and translated form, and new commentaries continue to be written. The most important and influential of the modern commentaries, both on the first section, the *Orah Hayyim*, are the *Mishnah Berurah* of Israel Meir Ha-Kohen, known as the Hafets Hayyim (1838–1933), and the *Hazon Ish* of Abraham Isaiah Karelitz (1878–1953), who is universally referred to by the title of his enormously popular book. Each of these authors was among the great leaders of traditional Judaism in his own day, and both alike succeeded, by focusing on the exhortation to moral and spiritual perfection, in breathing life into the dry bones of the *halakhah*, and making the code into a guide to religious living instead of merely a list of dos and don'ts.[4]

THE *ZOHAR*

Kabbalah is the name given to the main mystical tradition in Judaism, and even though relatively few Jews today would probably describe themselves as kabbalists the classical text of kabbalah, the *Zohar* ('Radiance') still enjoys a following, seven centuries after its appearance in late thirteenth-century Spain. Written in an artificial Aramaic, the book has the form of a commentary on the Torah, outwardly resembling the Midrash and purporting to go back to the time of the Tannaim. The work is a vehicle for the theosophical ideas of the kabbalah, centring on the doctrine of the *sefirot*, ten powers within the godhead produced by emanation from the ultimate and unknowable En Sof ('Infinite').

The *Zohar* spread from Spain around the Mediterranean, and after it was printed in Italy in the late 1550s it became even more widely accessible. It was regarded by many as a sacred book, and some North African synagogues contain two holy arks, one for the Torah and another for the *Zohar*. The book became enormously influential in Hasidism, a movement that arose in Poland in the eighteenth century, and it is said that the founder of the movement, the Baal Shem Tov, always carried a copy around with him. The opponents of the Hasidim, led by the Vilna Gaon, also accepted the sanctity of the *Zohar*. However this sanctity never became a matter of dogma, and nineteenth-century rationalism

---

[4] See Gersion Appel, *The Concise Code of Jewish Law: Compiled from Kitzur Shulhan Aruch and Traditional Sources: a New Translation with Introduction and Halachic Annotations Based on Contemporary Responsa* (New York, 1989–   ); Hayim Halevy Donin, *To Be a Jew: a Guide to Jewish Observance in Contemporary Life: Selected and Compiled from the Shulhan Arukh and Responsa Literature, and Providing a Rationale for the Laws and the Traditions* (New York, 1972); Boaz Cohen, *The Shulhan Aruk as a Guide for Religious Practice Today* (New York, 1983); Mosheh M. Yashar, *Saint and Sage: Hafetz Hayim* (New York, 1937); Simcha Fishbane, *The Method and Meaning of the Mishnah Berurah* (Hoboken, NJ, 1991); Shimon Finkelman, *The Chazon Ish: the Life and Ideals of Rabbi Yeshayah Karelitz* (New York, 1989).

was strongly opposed both to kabbalah as a whole and to the exaggerated respect paid to the *Zohar*. In recent times there has been a rediscovery of the spiritual riches of the kabbalistic tradition. Unfortunately, genuine interest in recovering an authentic Jewish heritage has become confused with a modern quest for esoteric exotica and a spiritual 'quick fix'. Study of the Jewish mystical tradition requires linguistic skills and painstaking work, as well as a sympathy with the aims of the earlier kabbalists. A large number of the publications about the *Zohar* and kabbalah available now are compiled by people lacking these resources, some of them little more than charlatans. These books have little or nothing to do with Judaism.

While there is an English translation of the *Zohar*, published in London in 1931, it is obscure and difficult to use. Anyone wishing to approach this key text and its ideas today would be advised to make use of the excellent annotated compilation originally published in Hebrew by Fischel Lachower and Isaiah Tishby and now available in an excellent English translation.[5]

THE *GUIDE OF THE PERPLEXED*

There is another class of books that have never enjoyed a sacred or canonical status, yet represent an important stream in Jewish thought and have exerted a great influence at various times, namely works of religious philosophy. The origins of this tradition are in Greek philosophy, but it has become so deeply embedded within Judaism that there are no real grounds for considering it an alien borrowing or a dilution of the Jewish spirit.[6]

This type of work has a long history: an early exponent was Philo of Alexandria in the early first century CE, a large body of whose works have been preserved by Christians, although among Jews he was forgotten. In the tenth century one of the giants of Jewish scholarship, Saadya (882–942), wrote his very influential *Book of Beliefs and Opinions*. Written in Arabic, like most of the medieval philosophical literature, this was heavily indebted to the contemporary Muslim school known as Kalam, and its aim was to set forth rational proofs of religious doctrines known

---

[5] *The Wisdom of the Zohar. An Anthology of Texts*, arranged by Fischel Lachower and Isaiah Tishby, tr. David Goldstein, 3 vols. (Oxford, 1989).

[6] The best recent introduction to the subject is Colette Sirat, *A History of Jewish Philosophy in the Middle Ages*, tr. M. Reich (Cambridge and Paris, 1985). The older book by Julius Guttmann, *Philosophies of Judaism* (New York, 1973), is still useful.

by revelation and tradition. Most of the subsequent Jewish thinkers stand in the Aristotelian tradition, but an important minority incline rather to Neoplatonism: the foremost representative of the latter trend is Solomon Ibn Gabirol (c. 1020–c. 1057), who is also known as a consummate Hebrew poet. His major philosophical work is the *Fountain of Life*, a discussion of the principles of matter and soul, but many of his philosophical ideas are to be found, mingled with mystical motifs, in his poems, particularly the long poem *The Royal Crown* (*Keter malkhut*).[7] Another influential work of medieval Jewish thought is the *Kuzari* (*The Khazar*) by Judah Hallevi (c. 1075–1141), also known as a Hebrew poet, which actually attempts, through rational argument, to demonstrate the inadequacy of reason as a source of knowledge of God compared to scriptural revelation.[8]

Of the Jewish Aristotelians the greatest is beyond a doubt Moses Maimonides (1135–1204), who also established a lasting reputation as a codifier of *halakhah* and a medical writer, although his older contemporary Abraham Ibn Daud (c. 1110–80) also made an important contribution to Jewish Aristotelianism with his 'Exalted Faith' (*Emunah Ramah*). Maimonides' *Guide of the Perplexed* (*Dalalat al-Ha'irin* or *Moreh Nevukhim*), has been widely regarded as the masterwork of medieval Jewish religious thought, and indeed it was received and cited with approbation by medieval Muslim and Christian thinkers. Its aim is to reconcile religious belief based on the Bible with the rational arguments about physics and metaphysics of Aristotle and his followers.[9]

The name of Maimonides is associated particularly with one of the best-known answers to the question 'what must a Jew believe?' In his commentary on the Mishnah he lists thirteen 'principles of our pure Torah and its foundations'.[10] These principles have become a sort of unofficial Jewish creed, and have made their way into the prayer book in two forms, as a creed beginning 'I believe with perfect faith that . . .' and as a hymn.

Maimonides may have been the greatest of the medieval Jewish philosophers, but he was by no means the last Jewish philosopher of note.

---

[7] See p. 145.

[8] Yochanan Silman, *Philosopher and Prophet: Judah Halevi, the Kuzari, and the Evolution of his Thought*, tr. Lenn F. Shramm (Albany, NY, 1995).

[9] Moses Maimonides, *The Guide of the Perplexed*, translated with an introduction and notes by Shlomo Pines (Chicago/London, 1963). See also Oliver Leaman, *Moses Maimonides* (London, 1989).

[10] See Menachem Kellner, *Dogma in Medieval Jewish Thought, from Maimonides to Abravanel* (Oxford, 1986).

Within the Maimonidean tradition Levi ben Gershom (Gersonides, 1288–1344) was a major figure, while Hasdai Crescas (c. 1340–1410) and his pupil Joseph Albo (c. 1380–1444) were critical of Aristotelianism. The modern era in Jewish thought was inaugurated by the disturbingly radical figure of Baruch Spinoza (1632–77), who was expelled from the Sephardi community of Amsterdam in 1656 for his heterodox views. Despite this, Spinoza had an influence on later, more orthodox, Jewish philosophers such as Moses Mendelssohn (1729–96). In the nineteenth and twentieth centuries several important works of religious philosophy were written, mainly by German Jews: they include Hermann Cohen's *Religion of Reason out of the Sources of Judaism* (published posthumously in 1919), Franz Rosenzweig's *Star of Redemption*, and Martin Buber's *I and You*.[11] Latterly German has been replaced, for historical reasons, by English as the main language of Jewish religious thought.

In reviewing rapidly the 'great Jewish books' which might be found in many Jewish homes we have only been able to skim the surface and mention the major works whose titles are household names. Others could be added which are equally well known among a more specialised readership, such as the *Tanya* of Shneur Zalman of Lyady, the fundamental text of Habad Hasidism. Nor should it be suggested that all these works would be found in a single home. On the contrary, it would be a very remarkable Jewish home which contained more than a few of them, because (with the notable exception of the Bible and prayer book) they represent distinct streams within Judaism. An Orthodox Jew who possesses well-thumbed copies of the Talmud and *Shulhan Arukh* and related halakhic works may never have opened the *Zohar* or Maimonides' *Guide*, while the latter works would appeal to very different types of readers, with an inclination to mysticism and rationalism respectively.

Moreover, mention of these classic Jewish works does not begin to exhaust the other, very different types of book we might find in a Jewish home. Novels, books of poetry, cookery books and history books all have their place on the Jewish bookshelf; grammars and dictionaries of Hebrew, too, both the biblical and the modern language. There is a burgeoning Hebrew literature from Israel which, even if it is inherently secular, has a great deal to say on Jewish subjects. There is also a literature in Yiddish which has come to be appreciated for its own sake and

---

[11] Hermann Cohen, *Religion of Reason out of the Sources of Judaism*, tr. Simon Kaplan (New York, 1972); Franz Rosenzweig, *The Star of Redemption*, tr. William W. Hallo (London/New York, 1971); Martin Buber, *I and Thou*, tr. W. Kaufmann (3rd edn, Edinburgh, 1970).

not only out of folksy nostalgia. The earlier literature such as the Talmud covered every conceivable subject: no topic or genre was ruled out because it was not 'serious' or 'religious' enough. To the modern literature, in all its diversity, Ignaz Maybaum applies the term 'European Talmud':

It covers the literature in which European Jewry discussed Jewish problems, wrestled with the spirit of its environment, succumbed to it, escaped it and finally assimilated it to the Jewish spirit and thus renewed the old legacy. This new literature is Jewish literature. Are Herzl's writings and diaries 'profane' literature? They are not as far as we Jews are concerned. Is Samson Raphael Hirsch's Bible commentary less Jewish than that of Rashi because the former was written in the nineteenth century? Hermann Cohen, Franz Rosenzweig, Mendele Mocher Seforim and Bialik, Ahad Ha'am and Solomon Schechter, these and numerous others are the rabbis of the European Talmud.[12]

These words were written in 1945. Time has moved on, and Jewish literature today is no longer only a European literature. It is American and Israeli as well. This is an open-ended 'Talmud' that grows and grows. Like the original Talmud, it does not seek final answers to perennial questions, but revels in a debate which respects the arguments of the other side, and finds as much value in analysing a problem as in solving it.

[12] Maybaum, *The Jewish Home*, p. 149.

CHAPTER FOUR

The Jewish religion

Jews today are more deeply divided than at any time in the past on the theory and practice of their religion. The divisions are visible in the existence of a multiplicity of synagogues in some towns, all proclaiming that they hold the key to true Judaism, and in occasional acrimonious disputes that have sometimes given rise to violence, particularly but not exclusively in Israel.

To understand these divisions it is necessary for us to look more closely at Jewish history over the last couple of centuries, and also at some of the main theological principles involved.

The French Revolution, with its demand for equal rights for all, symbolically marks the re-entry of the Jews into an active role in history. In fact the struggle for equal civil rights was to take a very long time, and in some countries it is still not over. Conversely, the ideas of the Enlightenment, which gave rise to this demand, had been around, and had been permeating Jewish society, for a long time before the Revolution. However, it is convenient to see the end of the eighteenth century and the beginning of the nineteenth as an important watershed in Jewish history. In a sense this was the end of the Jewish Middle Ages, at least in western Europe.

TRADITIONAL JUDAISM

The Jewish communities of the Middle Ages were essentially self-governing entities, with very little social, cultural or religious contact with their environment, although the various communities were attached to each other in a far-flung network. The rabbis were the guardians of the religious norms and traditions, and they issued rulings on questions affecting individuals or the community as a whole. In determining points of law the chief authority was the Babylonian Talmud, as interpreted and made more relevant in a large and constantly growing body of legal literature. The leaders of the community enjoyed various sanctions, and in the last resort could expel those who flouted their authority from the community, by invoking the *herem* or ban. In these circumstances tradition was universally respected, change was slow, the ultimate objective of education was to train worthy rabbis, and the profession of rabbi was honoured.

There was very little dissent, and each town normally only harboured one Jewish community. An exception was the rift between Karaites and Rabbanites. Karaism was a reforming movement that was strong between the ninth and eleventh centuries in the Middle East, and thereafter in the Byzantine Empire. It rejected the authority of the Talmud, and advocated a return to scripture. So acute was the rift between the Karaites and their Talmudically oriented opponents, the Rabbanites, that they formed separate communities in the same towns, which sometimes had to be separated by a wall.

Later, after the expulsion from Spain, separate communities of different origin were set up, for purely historical, not theological reasons, in the cities of the Ottoman Empire, and congregations of Sephardim and Ashkenazim existed side by side in some western European cities such as Amsterdam, Hamburg and London. In this way the ground was prepared for the pluralism that exists today. The distinctions were, however, more social than religious, and membership of a community was determined by descent rather than free choice.

A major shock was delivered to the old system by the revivalist movement known as Hasidism, which arose first in south-eastern Poland in the middle of the eighteenth century and spread very quickly throughout Poland. Hasidism challenged not only the authority of the rabbis, but their whole system of values, and it is hardly surprising that its fast-growing popularity was met by resistance on the part of the authorities, However, it was only in Lithuania, under the power of the redoubtable Gaon of Vilna and his disciples, that the bans pronounced by the Misnagdim ('opponents') against the new movement were effective, partly because they were backed up by appeals to the government. The success of Hasidism demonstrated that it was possible to question and even overthrow the traditional values.

A second challenge arose in the shape of the Haskalah, a self-consciously Jewish offshoot of the Enlightenment movement that spread eastward from Berlin during the nineteenth century. Its devotees, known as Maskilim, attacked and mocked the obscurantism and superstition of the rabbis and their abuse of their powers, and advocated secular values, and the replacement of the traditional education by modern, western-style schools. They were strong proponents of the Hebrew language, and both secular Zionism and modern Hebrew literature have their roots in the Haskalah.

As a successful Hasidic movement found itself in the position of the Jewish establishment all over Poland and even further afield, and as its leaders themselves confronted the challenge of the Haskalah, it became less radical in its stance, and from ridiculing Talmudic casuistry it began to concern itself with punctilious observance of the *halakhah*. Hasidim were strong supporters of the Mahzike Ha-Das ('Upholders of the Faith'), an organisation set up in 1879 in Galicia to support traditional values and combat modernism, and they are nowadays considered to be among the most staunchly traditionalist of Jews.

The massive migrations that have taken place since 1880, coupled with the Nazi genocide in Europe, have had the dual effect of destroying the old centres of traditional Judaism and of spreading it to new places, particularly in the United States and Israel, which are by far the largest centres of Jewish population today. Those immigrants who were most resolutely attached to the traditional style of Jewish life created their own communities where they could live in self-imposed isolation from the threats posed by the modern world, while others joined existing communities, on which they gradually came to exert a marked influence.

Because of the dramatic upheavals that have overtaken all the main centres of traditional Jewish life, traditional Judaism today is almost invariably associated with pockets of immigrant groups within western societies, and this heightens their air of exoticism and artificiality. There is almost nowhere left today where one can observe traditional Jewish life being lived in an organic and unaffected way within its traditional setting. Even the few surviving communities in Iran, Morocco and Tunisia are on the decline, while those of Galilee are too close to the hurly burly of Jerusalem to escape unscathed. The life of these, mainly Sephardi, communities is marked by an unself-conscious and unquestioning commitment to deeply rooted values, where legalism often yields to common sense, and mystical piety plays an integral part, visible in such practices as veneration of tombs of patriarchs and saints, often associated with pilgrimage.

Traditional Judaism today, particularly in Israel, is often designated by the Hebrew epithet *haredi*, meaning 'fearful' in the sense of maintaining an attitude of awe or veneration (an expression borrowed from Isaiah

66:5). The Haredi movement unites Hasidim and Misnagdim, despite their historic divisions. Haredim affect a distinctive style of dress: the men wear beards and sidelocks and black coats and hats, while married women have shaven heads, covered by a wig or headscarf, and wear modest clothing that hides most of their bodies. Haredim in Israel are increasingly violent in their hostility to modernising trends, and particularly to secular Zionism.

Since the political structures that supported pre-Emancipation Judaism no longer exist, neo-traditionalism has to find other structures in which to perpetuate the traditional forms of life and thought. This amounts to re-creating an imaginary, voluntary ghetto. Various strategies have been adopted, some of which (like the formation of political parties) represent creative compromises with modernity, while others involve theological developments. Many Ashkenazi Haredim support the Agudah, a political party which is Jewish traditionalism incarnate. The Agudah aims to make the voice of traditionalism heard where it counts, and to gain financial support for its activities, and notably for its impressive network of schools and colleges. Despite the hostility to Zionism which is deeply rooted within all Jewish traditionalism, the Agudah from the outset made its peace with the State of Israel, and plays an active part in Israeli politics, even participating in government coalitions, with a view to achieving its own aims. A 'Council of Torah Sages' supervises and guides the decisions of the movement, and through a new doctrine known as 'Knowledge of Torah' (*da'at torah*) the sages are invested with almost infallible authority to determine not only religious but political and even economic questions.

The characteristic and most important institution of traditional Judaism is the yeshivah or academy. In the yeshivah the focus of study is on the Talmud, which, despite its antiquity, is read as an authoritative guide to Jewish living today. Traditionally yeshivah education is reserved for men, but there are now some yeshivot catering to women. Yeshivot have proliferated in recent decades in Israel, thanks to a law exempting their students from military service, and although this has inevitably led to a lowering of standards, the best yeshivot are highly regarded and attract students from around the world. Many of these are *baalei teshuvah* or 'penitents', young Jews who have been brought up without much religious education, and are attracted by traditional values. The *baal teshuvah* movement has been assisted by, and has in turn contributed to, the introduction of new ways of teaching traditional Judaism in some yeshivot, and the yeshivah model has come to be imitated in some less traditional circles.

Haredi neo-traditionalism is a product of the Ashkenazi world. The history of the Sephardi communities of North Africa and the Middle East in their encounter with the modern world was completely different from that of the Ashkenazim of eastern and central Europe. While many Sephardi intellectuals, and even rabbis, were fascinated by the new ideas coming in from France, Italy and elsewhere, there was not the same polarisation and conflict that divided the Ashkenazim. The Sephardi world was never divided into opposing camps like the Hasidim and Misnagdim, modernists and traditionalists. On the contrary, successive waves of foreign influence have tended to enrich the tradition rather than challenge and unsettle it.

In Israel, however, the unique position of the Sephardi community has gradually led it to adopt its own form of neo-traditionalism, to some extent modelled on and influenced by its Ashkenazi counterpart but also nourished by elements of the Sephardi tradition such as a strong attachment to the mystical sources of Judaism which among Ashkenazim is more or less confined to the Hasidim. Up to the end of the First World War, under Ottoman rule, Sephardim constituted the backbone of the Jewish presence in the Land of Israel. Deeply pious and traditional, they clustered around the holy places of Jerusalem, Hebron and Galilee, of which they considered themselves the custodians. They were not immune to the influence of outside ideas, however, and a yeshivah, named Porat Yosef, was set up in Jerusalem, providing a new style of intellectual religious leadership for Sephardim not only in Israel but in the Diaspora as well. Under British rule immigration from Europe dramatically altered the numerical balance of Ashkenazim and Sephardim, but after independence in 1948 mass immigration from Arab countries brought in large numbers of Sephardim who were relatively untouched by the encounter with religious and secular Zionism and with western ideas. They were also socially disadvantaged, and after a difficult period of adjustment they began to clamour for recognition of their own cultural identity, a demand that found vigorous expression in the 'Black Panther' movement of the 1960s and 1970s. The waves of social and spiritual renewal converged in the formation of political activism under the leadership of rabbis and former yeshivah students, of which the most visible manifestation is the political party named Shas.

THE MODERNIST REFORM

In terms of religious belief and practice, the most far-reaching reform was that which began in Germany under the influence of the Enlightenment and the movement for political emancipation.

The new ideas manifested themselves at first in liturgical rather than in theological or legal reforms. The reason for this is presumably that with increased contact between Jews and Christians, Jews became aware of current Christian aesthetics of worship, and came to see their own traditional forms of public worship as falling short of what their Christian neighbours would expect. In the early nineteenth century the issues which provoked debate included prayer in the vernacular, the introduction of sermons and music, the shortening of the service and the decorum of worshippers. It was only later that a theoretical basis was sought for the reforms with the help of theologians and historians.

The first truly reformed congregation was the New Israelite Temple Association, set up in Hamburg in 1817. The reforms included a strict insistence on decorum, the introduction of choral and organ music, prayers in German and a German sermon. The liturgy was abbreviated, and the main emphasis was placed on the weekly Saturday morning service. The influence of Christianity is obvious. The reforms were at once condemned by the *beth din* (rabbinic court) of Hamburg, but they were imitated elsewhere.

There was no agreement, however, about how far to proceed with the reformation of Judaism or how fast, and the modernising movement was soon riven by acrimonious debates. The new ways found expression in a wide spectrum of formulations, ranging from the extreme theological conservatism of Samson Raphael Hirsch (1808–88) to the extreme liberalism of Samuel Holdheim (1806–60) and Abraham Geiger (1810–74). Characteristically, these three German rabbis had all enjoyed both a Talmudic and a secular university education, and much of the argument focused on how far it was permissible to allow the values of the surrounding culture to pervade Judaism.

Samuel Holdheim came from a background relatively untouched by modern trends, and received a traditional Talmudic education, yet became one of the most uncompromising of reformers. He formulated the influential view that changing times demanded changes in the law, even if the law is agreed to be of divine origin. He went further, however, than most of his colleagues could follow him when he transferred the Sabbath services in his Berlin temple to Sunday, abolished several festivals, and officiated at marriages between Jews and gentiles. Holdheim relied on the distinction between the religious and the national elements in Judaism: the latter (echoing Spinoza) he declared to be obsolete since the loss of the Temple in Jerusalem. In practice he was willing to abandon many purely religious observances: what were important were the beliefs and ethics of Judaism.

Abraham Geiger's religious philosophy was similar in many ways. He stressed the belief in progress: the Bible and Talmud represent an early, primitive stage in a revelation which is still continuing. Many traditional ceremonies (such as circumcision) are distressing to modern sensibility or incompatible with modern life. In any case, he argued, the law of God is essentially ethical, not ritual. Moreover, historical study shows that the rituals themselves have changed and developed, and there is evidence of this change in the Bible and Talmud themselves. Geiger became increasingly convinced of the need to 'dethrone the Talmud'. He supported the critical study of the Bible and wished to extend the critical method to the Talmudic literature as well.

Samson Raphael Hirsch's approach was completely different: an ardent radical, whose reforms of traditional practice often brought him into heated conflict with members of his congregation in Nicolsburg in Moravia, he would not allow any attempt to displace the Talmud from its traditional role. He frowned on biblical criticism and he deplored the overuse of the slogan 'progress'. It was the Jews, not Judaism, who were in need of reform, he argued. He hoped through education to breed a better understanding of Judaism, which would make radical reforms unnecessary.

The disagreements between Hirsch and Geiger and their respective followers found expression in polemics as bitter as those between modernists and traditionalists. From the literature it is clear that underlying the debate about observance and ceremonies is a genuine theological difference and, for once, an issue of belief. For Hirsch the belief in the inspiration and authority of the Bible, the Talmud and the whole corpus of rabbinic law became an article of faith. To budge from it even by an inch was to open the door to unrestrained reform. Maybe that is why he was particularly firm in his opposition to Zecharias Frankel (1801–75), a very conservative modernist who was himself an avowed enemy of what he termed 'negative reform leading to complete dissolution'. But articles of faith are alien to the whole spirit of authentic Judaism, which proceeds through debate and consensus – or so at least the reformers argued, and they dubbed the new conservatism 'Orthodoxy', a term borrowed from Christian theology, to highlight its dogmatic character. The name stuck.

Hirsch can be considered as the founder of modern Orthodoxy, and his books, such as the *Nineteen Letters on Judaism* and *Horeb*, are among the movement's classics. In 1851 he became the rabbi of the Adass Yeshurun congregation in Frankfurt am Main, a position he held for thirty-seven years, during which he transformed this small synagogue into the flagship of the new movement. However, whereas at the outset he claimed the support of the mass of German Jewry, over the years he was forced to recognise that the Orthodox were a shrinking minority, and, increasingly beleaguered, eventually he lent his support to the separation of the Orthodox from the united communities that had previously been the rule, and were increasingly dominated by reformers. This was a very contentious issue that split German Orthodoxy; the impact of the controversy can still be felt today.

The young Hirsch had had a vision of the best values in Judaism marching forward arm in arm with those of the German universities. The rapid growth of more radical Reform hardened his resistance to change, and his Orthodoxy became increasingly defensive and reactionary. In 1853, in response to the announcement that a new-style rabbinical seminary was to be established in Breslau, Hirsch published an open letter to the leaders of the seminary which was a tirade against the historical study of the Bible and the Talmud which he rightly perceived was undermining the fundamental belief that God had revealed the Torah to Moses on Mount Sinai. This commitment to a rigid and inflexible doctrine of revelation, increasingly difficult to maintain rationally, ultimately undermined Hirsch's conception of a fruitful marriage between Jewish and secular studies (known as *torah 'im derekh erets*), and stifled the radical elements in Orthodoxy that had made it so exciting in its early days.

For Orthodox Judaism today the Torah – meaning all the teachings of the Bible and the Talmud and subsequent canonical literature, and especially the practices codified in the *Shulhan Arukh* and other halakhic writings – is divinely revealed and immutable. There is little or no room in this view for open-minded biblical criticism or for historical analysis of the Talmud. Orthodoxy likes to claim that it is doing no more or less than continue the main stream of authentic Judaism as it has flowed down from ancient times. This claim makes it difficult for the leadership of Orthodox Judaism to guide the movement into new paths or even to present a coherent and interesting statement of its aims, the more so as

Orthodox rabbis often seem fearful of being savaged by their own followers and colleagues. Recently some leading Orthodox spokesmen in the United States and in Israel have found a distinctive voice, but they have difficulty making it heard in a movement that is dominated by neo-traditionalist tendencies, largely attributable to the enormous dominance of Jews of eastern European origin, who have no understanding of or sympathy for the cultural matrix from which the movement arose.

In the nineteenth century Orthodoxy steered a delicate middle course between Reform and traditionalism and earned the suspicion and hostility of both. Its social base and intellectual foundations, however, placed it firmly in the modernist camp. Subsequently developments sharpened the polemic between Orthodoxy and the more progressive wing of religious Jewry, while gradually eliminating the border that divided it from the more traditional elements. Today Orthodoxy, while remaining a substantial and vocal presence within world Jewry, is in considerable disarray, very largely because of uncertainty as to whether it is essentially a conservative modernising movement or a progressive traditional one. Orthodoxy still seems outwardly strong in western countries, particularly in those like Britain or France where it enjoys a position of institutionalised supremacy, but as a modernist movement it occupies an uncomfortable – some would say an impossible – position, vulnerable to attack both from the antimodernist right and from the antidogmatic left. Orthodoxy appears to be uncomfortably straddling the fence between traditionalism and modernism, allying itself openly with the traditionalists (who have come to be termed, misleadingly, 'ultra-Orthodox', as if they were a branch of Orthodoxy) yet conscious of competing for members with the more progressive movements.

Conservative Judaism (known in some countries as Masorti, 'traditional', presumably by comparison with the more progressive movements) occupies the middle ground in Jewish modernism. Although its roots are in Europe, in the 'Historical Positivism' associated particularly with Zecharias Frankel, it is really an American movement, that is closely associated with its main rabbinical college, the Jewish Theological Seminary in New York, which was founded in 1887 in a spirit of reaction against what were seen as the excesses of the Reform movement. The aim of the founders was to embrace the liberalism and pluralism of American Reform while safeguarding traditional practice.

The leaders of Conservative Judaism have always resisted the temptation to embody the ideals and principles of the movement in an authoritative statement. Certain strongly held beliefs, however, can be seen to be characteristic of the movement. In the first place, there is a firm commitment to the people of Israel and its religious values, coupled with a certain open-mindedness concerning the way these values should be interpreted. The intellectual founder of the movement, Solomon Schechter, declared that iconoclasm has always been a sacred mission of Judaism, and while he insisted that it was mistaken to say that Judaism had no dogmas, he felt that it had to be open to the demands of changing times. He coined the term 'Catholic Israel' to indicate a non-denominational approach which put the developing character of the Jewish people at the centre of the religion.

Schechter presided over the establishment in 1913 of the United Synagogue of America (later named the United Synagogue of Conservative Judaism), 'a union of congregations for the promotion of traditional Judaism', which now has well over 800 member congregations in the United States and Canada, and is itself a constituent of the World Council of Synagogues, established in 1957, and embracing synagogues in South America, Europe, South Africa and Israel.

The movement maintains a Committee of Law and Standards which attempts to rule on questions of religious practice, but the approach is not authoritarian, and although there is a deep-rooted reluctance to depart from established ways there is scope for openness and diversity.

This approach to *halakhah* differentiates Conservative Judaism sharply from Orthodoxy, even if in practice many Conservative and Orthodox Jews might agree entirely on matters of observance. One area where the divergence has clearly visible consequences is in the place of women in the synagogue. Mixed seating was a feature of Conservative synagogues from the early days of the movement, and women were eventually permitted to read from the Torah and to be counted in the number needed to make up a congregation for public worship. In the 1980s, after a long and divisive debate, women were accepted for rabbinical training in the Seminary. Many Conservative synagogues are now completely egalitarian.

The decision to train women as rabbis led to the creation of a breakaway organisation, now known as the Union for Traditional Judaism, which has a rabbinical school of its own.

Reform Judaism, like Conservative Judaism, is particularly associated today with the United States, while having its roots in nineteenth-century Germany and in the deep radicalism of men like Geiger and Holdheim, prepared to do away with any heritage from the past that stood in the way of the spiritual and moral regeneration of Judaism. Key elements of Reform Judaism as it developed in Europe were the 'normalisation' of Jewish life and the breaking down of barriers between Jews and gentiles, including the abolition of laws and customs that stood in the way of this process; a strong sense of the common ground between the Jewish and Christian religions and the mission of the Jews to bring the moral values of the Bible to the world in conjunction with the younger faith; and a strong commitment to the ideals of social justice identified with the biblical prophets and brought up to date to embrace such principles as the equal status of men and women within Judaism. The movement was consolidated and disseminated through a new-style rabbinate, trained in modern rabbinical seminaries to be familiar with the critical study of the sources and to be able to preach attractively in the vernacular. The reform of the religion was advanced through a series of rabbinical synods, whose decisions were taken back by the rabbis to their congregations.

Radical though European Reform was, its progress was hampered to a large extent by structures of society and state that were generally resistant to change and favourable to tradition and stability. America, on the other hand, to which increasing numbers of central and western European Jews were emigrating in the course of the nineteenth century, provided an ideal breeding ground for Reform. There was no presumption in favour of tradition; on the contrary, there was a strong feeling that the past must be left behind and transcended. Individualism and initiative were encouraged, and a spirit of common fraternity encouraged Jews who had never been allowed to feel entirely German to consider themselves American in every sense of the word, even while remaining committed to their own religion. The small numbers of Jews and the lack of rabbinic authorities in the pioneering days meant that an emphasis on traditional observance was lacking.

The first Reform congregation on American soil was set up in Charleston, South Carolina, in 1825, at a time when there were only some 5,000 Jews in America. By 1875 the number had swollen to a quarter of a million, and the majority of the newcomers were from German-speaking lands. In 1842 a group of immigrants founded a Reform congregation in Baltimore, but a more momentous event took place three years later, with the creation of Congregation Emanu-El in New York. Within a decade this congregation had a synagogue seating a thousand congregants, in which men and women sat together (a practice not yet established in Europe) and the decorous worship was accompanied by a mixed choir; it also had its own prayer book, devised by its rabbi and spiritual leader, Leo Merzbacher, who ironically had come from Europe with a certificate of Talmudic competence signed by the great opponent of modernism, Moses Sofer.

The man who may be considered the architect of American Reform was Isaac Mayer Wise (1819–1900). Although in many ways he was a conservative, who never abandoned his belief that the Torah was revealed by God and written down by Moses, Wise was thoroughly in tune with America and the opportunities it offered to Jews to combine loyalty to their country and their religion. Indeed in some ways he saw American democracy as a natural outgrowth of Judaism. After a period spent as a rabbi in Albany, New York, Wise was appointed in 1854 to a congregation in Cincinnati, Ohio, a rapidly growing centre which, under Wise's tutelage, was to become the powerhouse of American Reform Judaism. In 1873 a convention in Cincinnati set up the Union of American Hebrew Congregations, and soon afterwards a rabbinical seminary, the Hebrew Union College, was established. It is now one of the foremost Jewish academies in the world, with campuses in Los Angeles, New York and Jerusalem.

A conference of rabbis in Pittsburgh in 1885 formally adopted a kind of creed, known now as the Pittsburgh Platform. Its architect was Kaufmann Kohler, a leading progressive theologian of the movement. The purpose was to mark Reform Judaism off clearly from Orthodoxy and the nascent Conservative movement, on the one hand, and on the other from more radical movements like the Society for Ethical Culture, founded in New York in 1876/77, which rejected any claim to Jewish particularism or a special mission. The Pittsburgh Platform, while expressing respect for all religions, asserts that Judaism 'presents the highest conception of the God-idea'. The Bible reflects 'the primitive ideas of its own age'; modern advance in science, morality and social behaviour must take precedence over its demands, and the Bible's ceremonial regulations concerning diet, purity and dress are abandoned, as is any hope for a return to Palestine. 'We recognise in Judaism a progressive religion, ever striving to be in accord with the postulates of reason.' The Platform ends with a statement accepting the immortality of the soul and rejecting bodily resurrection, and another on the duty to resolve the injustices in society.

By 1937 the Pittsburgh Platform no longer seemed to represent the aspirations and beliefs of the movement, and a new statement, the Columbus Platform, was drawn up by Samuel Cohon. This adopted a more positive approach to ceremonial and observance and to the Jewish people and Palestine. A further statement, the 'Centenary Perspective', was composed in 1976 by Eugene B. Borowitz.

Today Reform claims to be the largest of the religious Jewish movements in the United States. American Reform is by far the most radical of the three main movements. Some of its attitudes have stirred up controversy, for example in revising the definition of Jewish identity to include the offspring of a non-Jewish mother and a Jewish father brought up as Jewish, and permitting the ordination of gays and lesbians as rabbis.

Outside the United States Reform Jews are a minority today, and they also tend to be much less radical than their American counterparts, with whom they are associated in the World Union for Progressive Judaism, created in London in 1926 and since 1973 based in Jerusalem. In Britain there are two separate organisations which co-operate in many ways: the Reform Synagogues of Great Britain and the slightly more radical Union of Liberal and Progressive Synagogues.

RADICAL ALTERNATIVES

The three main modernist movements, Orthodoxy, Conservatism and Reform, all share certain central presuppositions: in fact, despite their hostile rhetoric towards one another they are very close in many ways, that mark them off from traditional Judaism on the one hand and from the more radical versions of Judaism that will be discussed next. This rather sweeping statement would not be accepted by all modernist Jews: for example very many self-professed Orthodox Jews feel a close affinity with Ashkenazi traditionalism, at least in its more moderate forms. Many others, however, are uncomfortable with some aspects of traditionalism and feel themselves close to the more traditional wing of Conservatism. Again, many Conservative or Reform Jews would feel sympathy for some of the arguments and activities of Reconstructionism or secular Judaism, even if they do not share their basic ideology. What the various modernist movements share is a strong commitment to what are seen as the central spiritual values and theological beliefs, religious institutions and practices of Judaism as it has existed down the ages, together with a sense that the traditional heritage has to be interpreted and revised in the light of improved knowledge, technical advance and social changes. In their very different ways they all profess the belief in a single, beneficent God and in the authority of scripture, and they all maintain the institutions of the synagogue and the rabbinate. They are essentially conservative, and cautious in making reforms; though each movement has both more traditional and more radical wings, these tend to balance each other so that change, when it does occur, is rarely sudden and drastic.

The search for more radical alternatives is not a new development in Judaism; it has existed throughout Jewish history. One only has to think of the ancient Hellenisers and Epicureans, the gnostics and ecstatics of Roman times whose ideas fed into the medieval Kabbalah, or the many outbursts of messianic fervour, including primitive Christianity and Sabbateanism. Each of these was a response to a specific situation, and each expressed an impatience with received beliefs and values and sought a more drastic way out of what was seen as an intolerable Jewish or human predicament.

The radical alternatives that exist today are actually similar to those that existed at the end of the Second Temple period. The Epicureans were extreme rationalists who could not accept that there was a personal god who governed human affairs. At the other extreme were the various movements that found mainstream religion too lukewarm or remote, and looked for something more passionate and dramatic, involving an immediate contact with the divine. These latter movements tended to form close groups held together by esoteric beliefs and shared rituals. Similar later examples can be found in the twelfth century, and in the sixteenth and seventeenth (both periods that were marked by extremes both of rationalism and irrationalism). Today again, the radical movements range from extreme rationalists (so-called 'secular Jews') to various groups of an esoteric character. Of course there is a fundamental difference between these two types of response: the former is open and public and would like to win over all Jews to its views by means of rational argument, whereas the latter turns its back on reason and favours intimacy and mystique. We must therefore study them separately, but we should not forget that they are in a sense non-identical twins, both responding to the same stimuli and both sharing a rejection of mainstream beliefs.

'Secular Jews' is a term that refers to Jews who have chosen to abandon the belief in God. Secular Jews have not rejected their Jewish identity or their attachment to the Jewish people. On the contrary, they are to be found among the strongest supporters of Jewish causes.

Jewish atheism has its roots in the Haskalah, the Hebrew Enlightenment, in nineteenth-century eastern Europe, which shared the antireligious and anticlerical sentiments of the European Enlightenment in general, and in the Jewish socialism that emerged in the second half of that century. Both these movements nourished early Zionism, and a majority of the Jewish settlers in Palestine before the Second World War were militantly or implicitly atheist, while identifying strongly as Jews. Some of the prominent ideologists of Zionism, such as Ahad Ha'am, while rejecting Jewish religion as outmoded, call for a 'spiritual' revival: however, on closer inspection 'spiritual' turns out to mean something akin to 'cultural', even if these clarion calls are sometimes tinged with a romanticism that verges on the mystical. This is particularly true of Aaron David Gordon (1856–1922), a prophet of the return to the soil of the Land of Israel. Today, many Jews in Israel describe themselves as secularists (*hillonim*), and there is a lively and occasionally violent confrontation between secularists and religious Jews (*datiim*). However, secular Jews are also to be found in the countries of the former Russian Empire and wherever Jews from those lands have settled. Not all secular Jews by any means see themselves as socialist or as Zionist, though very many do identify as one or the other or both at once.

Within the institution of the non-religious kibbutz in Israel new quasi-religious festivals were introduced in the 1930s, combining references to the agricultural festivals of the Bible and the Zionist idea of returning to the land. Most of the early experiments failed to catch on, but non-religious kibbutzim have developed their own ways of relating to the traditional Jewish holy days. The Sabbath has been retained as a day of rest, and among the other festivals Passover, with its theme of liberation from slavery and oppression, has proved perennially popular. Kibbutzim have compiled their own forms of service for the Passover seder, telling the story of the exodus from Egypt without divine intervention.

It has been difficult for secular Jews to define their ideology in a positive sense, since, like atheists everywhere, they tend to see themselves in terms of what they are not, rather than what they are, and because of a shortage of institutions organised exclusively around a secular Jewish identity. By the last decade of the twentieth century, however, some serious efforts were beginning to be made to devise an intellectual underpinning for a secular Jewish identity.

Humanistic Judaism has emerged since the 1960s as a name for a form of Jewish secularism that is establishing not only an ideology but an organised structure, with leaders some of whom bear the title of rabbi. An International Federation of Secular Humanistic Jews was set up in 1985.

Reconstructionism represents an original halfway house between religious and secular Judaism. It is the creation of Mordecai Menahem Kaplan (1881–1983), an American Conservative rabbi who in 1922 founded the Society for the Advancement of Judaism. Reconstructionism combines the Conservative emphasis on the people of Israel with a rejection of the supernatural element in Jewish theology. The result is a system that places a high value on observance and community, but finally cuts the thread linking contemporary Jewish religion with the idea of a divinely revealed legislation. Jewish practices derive their authority not from God but from their historical status as the expression of the corporate will and identity of the people. The movement is thus in a direct line from Historical Positivism, and shares much common ground with Conservative and Reform Judaism, but in abandoning the belief in a personal, supernatural god it also moves closer to the secularist position. Despite the apparent attractions of such a compromise between tradition and modernity, Reconstructionism has failed to establish itself as a major strand in contemporary Judaism, although it is possible that many Jews share its main beliefs without having heard of the movement. The Reconstructionist conception of the synagogue as a community centre in which Jewish life in all its aspects (not just overtly religious ones) is preserved and transmitted corresponds to a widely held image in the Diaspora.

At the opposite end of the spectrum we find a proliferation of groups that have moved away from the soullessness of the larger organisations in search of an authentic religious experience drawing on various strands within the Jewish tradition. Most of these groups are deliberately small, and ascribe value to the individual person as a member of a group, rather than to the group as an organisation in which the individual's identity can become lost. A first step was taken in the proliferation of *havurot* ('fellowships') in the late 1960s and early 1970s. The first *havurah* was founded in Somerville, Massachusetts in 1968, and others soon followed, often in university towns. They devised forms of worship and spiritual togetherness with great freedom, and generally with an emphasis on equality of the sexes. So successful was the *havurah* movement that it was partially hijacked by the religious establishment, with synagogues setting up their own *havurot* not only for worship but for study or for social purposes.

Like Hasidism before it, the *havurah* movement reclaimed the spiritual heritage of the kabbalah, and indeed Hasidism itself became a major source of spiritual renewal for groups not formally attached to the historic Hasidic movement. The vocabulary of kabbalism and Hasidism has entered the language of proliferating groups existing on the fringes of Judaism, and increasingly reaching out to each other and beyond through the internet.

This account of the divisions within contemporary Judaism has deliberately emphasised the diversity that exists and the fluidity that characterises all the trends. There has been a good deal of movement in every direction, with children of Reform or atheist families discovering the attractions of traditionalism, and the offspring of traditional parents gravitating towards Reform Judaism or humanism.

CHAPTER FIVE

The family

THE FAMILY AS A UNIT

Jewish society is built upon two main units, the family and the community. What is the relationship between the two? It is very hard to say. They are two very different spheres of activity, and the rules and maxims that make up the Torah underline their difference by providing separate and sometimes conflicting guidance. No doubt some Jews find greater fulfilment in one or the other, and the balance may change in the course of an individual's life. But in the end both are equally necessary; to lose or minimise either is to sacrifice something essential and distort the character of Judaism. Louis Jacobs captures the dilemma acutely when he writes:

Rabbis are fond of preaching that Judaism demands far more than regular worship in the synagogue and that, for example, many of the highest ideals of the Jewish religion are realized in the Jewish home rather than in the synagogue. Worship in the synagogue is a sublime end in itself but it is also a means of inspiring Jews to lead a full Jewish life and much of life has its place outside the synagogue. There is a Torah for the synagogue, detailed rules, regulations, and attitudes to be adopted in the synagogue, but this is only part, albeit a significant part, of the Torah as a whole. The Torah is always described as 'the Torah of Life', that is of life as a whole.[1]

Students of religion have a tendency to look first and foremost at the public face of religion: at the meeting places and public buildings, public ceremonies and rituals, public statements embodied in homilies and creeds. When they are not studying the public face they think of the private face as represented by the solitary mystic, the hermit, turning his back on the turmoil, delusions and temptations of society and seeking God in the tranquillity of nature or the quiet of his innermost heart.

[1] Louis Jacobs, *The Jewish Religion. A Companion* (Oxford, 1995), p. 517.

This approach, derived consciously or unconsciously from Christian models, may not in fact be appropriate for the study of all non-Christian religions. Students of Judaism can certainly not afford to ignore the public face of Judaism, the worship of the synagogue and the communal institutions, which form the subject of the next chapter. They must be aware too of the voice of the individual,[2] that is heard pre-eminently in the biblical Psalms and in some of the other prayers recorded in the Bible. But a depiction of Judaism that confined itself to these two areas would be left with a gaping hole in the middle: the place that belongs to the family and the home.

The place of the family at the heart of Judaism reflects the solid, reassuring place of the family in a human society in which most people are born into a family, grow up in the bosom of a family, and look forward to creating a family of their own, in which the family is the unit that underlies the legal and fiscal structures, and where the family home is the commonest building-block of the urban landscape. That kind of society is less familiar to us today than it would have been to our grandparents, and their grandparents would very likely have known none other.

In truth the family has never had an easy time of it, because the interests of the family all too often seem to collide on the one hand with the demands of the individual and on the other with the claims of the collective – the state or society as a whole. Western civilisation has tended to glamourise those whose individual fulfilment is crushed by the institution of the family (*Romeo and Juliet* is just one of many fictionalised examples) or who pursue the claims of their destiny, very often in the service of the state or of the imagined good of the wider society, as soldiers or knight errants. These ideals are totally at odds with those of Judaism. Before the emancipation Jews were not called on to fight and die for the state, and had no reason to identify with its demands, which they generally experienced as hostile impositions. It was their private home life that gave them a sense of purpose and destiny, and that they did everything they could to protect and defend. In a conflict between the individual and the family they sided naturally with the latter.

During the age of emancipation, the nineteenth century, European and American Jews became assimilated to the ideals of the majority culture and subject to the same legal and political demands. They were conscripted or volunteered to serve in their countries' armies, and some

---

[2] What place there is for the individual in Judaism is a matter of debate. See Jacobs, *Religion and the Individual.*

had glorious military careers. Many found that the only way to better their lot (or in many cases simply to survive in an increasingly industrialised job market) was to put family life behind them, for a while or for ever. These developments were as important in undermining traditional family values as were the harsh blows of fate, the pogroms and persecutions, the impact of war on powerless civilians, and the unprecedented waves of migration. Throughout all these dramatic changes, however, Jews tended to cultivate a glowing and no doubt romanticised image of what family life had been like *before*, in a more innocent age.

Wherever and whenever they could, when the waves of violence receded, when money became more plentiful, when as immigrants they put down roots in a new land, these Jews made an effort to rebuild the structures of family life, and the networks of friends and neighbours that would support it. One fortunate sector of society, the wealthy Jewish bourgeoisie that grew up in the European cities, were pleased to find that the values of their adopted class coincided perfectly, in this respect, with those of their ancestors: bourgeois life was founded on the family and glorified its virtues. Well-to-do Jews in nineteenth-century Europe created a unique fusion of Jewish and bourgeois life, which can be studied in the writings and paintings of the period.[3] It was a life that was envied and imitated by less prosperous Jews. The atmosphere of a Jewish family gathering, a Passover seder for example, owes as much even today to this nineteenth-century Jewish bourgeoisie as it does to the medieval ghetto or to Jewish life in the Greco-Roman period.

Karl Marx accurately observed this willing fusion of Jewish and bourgeois values: 'Judaism reaches its climax in the perfection of bourgeois society,' he wrote.[4] However, he chose to focus on the negative aspects, as he saw them, of bourgeois life, and overlook the positive ones. He had many Jewish followers, particularly among the majority of Jews who were pitifully poor. Jewish socialists were generally favourable to the Marxist aim of destroying the foundations of bourgeois life, including the family. This programme found its most extreme expression in the deliberate abolition of the family unit in the kibbutzim of Palestine.

But even without going to such lengths many Jews in the twentieth century promoted or accepted the breakup of the family unit and the abandonment of family values. This is not the place to explore the intri-

[3] This point is well made by Ignaz Maybaum, *Jewish Existence* (London, 1960). Among many autobiographical works exemplifying this theme one of the most powerful is Stefan Zweig's *The World of Yesterday*.

[4] Karl Marx, *On the Jewish Problem* (1844). English translation by Helen Lederer quoted in Mendes-Flohr and Reinharz, *The Jew in the Modern World*, p. 267.

cacies of the conflicts provoked by this confrontation within Jewish society of two antithetical evaluations of family life, which is partly responsible for the alienation of large numbers of Jews from the religious establishment and for the distrust towards Zionism shown by most religious Jews until recent times. What is important is to underline that the place of the family within Jewish life is a subject of continuing debate, which in some ways has been confused rather than facilitated by the uneasy truce between the Jewish religious leadership and moderate Jewish socialism. One strategy of a successful establishment is to yield to some demands of its radical critics and to pay lip service to some of its principles, while rejecting far-reaching change. In describing Jewish family life we shall inevitably be presenting one side in this confrontation; the other side does not seem to have much that is positive to contribute to an account of Jewish family life.

If Jewish Marxists attack the family out of concern for the good of society, what of the other side of the pincer movement, individualism? Contemporary western civilisation encourages individuals, particularly the young, to seek their own fulfilment at the expense of institutions such as the family that might thwart them. Young Jews are naturally receptive to this message. Jewish society favours upward economic mobility. Jewish parents make sacrifices so that their children will do well. All too often that means that the children will leave home and adopt a very different lifestyle to that of their parents. In any case there is little in the traditional social and religious structures to bind young Jews between the age of Bar or Bat Mitsvah and the birth of their first child (which is why in traditional society this gap was often reduced to a minimum, whereas today it can last many years). Jewish society has its own strategies to deal with this danger. Many opportunities have been created for young Jews living outside the family to meet other Jews and share various types of activity. Even if the worst comes to the worst, and a non-Jewish marriage partner appears, there are various expedients that can minimise the disaster. For their part, Jewish singles have developed their own frameworks for Jewish growth and self-expression, such as the *havurah* ('fellowship'), a group (which may be more or less structured) that meets on Sabbaths and other occasions to share a Jewish life without the constraints of the family and the family-based synagogue.

The Jewish family is extensive and has rather flexible boundaries. Family ties embrace not only those related to one another by blood, but also those related by marriage, including the marriage of other family members. (Those related by marriage are known as *mehutanim*.) In the past Jewish families were commonly very large, and a couple might find themselves living under one roof not only with their children but also their parents and even other family members who were single or who for some other reason had no home of their own. Nowadays this arrangement is less usual, as family units generally have become smaller and it is easier for individuals on their own to fend for themselves, but a sense of the wider family remains strong, and it is still quite common for members of the extended family to gather together for special occasions such as the Passover seder.

In the traditional family precise and differentiated roles were attributed to men, women (married and unmarried) and children. Responsibility was distributed between men and women, the latter by and large taking more responsibility for the day-to-day running of the home (and in some cases the family business), while the overall and long-term responsibility fell upon men. Study of Torah was a religious obligation binding on men in particular, and it was considered meritorious (and still is in traditional circles) for a man to devote himself entirely to study and count on his wife to support the family. As for children (defined as boys up to the age of thirteen and girls up to twelve), they carried no formal responsibility, being under the legal age, but were expected to play their part within the family, obey their parents, and (particularly in the case of boys) commence their studies. Men, women and children also had distinct religious rituals allotted to them: for instance on Sabbath Eve the woman of the house lit the lamps and her husband recited the Sabbath blessings (*kiddush*), while at the Passover meal or seder the Four Questions (*mah nishtanah*) were recited by the youngest child present.

Today inevitably for most Jews these ancient structures have become weakened, modified or demolished altogether. The 'new man' and the emancipated woman have made their appearance, and home life is more of an equal partnership with many of the roles being shared. Nevertheless, the ritual aspects of the old division, together with some social features, have proved remarkably resistant to change. It is still common, even in emancipated families, to see the mother light the Sabbath lights and the father say *kiddush*, while children still play their traditionally prominent role during the Passover seder and (girls now generally included) are still expected to study Hebrew and learn about Jewish history and religion, whether in classes at the synagogue or at a Jewish school.

THE JEWISH HOME: SPACE

The Jewish home provides the physical setting for the life of the Jewish family, and indeed is inseparable from it: it is the family that gives a Jewish home its special character. Nevertheless, there are some external signs that mark out the Jewish home, and the most visible is the *mezuzah*, a handwritten parchment contained in an elongated case marked with the Hebrew letter *shin* (for *Shaddai*, an old name of God), and fixed to the doorways of the house. Although these are sometimes described as amulets or talismans, and one sometimes sees pious Jews kissing them on entering or leaving a house, there is nothing magical about them, but they are a reminder of the words of the Torah which are actually inscribed on them: 'You shall write them [the words of the Torah] on the doorposts of your house and upon your gates' (Deuteronomy 6:9). The meaning is understood to be that everything that is done by Jews either inside or outside the home should be marked by an attentiveness to the Torah. It is in obedience to an adjacent verse ('You shall bind them as a sign on your arm and they shall be as frontlets between your eyes', Deuteronomy 6:8, cf. Exodus 13:9) that traditional Jews when they say their weekday morning prayers put on *tefillin* or phylacteries: leather boxes containing similar handwritten texts, and attached to the forehead and upper arm with leather straps.

The fixing of the *mezuzah* on a new home is an occasion for rejoicing. There is a short religious service, known as *Hanukkat Ha-Bayit* ('dedication of the house'), an expression taken from Psalm 30, which is recited on this occasion.

Each room in a Jewish home has its own particular character, but no other room is so stamped by its Jewish identity as the kitchen, particularly in Orthodox and traditional homes, where a rigorous separation is made between milk and meat products, extending to keeping separate cooking utensils, china and cutlery for each, and in very particular households separate fridges and dishwashers. Since during the festival of Passover many of these utensils cannot be used but must be replaced, it can be an expensive operation to equip a Jewish kitchen.

All food served in an observant Jewish home must conform with the rules of *kashrut*. These rules have become very complex over the years, and they are observed more scrupulously in some households than in others. Broadly speaking the rules can be divided into two groups, those determining which species of animal may or may not be eaten, and those concerned with the manner of death, preparation, cooking and serving.

The lists of forbidden and permitted animals are taken from the Torah (Leviticus 11 and Deuteronomy 14:3–21). There are three main classes of permitted animals: quadrupeds, birds and fish. Kosher quadrupeds have to conform to two criteria: they must have cloven hooves and chew the cud. The only animal that has cloven hooves but does not chew the cud is the pig, which may be the reason why the pig has been viewed as the non-kosher animal *par excellence*. Cattle, sheep, goat and deer all come into the category of permitted animals. Horses, which have undivided hooves, as well as animals with paws such as rabbit and hare, are forbidden. As for birds, rather than provide general guidance the Torah lists the ones that are forbidden. As it happens they seem to be birds that kill other animals or fish or that eat carrion. The implication is that all other birds are permitted, but since some doubt exists as to the identity of some of the birds on the list scrupulous Jews only eat domesticated birds that are known by tradition to be kosher, such as chicken, duck, goose, turkey and pigeon. Fish have to have fins and scales, a curious rule, since there do not seem to be any fish that have scales but not fins. By and large this rule causes no difficulties, but rabbis continue to argue over some doubtful cases, such as sturgeon, swordfish and turbot. All other animals are forbidden, except for certain kinds of locust that are specifically permitted.

Animals that are not kosher are called *terefah* (*tref* for short). Even a small quantity of *terefah* can contaminate a dish or foodstuff, and so scrupulous Jews are very attentive to the ingredients of prepared foods, such as biscuits that may be made with animal fat. If a pot or pan in which non-kosher food has been cooked is subsequently used for cooking kosher food it will render it *terefah*, but the utensil may first be cleansed in boiling water. (China and porcelain vessels cannot be cleansed.)

Animals that have been killed by other animals or that have died of their own accord are specifically forbidden (Exodus 22:30; Leviticus 11:39; Deuteronomy 14:21), as is the consumption of the blood of any animal (Leviticus 7:26–27; 17:10–14). This means that only those permitted animals and birds that have been properly slaughtered may be eaten. Elaborate rules have been developed for *shehitah* (slaughter). The butcher or *shohet* must be a person of moral integrity, and his knife must be extremely sharp and free from the slightest nick, so as to avoid inflicting pain on the animal. The animal's throat is cut with a single continuous movement, and the blood is immediately emptied out. An animal that has certain defects or diseases, even if properly slaughtered, is considered as *terefah*, so the butcher will examine the organs, particularly the lungs, with great care, and if necessary will consult a rabbi. Not all parts even of animals that have passed all these tests may be eaten. In particular, the sciatic nerve which runs through the hindquarters is not eaten, by very ancient custom (Genesis 32:32), and since removing it ('porging') is a difficult process, the meat of the hindquarters is not eaten at all in some places, such as Britain. Before the meat may be eaten the remaining blood is drawn out by salting. (Grilling over a naked flame is an acceptable alternative method in the case of liver.) Fish do not need to be killed in a special way or salted, as their blood is not considered to fall under the prohibition.

There is a further set of rules, based on a curious prohibition on eating 'a kid seethed in its mother's milk', which is repeated three times in the Torah (Exodus 23: 19; 34:26; Deuteronomy 14: 21). The rabbis understood this to mean that no kind of meat may be cooked in any kind of milk. As an extra precaution, they forbid the eating of meat and milk products at the same meal, even if they have not been cooked together. This rule in its turn has been extended, so that one has to wait a certain length of time after eating meat before eating dairy products; some people wait as much as six hours. And, as we have already mentioned, it is common for Orthodox Jews to keep separate sets of pots, dishes and cutlery for use with meat and dairy foods.

One way round most of these demanding requirements is not to eat meat, and indeed there are many vegetarian Jews and there are even Jewish vegetarian organisations. Even vegetarians, however, must be on their guard against eating certain foods which transgress against one or other of the food laws, such as an egg with a blood spot, cheese made with animal rennet, or gelatine.

The place of the kitchen in Judaism is captured brilliantly by Lionel Blue:

And the changes of the liturgical year are marked out for the Jew by smell and taste, by the aromas of the kitchen. Through the most basic senses, he feels the changing moods of the spirit. Theologies alter and beliefs may die, but smells always remain in his memory, calling him back to his own childhood and to the childhood of his people. Whatever prayers he may forget, the gastronomic cycle always remains. Passover is the bread of poverty, with tears of salt water, and the horseradish of bitterness. Ruth is cream and cheesecake, and the New Year is the sweetness of apples and honey. Esther comes with poppy seed, and the Maccabees with nuts. The delightful litany only halts to mark the destruction of the past, or days which commemorate the sins of the present. On these tragic and sad days there is a total fast, and the kitchen, the heart and soul of the Jewish home, misses a beat, and a darkness covers this little world.[5]

From the kitchen it is but a short step to the table. In an age when the dignity of the dining room in many homes is being eclipsed, in Jewish homes it still retains its centrality. It is not a formal and secluded room from which children are excluded. At least once a week the whole family gathers round the table for a festive meal with its traditional recipes and rituals. If we imagine this table prepared for the evening meal of the Sabbath or a festival, we must envisage it impeccably laid, with a clean white tablecloth and the finest china and cutlery the family can afford. Our attention may be caught by a pair of silver candlesticks and a silver wine goblet, and an embroidered cloth covering a plaited loaf of bread (*hallah*).

In some homes we may notice some skullcaps, plain or ornamental, for the men and boys to wear while saying the blessings before and after the meal. This is a subject where widely differing views prevail. The covering of the head while praying is not mentioned in the Bible (except that the high priest wore a mitre as part of his official vestments), and as late as the thirteenth century it seems that rabbis in France recited blessings bareheaded. By that time, however, the Babylonian custom of covering the head to pray had gained wide acceptance, and many traditionalist and Orthodox Jews keep their heads covered throughout the day, whether indoors or out. Other Jews cover the head only while in a Jewish home, and others again keep it covered while eating, particularly on Sabbaths and festivals. Reform Judaism was at first opposed to the custom of covering the head, but today many Reform and Liberal Jewish men cover the head to pray. Many women, too, now cover their heads to pray.

It has been said that in the Jewish home the father is a priest and the table an altar. This is the time-honoured ritual of Friday evening or Sabbath Eve. The mother lights the lights, traditionally at a specified time before sunset, but in non-Orthodox homes it is often done at the beginning of the meal. In the past oil lamps were often used, sometimes hanging lamps with seven wicks, to represent the seven days of creation, but today it is usual to light a pair of candles. The children are blessed by their parents, and there may be a song symbolically welcoming angels into the home, and the father may read aloud the praise of the valiant

---

[5] Lionel Blue, *To Heaven, with Scribes and Pharisees* (London, 1975), pp. 39–40.

wife in Proverbs 31:10–31. During the festive meal it is customary to sing table songs (*zemirot*), and afterwards the grace or benediction after food (*birkat ha-mazon*) is sung. The singing is jolly rather than reverential, and the general mood is one of informality and joyfulness.

The Friday evening meal is the high point of the week in a Jewish home, but there are other meals that have their accompaniment of ritual. Traditionally the Sabbath has three meals: the second is lunch on Saturday, and the custom exists in some circles of celebrating a third meal on Sabbath afternoon to intensify and prolong the Sabbath mood. The major festivals are marked by formal meals too: the three 'pilgrim' festivals Pesah (Passover), Shavuot (Pentecost) and Sukkot (Tabernacles) and the two solemn holy days, Rosh Ha-Shanah and Yom Kippur.

The Passover evening meal is unique. The mood is like no other festival, and the preparations may take several days or even weeks. Scattered family members make a point of gathering together for the festival, and it is customary to invite additional guests. The basic rules of the celebration are found in the Torah (Exodus 12–13), but they were considerably elaborated in the Greco-Roman period, and the meal as celebrated today retains noticeable elements from a Roman banquet. These include the custom of reclining on a cushion, and of dipping herbs in salt water or sweet paste.

The bedroom is an area that in the ancient codes is as strictly regulated as the kitchen, but since nowadays such regulations tend to be regarded as an unwarranted intrusion on privacy the rules concerning sexual activity are much less discussed and probably less strictly observed (though this is not easy to ascertain) than the rules of *kashrut*.

The first and greatest restriction concerns who may legitimately have sexual intercourse with whom. In practice this excludes all relations except for those between married couples, and thus incest, group sex and under-age sex are all ruled out by definition. Sexual acts between males are also forbidden, on the basis of a biblical prohibition (Leviticus 18:22, 20:13), but the codes do not dwell on this topic. Lesbian sex, which is not mentioned in the Bible, is forbidden by the codifiers under the rather vague heading of 'Egyptian acts' (Leviticus 18:3). Recently strong arguments have been put forward in progressive circles in favour of tolerating or permitting homosexual acts by both sexes, at least within stable relationships, but Orthodox authorities and a weighty body of Conservative opinion are opposed to this reform. Solitary sex is forbidden for males, who are also encouraged to avoid anything that might lead to it. (The *Zohar* describes it as the most defiling of all sins.) Since this ban is based on a biblical prohibition on 'wasting seed', many authorities hold that it does not apply to women.

Even within marriage sexual activity is closely regulated by the rule books. It is forbidden during the wife's menstrual period and for the seven following days, when she is in a state of ritual impurity according to biblical law (Leviticus 18:19; cf. 15:19–31). She is similarly 'impure' after giving birth (Leviticus 12). During these periods the woman is termed a *niddah*, and the whole subject of *niddah* impurity and the consequent prohibitions is discussed with almost obsessive interest in the various rule books. Nowadays many of the restrictions have been tacitly or explicitly abandoned. The main one, which is supposed to be observed by Orthodox Jews, is to refrain from sexual intercourse, and at the end of the period the wife is to immerse herself in a ritual bath (*mikveh*). After that, normal sexual relations may resume until the next menstrual period.

'Normal sexual relations' are also governed by various rules, specifying for instance that they must be conducted with sobriety and modesty, in darkness, and with the husband uppermost. They are not permitted if the wife is unwilling, or if she is too eager. On the other hand the husband is to have regard to the wife's pleasure, and he is not allowed to deny her sexual intercourse altogether.

While the bathroom has no specified role in the Jewish home (private bathrooms were virtually unknown when the rules evolved), cleanliness is undoubtedly a virtue among Jews, and ritual washing and bathing occupies an important place in traditional observance. Even progressive Jews or secular kibbutzniks will tend to take a bath and dress in clean clothes in readiness for the Sabbath and festivals. The *mikveh* (ritual bath) used to be a feature of every Jewish community, and its demise in modern times has no doubt been favoured by the availability of bathing facilities at home. In addition to full immersion, which requires a *mikveh*, handwashing is mandatory or customary in various circumstances, such as on getting up in the morning, before eating bread, after sexual intercourse and after a burial. In some Jewish homes you will see a small pitcher with two handles, which is used for pouring water over the hands, since water straight from the tap is not adequate for ritual washing.

THE JEWISH HOME: TIME

Time in the Jewish home is regulated by the regular succession of days, weeks and years. On a longer scale it is measured by the lifetime of each member of the family.

The Jewish day begins technically at sunset, which is why the Sabbaths and festivals are marked by lighting candles or oil lamps in the home a little before sunset. Technically the Sabbath ends when three stars have appeared in the sky.

The rhythm of the day is marked for observant Jews by the succession of prayers. There are actually two different cycles: the Shma (which is technically a scriptural reading rather than a prayer) is recited twice daily, in the evening and in the morning, while the statutory prayer or *tefillah* (commonly known as Amidah, 'standing', because it is always recited standing up) is recited three times each day, evening, morning and afternoon (in obedience to a hint in Psalm 55:17). Both the Shma and the Amidah form part of the service of the synagogue, and many Jews prefer to say them, where possible, with a congregation. Nevertheless, strictly speaking there is an obligation for each Jewish man (and woman in the case of the Amidah) to say them even if alone.

The week is made up of seven days, six working days followed by a day of rest, the Sabbath. This pattern is very ancient, as we read in the Torah: 'For six days you shall labour and do all your work, and the seventh day is the Sabbath of the Lord your God, when you shall do no work' (Exodus 20:9–10). The whole week seems to lead up to the Sabbath, and in fact in Hebrew the other days do not have names of their own, but are simply numbered 'first day' (Sunday), 'second day' (Monday) and so on.

Friday is a day of preparation for the Sabbath, particularly in the home, which must be cleaned and tidied, and where the Sabbath meals must be prepared in advance, since no cooking must be done once the Sabbath has begun. (Hot food may however be kept warm.) The table is laid for the evening meal, as we have seen, with a clean white table-cloth, with the best tableware, and with the special candlesticks and wine goblet. The members of the family bathe and dress in clean clothes.

The arrival of the Sabbath is likened to the entry of a bride or a queen. Some sources speak of a Jew possessing an 'additional soul' on the Sabbath, and of the angels that enter the home at this time. It is a time not only of rest from work but of joy and pleasure, which is why there is an emphasis on eating and drinking, and it is considered a particularly propitious time for marital relations.

Sabbath joy is more than the spontaneous relief of hardworking people who are enjoying a break from their labours. It has something of a religious character, and is known in Hebrew as *oneg*, in allusion to a passage of the Prophet Isaiah (58:13–14):

If you turn back your foot from the Sabbath, from doing your own will on My holy day, and call the Sabbath a joy and the Lord's holy day honoured, and if you honour it by not doing your own ways, finding your own will, speaking your own word, then you will rejoice in the Lord, and I shall let you mount upon the high places of the world, and feed you with the inheritance of your father Jacob. The word of the Lord has spoken.

The joy of the Sabbath is thus not an expression of material enjoyment and crude merrymaking, but is closely linked to observing the command to 'Remember the Sabbath day to keep it holy' (Exodus 20:8).

The primary reason given for the observance of the Sabbath in the Torah is as a commemoration of the creation of the world, when God is described poetically as resting on the seventh day. 'For in six days the Lord made heaven and earth and the sea, and everything that is in them, and rested on the seventh day; therefore the Lord blessed the Sabbath day and declared it holy' (Exodus 20:11; cf. Genesis 2:2–3). All forms of work are forbidden, and this is understood to include writing and handling money, as well as switching on a light or electrical appliance and driving or riding in a motor vehicle. For those who observe the rules stringently the Sabbath really is a time apart from weekday life, when the very rhythm and texture of living are different. Conservative Jews tend to make some concessions, for example by switching on lights or driving to synagogue, and Reform Jews are more permissive still, but all alike strive to make the time of the Sabbath different from the rest of the week. The Sabbath is a holy day, and 'holiness' (*kodesh*) in Hebrew has more of the sense of difference than of spiritual elevation, though this too has its place in Sabbath observance, particularly for the more mystical wing of Judaism. The kabbalists, in welcoming the Sabbath as a bride, imagine that they are welcoming the Shekhinah, the presence of God. On this day the male and female elements in the Godhead are united, hence the souls that enter children conceived on the Sabbath are particularly sublime.

The Hasidim take the rejoicing on the Sabbath particularly seriously. Before the beginning of the holy day they purify themselves by immersion in the *mikveh*, and they dress in special clothes. Setting aside an old prohibition, they are fond of dancing on the Sabbath, and they experience the holiness of the day with great intensity. When they eat the Sabbath meals in the presence of their leader, the Tsaddik, he passes around to his followers food from the dishes he has tasted. Hasidim are particularly aware of the mystical dimension of the Sabbath at the third meal, in the afternoon. As the light fades they listen to the teaching of the Tsaddik, communicated to him by the Shekhinah. They also have an additional meal after the departure of the Sabbath, to escort it on its way.

The end of the Sabbath, when three stars have appeared in the sky, is marked by the ceremony of *havdalah* ('distinction'). As the Sabbath is welcomed with light and wine, so it is seen out with light and wine, and additionally with fragrant spices. The special spice-boxes are often beautifully made, and the candle is plaited so that it has several wicks. The prayer for this occasion praises God 'who makes a distinction between holy and profane, between light and darkness, between Israel and the other peoples, between the seventh day and the six working days'. Afterwards it is customary to sing songs in praise of Elijah, the harbinger of the Messiah. With this joyful and attractive ceremony the Sabbath fades gradually once more into the mood of the working week.

The Jewish year is essentially lunar, and indeed in ancient times the day of the new moon (Rosh Hodesh) was important enough to be compared to the Sabbath (e.g. 2 Kings 4:23, Isaiah 1:13) although nowadays it is a minor observance. Work is permitted, although there is an old tradition that women have a holiday from work, and there is a tendency now to see Rosh Hodesh as a women's festival. Beginning in the United States in the early 1970s, Orthodox women's prayer groups are held on Rosh Hodesh, and groups of women gather to perform rituals celebrating rebirth and renewal. Originally the occurrence of the new moon was determined by observation; the calendar was fixed by calculation in the fourth century, and still corresponds to the observable phases of the moon. Each month has either twenty-nine or thirty days.

The calendar is not purely lunar, however, for if it were the festivals would move round the cycle of the seasons, whereas Passover must fall in the spring, the season at which the exodus from Egypt took place. This adjustment is achieved by 'intercalating' an additional month seven times in every nineteen years. The additional month is inserted before the month in which Passover falls.

All Jews today share this calendar (with the exception of the few remaining Karaites, whose calendar is a little different). There is, however, a discrepancy with regard to the so-called 'second days' of festivals. Jews in Israel follow the biblical rules with regard to the three 'pilgrim festivals', Passover (the first and seventh days are full festivals), Pentecost (one day) and Tabernacles (the first and eighth days are full festivals). According to ancient custom, Jews outside Israel added an extra day to each of these, probably because of uncertainty before the calendar was fixed. Today Reform Jews in the Diaspora have reverted to the biblical dates, and some Conservative rabbis are in favour of doing likewise. New Year, however, which was a one-day festival in the Bible, is celebrated for two days both within and outside Israel, except among some Reform Jews, who prefer to follow the biblical practice.

The cycle of the year in the home is marked by the two major religious observances of Passover in the late spring and Rosh Ha-Shanah (New Year) at the end of the summer, five and a half months later. The home is cleaned and prepared in readiness for both festivals, but Passover requires more thoroughgoing preparation because of the religious requirements of the festival. According to the Torah, 'no *hamets* or leaven shall be seen within your limits' (Exodus 13:7; cf. 12: 15, 19). *Hamets* is understood to refer to grains that have sprouted or cereal products that have become leavened. The house, and particularly the kitchen, is therefore subjected to a very thorough springcleaning. Old food is thrown out and fresh food is brought in, and bread is replaced by unleavened bread, *matsah*, for the period of the festival, which lasts seven days according to the Torah (eight days in many homes outside Israel). All Jewish festivals have their own recipes and flavours, but Passover food is a world of its own, to which whole books have been devoted. Pots and pans, plates and dishes, knives and forks must all be specially treated, discarded or withdrawn from use, and some households keep a special set of kitchen utensils and tableware to be used only at Passover. According to old custom a '*hamets*-hunt' takes place the evening before the festival commences, with a few crumbs being left deliberately to be found and ceremoniously swept up, to be burnt the next morning.

Traditionally all members of the family should prepare themselves by having their hair cut and by bathing. Technically first-born sons are supposed to fast on the day leading up to the seder, in remembrance of the killing of the Egyptian first-born (Exodus 12:29), although this fast is not much observed today.

On the morning preceding the festival the preparations intensify. The last *hamets* is burnt, and after mid-morning no more *hamets* may be eaten. The evening meal, the seder, is a feast, and for many Jewish homes this is the largest and most festive dinner of the year. Special dishes are prepared for the meal itself, and each family has its own favourites. It is common to begin the meal with hard-boiled eggs in salt water.

Symbolic foods adorn the table: three sheets of *matsah* (unleavened bread), serving as a reminder that the Israelites left Egypt in such haste that there was no time to let the dough rise; *maror* or bitter herbs, commonly represented by horseradish, because the Egyptians embittered the lives of the slaves; *pesah* (Passover offering) is a lamb, appointed in the Torah to be eaten as the meal of the day. Nowadays lamb is avoided for the actual meal, but a roasted shank bone reminds the company of the days when the sacrificial offering was made. A roasted egg is another reminder of the sacrifices. There are also green leaves (*karpas*), because this is the spring time, salt water for the tears of the afflicted, and a sweet reddish-brown paste called *haroset* which is said to evoke the mortar used by the slaves in construction work.[6] Each of these foods has its place in the ritual.

Wine plays a special part in the seder. Each participant is supposed to drink at least four glasses, and an extra goblet is placed on the table for the prophet Elijah, who according to folk belief will come again to herald the Messiah.

The participants in the seder dress as they would for a formal dinner or special occasion. In some Ashkenazi families it is still the custom that the head of the household, who will lead the ceremonies, wears a *kittel*, a white tunic that is one of the burial shrouds.

The book of words containing the Bible readings and prayers, and often useful reminders about the conduct of the seder, is known as the Haggadah ('recitation'). The text is very old: although some songs were added in the Middle Ages the main text goes back to the time of the early rabbis.

The rituals of the seder are strictly laid down by tradition and followed in due order. The first of the four glasses of wine is for the *kiddush* of the festival, which opens the proceedings. Those present then wash their hands (an ewer and basin are passed round the table for this purpose). Then the leader, normally the master of the house, dips some parsley or another salad vegetable in salt water and passes it around to everyone. He takes the middle *matsah* of the three, breaks it in half, and sets one half aside. This is the *afikoman*, the symbolism of which is now shrouded in obscurity. The custom is for the children during the meal to steal the *afikoman* (often it is hidden for them to find) and hold it to ransom, as the seder cannot continue without it. The narration proper then commences, in response to four questions usually asked by the youngest child:

Why is this night different from all other nights?
On all other nights we eat either leavened or unleavened bread: why tonight do we only eat unleavened bread?

---

[6] For some recipes see Claudia Roden, *The Book of Jewish Food* (London, 1997).

Tishri		Heshvan		Kislev		Tevet		Shevat		Adar	
1	ROS HA-SHANAH (New Year)	1		1		1	◊◊◊◊◊◊◊◊	1		1	
2		2		2		2	◊◊◊◊◊◊◊◊	2		2	
3	Fast	3		3		3		3		3	
4		4		4		4		4		4	
5		5		5		5		5		5	
6		6		6		6		6		6	
7		7		7		7		7		7	
8		8		8		8		8		8	
9		9		9		9		9		9	
10	YOM KIPPUR (Day of Atonement)	10		10		10	Fast	10		10	
11		11		11		11		11		11	
12		12		12		12		12		12	
13		13		13		13		13		13	Fast of Esther
14		14		14		14		14		14	PURIM
15	SUKKOT (Tabernacles)	15		15		15		15	New Year of Trees	15	
16		16		16		16		16		16	
17		17		17		17		17		17	
18		18		18		18		18		18	
19		19		19		19		19		19	
20		20		20		20		20		20	
21		21		21		21		21		21	
22	SHEMINI ATSERET	22		22		22		22		22	
23	SIMHAT TORAH*	23		23		23		23		23	
24		24		24		24		24		24	
25		25		25	HANUKKAH ◊	25		25		25	
26		26		26	◊◊	26		26		26	
27		27		27	◊◊◊	27		27		27	
28		28		28	◊◊◊◊	28		28		28	
29		29		29	◊◊◊◊◊	29		29		29	
30				30	◊◊◊◊◊◊			30			

■ High holy days □ Other festive days

■ Pilgrim festivals □ Minor fasts and solemn periods

*Extra day of festival not observed in Israel or by Reform communities

4. The Jewish calendar

Nisan		Iyyar		Sivan		Tammuz		Av		Elul	
1		1		1		1		1		1	
2		2		2		2		2		2	
3		3		3		3		3		3	
4		4		4		4		4		4	
5		5	Israeli Independence Day	5		5		5		5	
6		6		6	SHAVUOT (Pentecost)	6		6		6	
7		7		7	*	7		7		7	
8		8		8		8		8		8	
9		9		9		9		9	Fast	9	
10		10		10		10		10		10	
11		11		11		11		11		11	
12		12		12		12		12		12	
13		13		13		13		13		13	
14	Fast of the Firstborn	14		14		14		14		14	
15	PESAH (Passover)	15		15		15		15		15	
16		16		16		16		16		16	
17		17		17		17	Fast	17		17	
18		18	Lag Ba-Omer	18		18		18		18	
19		19		19		19		19		19	
20		20		20		20		20		20	
21	PESAH (Last Day)	21		21		21		21		21	
22	*	22		22		22		22		22	
23		23		23		23		23		23	
24		24		24		24		24		24	
25		25		25		25		25		25	
26		26		26		26		26		26	
27	Holocaust Remembrance Day	27		27		27		27		27	
28		28		28		28		28		28	
29		29		29		29		29		29	
30				30				30			

On all other nights we eat all kinds of herbs: why tonight do we eat bitter herbs?

On all other nights we do not dip our herbs even once: why tonight do we dip them twice?

On all other nights we eat either sitting or reclining: why tonight do we all recline?

The reply begins:

We were Pharaoh's slaves in Egypt. The Lord our God brought us out from there by power and force. And if the Holy One, blessed be He, had not brought our ancestors out of Egypt, then we, our children, and our grandchildren would continue to be enslaved to Pharaoh in Egypt. That is why, however wise or clever or old we are, however knowledgeable in Torah, we must obey the command to talk about the Exodus from Egypt. The more one talks about it, the more praiseworthy it is.

There follows a lengthy series of comments on the biblical account of the Exodus, and in some homes, not content with reciting the traditional texts, the participants add their own explanations, and their own comments on the theme of liberation, because the theme of Passover is not only the historical exodus but everything it symbolises, including the contemporary political implications of freedom as well as its moral and spiritual dimensions, and also the future redemption. The three main symbols, the roast lamb, unleavened bread and bitter herbs, are each singled out and explained, and then the Hallel is recited, consisting of Psalms 113 to 118, followed on this occasion by the 'Great Hallel', Psalm 136.

The Hallel is interrupted by the meal. (Originally the meal was eaten at the beginning, before the four questions, which are evidently a response to it.) There is a series of blessings before the meal, on wine (the second glass), handwashing, bread and *matsah* (of course *matsah* is used for both of these, since leavened bread is strictly forbidden), and *maror* (bitter herbs). Pieces of horseradish are generally used for *maror*; first they are dipped in the sweet paste, *haroset*, and then they are eaten in the form of a sandwich between two pieces of *matsah*. After the meal, when the *afikoman* has been bought back from the children, it is broken in pieces which are either eaten or kept until the next Passover. Then grace after meals is sung, followed by the drinking of the third glass of wine.

After the end of the Hallel there are some prayers, and then the fourth glass of wine is drunk, at which point the proceedings are technically over, and the following concluding hymn is sung:

The Passover seder is concluded
According to custom and ordinance.
As we have been found worthy to celebrate it
So may we be found worthy to celebrate it again.
Pure One, dwelling in Your habitation,
Raise up the countless congregation.
Take and lead the saplings of Your stock –
Redeemed with joyous song – to Zion.
NEXT YEAR IN JERUSALEM!

The evening does not end here, however, but a cheerful singsong ensues, a reward for the children who have stayed awake this long.

Those families that keep the festivals for two days will have a second seder the following night; the rest have only one seder, and for these at the end of the first day, which is marked in the home by a festive midday meal, full festival changes to *hol ha-moed*, an in-between time that shares in the sanctity of the festival but on which work, at least of the more essential kind, is permitted. The special food laws continue to be observed, and only unleavened bread may be eaten. The cakes and biscuits cannot be made with flour; delicious pastries are made with other ingredients, notably almonds and cinnamon. The seventh day (seventh and eighth for those who keep two days) is a full festival, with further feasting.

On the second evening, according to an ancient custom, there begins a period of seven weeks known as the 'Counting of the Omer'. (The *omer*, 'sheaf' was a harvest offering that was formerly brought to the Temple on the second day of the festival: Leviticus 23:9–14.) It is customary to count the days and weeks aloud, and some families have an '*omer* board' which helps them to keep count. For reasons which remain unclear the counting of the *omer* became a period of sadness, during which weddings do not take place. Orthodox Jews do not shave or have their hair cut. The thirty-third day (known as Lag Ba-Omer) is, however, a joyful day, when marriages are permitted. The origin and significance of the day are obscure; it has attracted various folkloric practices, particularly among kabbalists, who consider it to be the anniversary of the death (or as they euphemistically say the 'marriage') of one of their greatest saints, Simeon bar Yohai, whom they consider to be the author of their holy book, the *Zohar*. At his grave in the Galilean village of Meron they dance around fires singing hymns in his honour, and three-year-old children have their hair cut for the first time. In the West there are no particular observances for Lag Ba-Omer.

After the end of the seven weeks of the *omer* comes the festival of Pentecost or Shavuot, which is understood to commemorate the giving of the Torah at Mount Sinai. There are no specific rituals in the home, but it is customary to decorate the home with greenery and flowers, and to serve dairy products such as cheesecake or *blintses* (cheese pancakes). As on the other pilgrim festivals and Rosh Ha-Shanah, all work is forbidden and a mood of joyful rest pervades the home.

In the course of the summer three weeks of solemnity are observed, beginning with the fast of Tammuz (which usually falls in July) and ending with the fast of the ninth of Av. Weddings are not celebrated during these three weeks, and some Jews also refrain from buying new clothes, wearing clean clothes, having their hair cut, or eating meat or wine on weekdays. (Others only apply these restrictions during the last nine days, while many, perhaps most, ignore them entirely.)

As the summer proceeds towards its end Jews become increasingly aware of the approach of the most solemn festivals of the year, Rosh Ha-Shanah and Yom Kippur. Penitential prayers (*selihot*) are recited, and it is customary to visit the graves of parents or close relatives at this time. Rosh Ha-Shanah means 'New Year' (although in the Torah the year is said to start in the spring, in the month of Passover). This New Year festival is not, however, a time of uproarious celebration, but of serious reflection and self-examination. It is also known as Yom Ha-Din, 'Day of Judgment': it is taught that at this time all Jews are judged in relation to their actions during the preceding year, and that on Yom Kippur, the Day of Atonement, nine days later, their fate is sealed. The synagogue liturgy of these Days of Awe is sternly adorned with allusions to God's majesty and all-seeing justice. Yet in the home something of the sweetness of the festival comes out, in the usual festive family meals, and particularly in the custom of dipping the bread at the beginning of the meal into honey rather than salt, and then of eating apple dipped in honey, accompanied with the wish to be granted 'a good, sweet year'. The loaf itself is plaited in a round shape rather than the usual elongated form, perhaps to indicate that like the year it has no real beginning or end.[7] But the joyful theme yields to a more sombre mood of repentance in the Ashkenazi folk ceremony of *tashlikh*, when Jews go to water, preferably to a river or the sea where there are fish, and shake their clothes as if to cast off every trace of sin, while reciting appropriate biblical verses, such as Micah 7:18–20, which contains the words 'and you shall cast (*tashlikh*)

---

[7] For other food customs observed on this festival see Roden, *The Book of Jewish Food*, pp. 27–8.

into the depths of the sea all their sins'. The origin of this practice is unknown, and there is no mention of it before the fifteenth century: it may represent a Jewish adaptation of a pagan ritual.

The days from Rosh Ha-Shanah to Yom Kippur are known as the Ten Days of Penitence, and their mood is unrelievedly chastened. This is the last opportunity to make amends for sins of commission or omission in the hope of obtaining a favourable judgment before the heavenly ledgers are finally closed. Some rise early to recite penitential prayers, and read improving tracts. It is recommended to seek forgiveness from all those one may have wronged during the year just elapsed, so as to be able to concentrate one's efforts on atoning for sins against God. The third day of the month is a minor fast, known as the fast of Gedaliah. On the morning preceding Yom Kippur some still perform the colourful ceremony known as *kapparot*, 'atonements'. A white fowl is taken, a cock for a man or a hen for a woman, and waved three times round the head, with the words: 'This is my substitute, this is my vicarious offering, this is my atonement. This fowl will go to its death, but may I enjoy a long, pleasant and peaceful life.' The bird is then slaughtered, and the meat is given to the poor, or it is eaten and its value given to the poor in money. Once widespread, this folk custom was vigorously opposed by Sephardi rabbis, but it has retained its popularity among Sephardim as well as Ashkenazim to this day, testifying, like *tashlikh*, to the persistence of folklore. Pious Jews also bathe in the *mikveh* on the eve of the fast, perhaps as a symbol of the washing away of sins, or in recollection of a celebrated play on words ascribed to Rabbi Akiva: the prophet Jeremiah (17:13) calls God the *mikveh* (meaning 'hope') of Israel. 'As the *mikveh* cleanses the unclean, so does the Holy One, blessed be He, cleanse Israel.'[8]

The great fast of Yom Kippur is the one day of the Jewish year in which the home plays no part. Eating and drinking, washing, the use of unguents and the wearing of leather shoes, and even sexual relations are forbidden. The scene of activity shifts to the synagogue, and it even used to be customary for worshippers to remain there all night in prayer, turning their backs on the comfort of home and bed. The solemn fast is framed, however, by two family meals, and it is taught by way of discouraging asceticism that it is as praiseworthy to dine well beforehand as it is to fast. A candle is lit that will burn throughout the twenty-five hours of the fast.

---

[8] Mishnah, *Yoma* 8:9.

Immediately after breaking their fast some families make a point of making a start with the construction of the *sukkah*, in readiness for the festival of Tabernacles (Sukkot), which follows only five days later. A *sukkah* is a simple, impermanent structure roofed with greenery thin enough to allow the stars to be glimpsed. It must be built out of doors, so as to be exposed to the elements, but it is permissible to build it on a roof or an open balcony. It is made in obedience to the Torah, where God states (Leviticus 23:42–5): 'You shall live in huts (*sukkot*) for seven days; all native-born Israelites shall live in huts, so that future genera-tions may know that I made the Israelites live in huts when I brought them out of the Land of Egypt.' Theoretically, therefore, one should take all one's meals in the *sukkah* and even sleep in it for the seven days of the festival. (There is no obligation to do either if the rain is coming in.) In accordance with the principle of 'adorning the precepts' (*hiddur mitsvah*) it is customary to decorate the *sukkah* with flowers and fruit, and it is also customary to invite guests to share the joy of the *sukkah*. There are also invisible holy guests (*ushpizin*, from the Latin *hospites*, 'guests'), the biblical heroes Abraham, Isaac, Jacob, Joseph, Moses, Aaron and David, whose presence is welcomed on successive evenings with elaborate greet-ings composed by Isaac Luria, the kabbalist of Safed in the sixteenth century.

The festival week of Tabernacles concludes with the riotous joy of Simhat Torah (Rejoicing in the Torah). Although the proper place for this celebration is the synagogue, where the scrolls are lodged, the joy-fulness is so intense that it spills over into the home and even the street, with singing and dancing, and a certain amount of alcoholic indulgence.

Tabernacles marks the end of an intense and often draining period of mingled festivities and solemnities, and it is with some sense of relief that the Jewish family looks forward to the relatively quiet period that follows. The gloom and darkness of winter are relieved by the eight-day joyful-ness of Hanukkah (meaning 'dedication'), commemorating the rededi-cation of the Jerusalem temple by the Maccabees after it had been desecrated by the Seleucid hellenisers in the second century BCE. Hanukkah is a minor festival: there is no feasting, and it is not a holiday from work. The main way it is observed is by lighting oil lamps or candles, one on the first evening, two on the second, and so on, until on the eighth evening eight lights are lit. On each evening an additional 'servant' light (*shammash*) is used to light the main lights. Special lamps or candle-holders (known by the name of *menorah* or *hanukiyyah*) are used, sometimes devised in fanciful styles, and they are placed in a window so as to shine out into the darkness. The lighting of the lamps is accompanied by special prayers, and the singing of a much-loved hymn, *Ma'oz Tsur*, 'Fortress, Rock of my salvation, it is pleasant to sing your praise. Restore my house of prayer, and there we shall offer thanksgiving...' A special blessing praises God for 'performing miracles on those days at this season'. Among the ancillary customs that have grown up, children are given gifts of cash, and play gambling games with little spinning tops inscribed with four Hebrew letters, while their parents may play cards. Fried foods, such as *latkes* (potato pancakes), doughnuts or fritters, are eaten.

A few weeks after Hanukkah comes another minor observance, the 'new year of trees', the 15th of Shevat or Tu Bi-Shevat, celebrated by tree-planting and by eating fruits, particularly those that come from the land of Israel.

The month of Adar (February/March) is described as the happiest month of the year, because on the 14th there falls the joyful celebration of Purim. This is the month that is repeated in intercalated years, and when this happens Purim falls in the second Adar, so that it is always a month before Passover. Purim, like Hanukkah, is a minor festival, but its theme is a major one for Jews: deliverance from persecution. Tradition lays down various observances, such as a fast on the preceding day and a feast on the day itself, charitable gifts, and taking food to friends or neighbours, but the most striking features of the home celebration are the licence, indeed encouragement, to drink to the point of oblivion, and a riotous carnival atmosphere, with the wearing of masks and fancy dress (even cross-dressing, forbidden in the Torah, is tolerated). Children act out the story of Queen Esther, and three-cornered pastries filled with poppy seeds, known as 'Haman's ears' or 'Haman's pockets', are traditionally eaten.

RITES OF PASSAGE

The lifetime of each Jew is marked by joyful or sad ceremonies marking moments of transition from one status to another. Some of these ceremonies find an echo in the synagogue and the wider community, but their primary focus is generally within the home.

The Jewish home is built upon the institution of marriage. It is considered a binding obligation to 'be fruitful and multiply', which is said to be the first commandment uttered by God to mankind (Genesis 1:28; cf. 9:1, 7); but marriage is also praised as conferring joy, love and harmony.

Both the institution and its ceremonies have evolved considerably over the centuries. In the West, under Christian influence, there is a certain tendency for marriages to be performed in synagogue with a rabbi officiating and delivering an address, and with bridesmaids and a best man. Traditionally, however, the couple marry each other with no need of an officiant, and the ceremony may take place at home or even in the open air. It is performed under a canopy known as a *huppah*, and the term *huppah* has come to be used of the marriage itself. There are many variations in the details, but the following account, based on the Orthodox marriage ceremony, includes the most widely followed practices.

A marriage document or *ketubah* is first drawn up and witnessed, stating the date and place and recording the husband's acceptance of his obligations towards his wife, and the amount that he will pay her if he divorces her. It includes these words: 'I faithfully promise that I will be a true husband to you, I will honour and cherish you, I will work for you, I will protect and support you, and will provide everything that is necessary for your due sustenance, as it is fitting for a Jewish husband to do.' (Reform Judaism favours a reciprocal marriage ceremony and an egalitarian *ketubah*.) This legal document, traditionally drawn up in Aramaic, is sometimes richly illuminated. It is signed by two witnesses. Without a *ketubah* it is not strictly legal for husband and wife to live together.

Marriage is an occasion for rejoicing, but it is also a solemn moment for the bride and bridegroom, and they are supposed to fast from dawn until the end of the ceremony. Mindful of the serious responsibilities they are undertaking, when they say their prayers they include a confession of sins and some penitential passages. It used to be customary for the bridegroom to wear for the first time during the ceremony the *kittel*, the death-robe which he would put on each year at the Passover seder and the Day of Atonement, and in which he would be buried: this shroud was a gift from his bride. 'It is truly a unique wedding gift. It serves to remind us that in the midst of life we are near death.'[9]

The bride and bridegroom are escorted to the *huppah* by their parents, who stand under the *huppah* with them, the bride and groom facing towards the east. The ensuing ceremony is in two parts, representing two stages which in ancient times were completely separate, the betrothal (*erusin* or *kiddushin*) and the marriage proper (*nisuin*). After some opening songs and prayers, the officiant says the blessing over wine and then recites the benediction for betrothal. The bride and groom sip the wine,

---

[9] Maybaum, *The Jewish Home*, p. 125.

and the groom places a ring on the bride's right forefinger, saying: 'Behold, you are betrothed to me by this ring according to the law of Moses and Israel.' (In egalitarian marriages there is an exchange of rings.) The *ketubah* is then read out, and this concludes the first stage, the betrothal ceremony. In the second stage seven benedictions are recited, linking the marriage on the one hand to the creation of mankind and on the other to the future redemption. The seventh blessing runs as follows:

> Blessed are you, Lord our God, king of the universe, who created joy and gladness, bridegroom and bride, mirth and song, jubilation and merriment, love and companionship, peace and friendship. Soon, Lord our God, may there be heard in the cities of Judah and in the streets of Jerusalem sounds of joy and gladness, the voices of bridegroom and bride, jubilant voices of bridegrooms from their bridal canopy and of young people feasting and singing. Blessed are you, Lord, who make the bridegroom rejoice with the bride.

After another sip of wine the bridegroom breaks a glass, an ancient custom whose significance has been lost. It may have been intended originally to avert the forces of evil – or perhaps it is to remind the couple and their guests of the fragility of all happiness. Technically the marriage is incomplete without being consummated by sexual union, symbolised by the bride and bridegroom spending some moments together after the ceremony. (This is known as *yihud*, 'unification'.) The marriage is also incomplete without feasting and dancing. (In very traditional circles the men and women dance separately.) The meal ends with a special grace, followed by a repetition of the seven blessings.

A good marriage is a blessed ideal, but Jewish law recognises that sometimes it cannot be achieved, and makes provision for divorce. The Jewish attitude to divorce is pragmatic: whatever the attitude may have been in earlier times, today it is seen as a matter for regret and is only practised as a last resort, when the marriage has irretrievably broken down. However, the sources speak of it in a matter-of-fact way, and no particular stigma attaches to a divorcee. As with the marriage, so with divorce: it is a matter for the couple themselves and not the state or the court. A rabbinic court is, however, invoked to ensure that the instrument of divorce, a document known as the *get*, is correctly drawn up and delivered, since any technical fault may render the divorce invalid and prevent a subsequent remarriage. The *get* is written by a qualified scribe, and is delivered by the husband to the wife in the presence of two witnesses, who sign the document. Once the *get* has been duly delivered the parties are free to remarry, just as widows or widowers are.

The birth of a child is a happy event. In fact, as we have seen, it is considered to be mandatory to have children (defined minimally as a son and a daughter), and to have a large family has traditionally been seen as a blessing. Even Orthodox authorities, however, do not rule out birth control entirely, once the basic command to reproduce has been complied with, although they tend to limit it to cases where the wife's life might be endangered by a pregnancy. Conservative and Reform rabbis are more lenient.

Traditional Judaism has been more welcoming of boy children than of girls. The Torah prescribes that a mother is ritually impure for seven days after giving birth to a son and for twice as long for a daughter, and there is even a view, also rooted in the Torah, that the periods should be forty and eighty days respectively. After the birth of a son there is the excitement and festivity of the circumcision ceremony, when the child receives his name, together with a series of feasts on the Friday evening after the birth, a week after the circumcision, and at the age of one month in the case of a first-born, but there is no such public rejoicing over a daughter. The Talmud records a statement: 'Happy is the man who has male children, and woe to the man who has female children.' Naturally this kind of sexual discrimination is anathema to the more liberal wing of Judaism, and even within Orthodoxy some feminists have rebelled against it and devised ceremonies to mark the birth of a girl.

Circumcision, a minor surgical operation involving the removal of the prepuce, is a religious obligation devolving upon the father (though he is usually only too happy to delegate it to a specialist circumciser, termed a *mohel*). It is an occasion for rejoicing: it is customary to assemble a gathering of family and friends, and to serve a festive meal afterwards. Circumcision is a visible sign of the covenant between God and the Jewish people (although it should be noted that a son of a Jewish mother who for whatever reason is not circumcised is still Jewish). It is known in Hebrew as *brit milah*, 'covenant of circumcision', or more commonly simply as *brit*, 'covenant'. It is therefore the first stage of a process that will be completed at the age of thirteen when the child comes of age legally, and takes upon himself the obligations laid down in the Torah. This being so, it is hardly surprising that both occasions are marked by festivity and joyfulness. It used to be a custom to embroider the baby's swaddling band with his name and the date of the circumcision, and the hope that he may achieve Bar Mitsvah, marriage and good deeds (a form of words taken from the blessings recited on this occasion). The band was donated to the synagogue, where it was used to bind the scroll of the Torah.

The proper age for circumcision is the eighth day, that is the same day as the birth but a week later (see Genesis 17:12, Leviticus 12:3). However, this is understood as a minimum age, and the circumcision may be deferred for reasons of health.

Circumcision may be performed at home, in synagogue, or in any other place. (If the eighth day falls on Yom Kippur it is performed in synagogue, since that is where the congregation is assembled.) A couple, sometimes an engaged or childless couple, are designated as godparents, and they hand the baby to the *sandek*, the person who will hold the child during the proceedings. Before the circumcision the *mohel* recites a blessing, and afterwards the father and the *mohel* both recite special blessings. The child is then given a Hebrew name, in the form of a patronymic – N son of N. This is the name by which he will be named all through his life in synagogue, and which will be inscribed on his *ketubah* and his tombstone. The baby is given a drop or two of wine, and the father and mother drink some wine. (In traditional circles the mother is not present in the room, and the goblet of wine is taken out to her.) After the festive meal which follows there is a special form of grace, invoking blessings on the parents, the child, the *mohel* and the *sandek*.

An ancient rite which is still observed by traditionalists is the 'redemption of the first-born son' or *pidyon ha-ben*. It is performed when the child is thirty days old, since before that time the life of the new-born child is not considered to be decisively established. In the Torah God gives this instruction to Moses: 'Dedicate to me every first-born, the first fruit of every womb among the Israelites, whether of human or beast: it is mine' (Exodus 13:2). This instruction is understood to apply only to male children: a daughter does not have the status of a first-born. The child is ceremonially purchased back (the original meaning of 'redemption') from a priest (*kohen*) who is invited to share in a festive meal. The priest asks the father whether he prefers to hand over his son or five pieces of silver. The father hands over five coins, and various blessings are recited.

It is interesting to compare the destiny of the two rituals, circumcision and the redemption of the first-born. Both are very ancient, being grounded in the Torah. Both concern new-born babies, an area in which superstition is rampant. Both are open to similar rational objections: they are remote from real life in the modern world, and are blatantly sexist. Additionally, circumcision is aesthetically repugnant to many people, and carries with it a small but real risk to the health of the child. For this reason, if one of the two had to die out, it might have been supposed it would be circumcision. And yet circumcision, even after coming under outspoken attack in the nineteenth-century Reform movement and having betrayed countless Jewish men and children to death at the hands of the Nazis and their collaborators, is maintained by the vast majority of Jewish families today (even if they often resort in the West to the services of a surgeon rather than a *mohel*), whereas the redemption of the first-born is all but forgotten. The answer probably lies precisely in the role of circumcision as a factor in Jewish identity. It has come to be seen as the outward mark of a Jewish man, and it may be that in an age when other visible signs of Jewish identity have progressively disappeared it became all the more important to hang on to this one. Even so critical a Jew as Spinoza could say: 'Such great importance do I attach to the sign of the covenant that I am persuaded that it is sufficient by itself to maintain the separate existence of the nation for ever.'

The period of childhood runs officially up to the age of twelve for a girl and thirteen for a boy. Traditional Judaism imposes very few restrictions on children. They are not considered legally responsible (their parents carrying the responsibility for their actions). In traditionalist circles no distinction is made between boys and girls until the age of three. From this age a girl is protected from being alone with a male aged nine years or over, and a boy's hair will now be cut short, with the exception of the side-curls that are left hanging over the ears, in obedience to an instruction in the Torah (Leviticus 19:27). He will begin to wear a skullcap (*kippah*) on his head, and a fringed undergarment (*tallit katan*) under his shirt, and his education will commence. These customs are not observed by the majority of western Jews.

The education of children is the responsibility of the parents, and specifically the father. The instruction to teach the Torah 'to your children' is repeated twice in the Shma. Unfortunately the Hebrew word for 'children' is ambiguous: it can also mean 'sons', and there is disagreement both about the original meaning of the instruction and about the way in which it should be carried out today. Many traditionalists argue that only sons should be educated, since the full weight of Jewish observance falls on them. Traditionally it is true that Jewish education was largely confined to males. With the breakdown of male dominance of the religion among Reform and later among Conservative Jews the education of girls has gradually come to be accepted, at least in the West, and changing attitudes have begun to percolate into Orthodox circles too. Nowadays a majority of Jewish girls receive some form of education about Judaism, although at the more traditional end of the spectrum it may not be strictly comparable to that dispensed to boys, either in quantity or in content. In some respects traditionalist girls may receive a broader education than boys, who are expected to concentrate on the study of the Talmud and the minutiae of the *halakhah*.

The passage from childhood to adulthood at twelve or thirteen is marked, at least for boys and increasingly for girls too, by family celebrations that can sometimes reach exorbitant proportions. From this age, early though it may seem, Jews are technically of marriageable age, and in traditional societies the broking of a suitable match becomes a prominent preoccupation of the parents, particularly for daughters. The professional matchmaker (*shadkhan*) used to be a familiar figure in the ghetto; his activity has been replaced not only by the amateur efforts of family and friends but by specialised Jewish dating agencies. Jewish youth clubs, of a religious, political or sporting nature, play their part in helping to bring about suitable matches, which in practice means ensuring that Jews marry other Jews. There is understandable anxiety about the future of Judaism in an open society, particularly in the absence of any real tradition of growth through conversion, and exogamy (generally referred to as 'marrying out', 'intermarriage', or in a vaguer way as 'assimilation') is seen instinctively by many as the main threat. This is the reason why membership of Jewish youth clubs is frequently restricted to Jews, a restriction that occasionally gives rise to misunderstanding and even resentment. In Israel the state makes no provision for marriage between members of different religious communities; although this policy is no doubt effective up to a point in limiting exogamy, it is perceived by many as an intolerable curb on personal freedom, and there are increasingly vocal demands for it to be abandoned. In any case, Jewish Israelis who are determined to marry non-Jews may do so abroad, in which case their marriage is recognised in Israel. Young Jews sometimes complain of the pressures that are put on them to marry, and specifically to marry Jews. Even homosexuality is not taken very seriously as a valid reason for not marrying. Orthodox authorities tend to insist that homosexuals are subject to the requirement to 'be fruitful and multiply', and in current debates about homosexuality and Judaism one often has the impression that the sin of wilful childlessness is a more cogent objection than the Torah's prohibition on sexual relations between men.

One way round the threat to the Jewish family posed by exogamy is to welcome the non-Jewish marriage partner into the wider family, and provide pressure and support for the children of the marriage to be brought up as Jews. As recently as a generation or two ago it was not uncommon for Jewish parents to go into mourning for a child who 'married out', and cut off all relations. Rabbinic authorities refused to entertain applications for conversion to Judaism on the grounds of marriage, invoking an old law stating that conversion could not be countenanced if the convert received a benefit as a result. Nowadays these attitudes have virtually disappeared, at least in the West. Traditional law recognises the children of a non-Jewish father and a Jewish mother as Jews in every respect. Such Jews are an ever-growing element within Jewish communities today, and attitudes and institutions are having to adapt to accommodate them. Their non-Jewish parents are increasingly welcomed, and even encouraged to play a part in the life of the community as they do in the family. The more radical wing of the Reform movement (and this includes the numerically dominant American Reform movement) goes further, and recognises the children of a Jewish father and a non-Jewish mother as Jewish, under certain conditions. Some Conservative Jews are sympathetic to this realignment, which in addition to its practical benefits in terms of Jewish demography eliminates a provision which is easily attacked as needlessly discriminating between the sexes.

As for the expedient of conversion, this is positively encouraged by many rabbis, in preference to 'marrying out', and the vast majority of cases of conversion heard by rabbinic courts fall into this category. The preparation of prospective converts is slanted towards the setting up of a Jewish home, and the Jewish marriage partner is encouraged to share in the convert's studies. Although it would be wrong to deny that some prejudice, the legacy of centuries, still exists among Jews against converts, it is breaking down very fast in the face of the contemporary situation, and members of Reform congregations will freely admit that converts are among the most knowledgeable, active and committed members of the community.

The emphasis on having children is not simply a matter of natural instinct, obedience to the Torah, or concern for the future of the Jewish community. In many people's minds a function of children is to look after their parents in sickness or old age, to ensure that they are properly buried, and to recite the Kaddish prayer in their memory. There is an obligation on children, throughout their lives, to 'honour and fear' their parents. This is explained as encompassing such things as standing up when they come into the room, ensuring that they are clothed and fed, not contradicting them, losing one's temper with them, or putting them to shame, and speaking of them with respect, even after their death.

Death is part of life, and it is accepted in Judaism as an inevitable aspect of the human condition. Everything possible must be done to promote health and save life, and killing is viewed with abhorrence; but Jewish teachers have insisted that one should not be afraid to die or be angry about it, but should accept one's death, whatever the circumstances. On hearing news of a death the Jew is supposed to respond with the words 'Blessed be the true judge', affirming one's confidence in the justice of God's decrees, however hard it may be to accept the individual verdict.

A Jew who senses the approach of death and is able to do so recites a confession. The following form of words is found in prayer books, and Nahmanides (1194–1270) says that it was already old in his day:

I acknowledge before you, Lord my God and God of my ancestors, that both my cure and my death are in your hands. May it be your will to send me a perfect healing. Yet if my death is fully determined by you, I will lovingly accept it from your hand. May my death be an atonement for all the sins, iniquities and transgressions that I have committed before you. Grant me some of the great happiness that is stored up for the righteous. Make known to me the path of life. In your presence is fullness of joy; at your right hand bliss for evermore.

Other prayers may be said, and as the end approaches those present recite the following verses aloud, concluding with the opening words of the Shma, the declaration of God's unity that all pious Jews long to say as they expire:

The Lord reigns, the Lord reigned, the Lord shall reign for ever and ever.
Blessed be the name of His glorious reign for ever and ever.
The Lord, He is God.
Hear, Israel, the Lord our God, the Lord is One.

A dying person should never be left alone, and those present have an obligation to treat him or her with consideration and respect, and to avoid doing anything that might hasten death. Euthanasia is considered to be murder, although some rabbis have argued that there is no obligation to keep someone alive mechanically who is not capable of independent life, particularly if the patient is in pain. It is also widely accepted that pain-killing drugs may be administered even if they have the indirect effect of hastening death.

According to classical halakhic sources, the cessation of breathing marks the moment of death. Since the concept of 'brain death' emerged in the late 1960s there has been some rabbinic discussion of the possible need to revise the old definition, particularly in relation to the vexed question of organ transplantation.

Once death has been established the eyes of the corpse are closed, preferably by a son, and it is carefully placed on the floor. A dead body must be handled with the same respect as is due to a living person. It is not stripped naked, but is always decently covered, and it is not disturbed more than is necessary. It is not left alone, but traditionally 'watchers' (*shomrim*), who may be relatives or friends, stay with it until the burial, reciting psalms.

Mourning is governed by very strict rules. Those who have observed them tend to agree that they are a help rather than an intrusion. They provide reassurance, and a framework for conducting oneself at what can otherwise be a time of aimlessness and uncertainty. The object of the rules is not to stifle or contain grief, but rather to provide support to the mourners and to help them over their time of trial and back into normal life.

The definition of a mourner is a father, mother, son, daughter, brother, sister, husband or wife of the deceased. Children under Bar/Bat Mitsvah age do not observe mourning, and there is no mourning or formal burial for an infant under thirty days old. (Informal rites of grieving for still-born babies and for infants are now being devised, because of a recognition that the parents need some means of channelling their grief.) Sons or daughters are distinguished from other mourners in a number of ways. For example, mourners have their clothes torn as a mark of grief: for sons and daughters this is done on the left, near the heart, while for other mourners it is done on the right side. (Nowadays, since people tend to object to expensive clothes being torn, the tearing is often done on a tie or a ribbon. Reform Judaism has abandoned the practice of tearing altogether.) The period of mourning extends to a year for one's parent; other mourners only mourn for a month.

Mourning proper only begins from the funeral. In the period between death and burial the mourner is known as an *onen*, and is not subjected to many particular rules, but, on the contrary, is relieved of religious obligations such as reciting prayers or saying the blessings before and after food. An *onen* should not drink wine, eat meat, indulge in luxuries or pleasures, or conduct business or professional activities. The main concern of the *onen* is to make arrangements for the funeral.

On returning home from the cemetery the mourner (who is now known as an *avel*) is offered a plate of food, which generally includes hard-boiled eggs and other round foods. It is customary to light a candle which will burn for the next seven days. Some people cover the mirrors in the house of mourning, or turn them to face the wall.

Mourning comes in three stages. The first, and most intense, lasts for seven days, and is known as Shivah ('seven'). In fact, since the day of the funeral counts as the first day and Shivah ends one hour into the seventh day, it actually lasts rather less than six days; moreover on the Sabbath no outward signs of mourning are observed. If a festival falls during the period the Shivah ceases and is not resumed. During Shivah the mourners remain at home and sit on low stools (whence the popular expression 'to sit Shivah'). They do not work or attend to their business affairs, have sexual intercourse, bathe, use cosmetics or creams, shave or have their hair cut. It is customary not to study Torah. After three days the rules are relaxed a little, and those who must go back to work may do so. Prayers are held in the house of mourning, and friends gather, to offer condolences, show solidarity, and provide a congregation so that the Kaddish may be said. The mourners are not expected to act as hosts: friends often bring food, and take it on themselves to serve it, and to underline this reversal of the norms there is a tradition, still observed by some, that a mourner receives greetings but does not initiate them.

The next period, Shloshim ('thirty'), continues until the morning of the thirtieth day after the funeral. During this phase mourners continue to refrain from shaving and having their hair cut, they do not listen to music and do not attend weddings or parties. (The restrictions on shaving and hair-cutting are often ignored today, and even Orthodox Jews sometimes cease to observe them after the Shivah.) At the end of the Shloshim mourning is at an end, except for children of the deceased who continue until twelve months after the death.

The date of death is commemorated each year by lighting a memorial candle and reciting Kaddish. This is known among Ashkenazim by the Yiddish name *yortsait* or *yahrzeit* ('year-time'). In Britain it is customary to say to mourners at this time, 'I wish you long life'.

As the preceding pages show, there are ample opportunities not only on special occasions but in daily life too for Jews to remind themselves of their distinctive heritage and destiny. The various rituals have the power to bring Jews closer to God, and also closer to their family and friends, and indeed to their ancestors too. In traditional Jewish life these reminders are ever-present. Boys and men wear a head-covering and fringes all the time, and the very traditional wear distinctive clothing. Women observe the rules of *tseniut*, 'modesty', keeping their bodies covered with the exception of hands and faces. Married women have shaven heads, and many wear a wig known as a *sheitel*. There are blessings to be said not only over different kinds of food and drink, but for example on seeing an unusual sight, or on hearing good or bad news. The majority of Jews, however, do not adhere to the whole of this rich and distinctive tradition. Many lead lives which are almost indistinguishable from those of their gentile neighbours.

CHAPTER SIX

The community

THE JEWISH COMMUNITY AND HOW IT WORKS

If the family and the home constitute one focus of Judaism in the world, the community and the synagogue constitute the other. The difference between the home and the synagogue is the difference between the private and the public sphere. These two are impossible to separate in the life of the individual Jew. The life of the home leaves spaces which are to be filled by the synagogue and public observance. The home observances of Yom Kippur, for example, the two family meals, frame the long hours of synagogue worship. Equally the synagogue leaves room for the home. And the two spheres sometimes break in on each other: when the family go to synagogue and pray together, as they now can in Reform and Conservative synagogues, and particularly when they gather to celebrate a family occasion such as the birth of a baby, a Bar Mitsvah or a marriage; or when the community gathers in a house of mourning to express their solidarity with their grieving fellow members and to make up a minyan for the recitation of the Kaddish.

The concept of the minyan is at the heart of the traditional distinction between private and public. The Hebrew word *minyan* simply means a number, but it is used to refer to the number required to make up a congregation for public worship. The old rule is that a minimum of ten adult male Jews are required for the recitation of certain prayers, particularly the Kaddish. Conservative rabbis, seeking to remedy some of the more offensive distinctions between the sexes in the old *halakhah*, allow adult women to be counted in the minyan. Of course in large communities the congregation is often far greater than a bare minyan: it may consist of hundreds or exceptionally even thousands of worshippers. But even in large gatherings the concept of minyan has its role to play. The worshippers do not all arrive simultaneously, and it is convenient to have a clear and incontrovertible definition of when enough people have arrived to allow public worship to begin. Traditionally it has been considered meritorious to be one of the minyan, that is to be among the first ten men to arrive at the synagogue. To make up a minyan is particularly important in small communities, where public prayer may have to be suspended if the crucial number of ten is not reached. Hence the old institution of the 'minyan man', a poor Jew who was paid to attend services and make up the numbers. Reform Judaism has abolished the whole concept of the minyan: prayers may be said with any number present, and services begin at advertised times. This obviates some problems, particularly for small communities, but at the cost of blurring the distinction between private and public.

Apart from the regular worship of the synagogue a minyan may gather in any suitable place to say the public prayers. The obvious example of this is the minyan that gathers in a house of mourning. Another, more joyful, example is the recitation of the seven blessings at dinner on one of the seven days following a wedding. In fact in the ordinary grace after food the presence of a minyan is marked by a special opening formula. But a group of people who happen to be together for whatever purpose, for example for a meeting, or because they work nearby, may decide to constitute a minyan to say their prayers together.

This minyan may sometimes develop into a fixed gathering that becomes in a sense an alternative to the regular synagogue worship. It may grow in time into a fully fledged synagogue: many synagogues have begun in this way. But the members may well feel that 'small is beautiful', and foster the intimacy of a small minyan.

The synagogue is the visible side of the Jewish community. The community in turn is made up of a number of families and individuals. The word 'synagogue' in fact can be used to refer to the community rather than the building. Despite what is sometimes said to the contrary, this is not a modern development aping the Christian use of the word 'church', but goes right back to the origins of the word 'synagogue', which is a Greek word originally meaning an assembly. In Greek Jewish texts from the ancient world (especially outside the Land of Israel) 'synagogue' usually means the community of the Jews.

Each synagogue is autonomous, since Judaism acknowledges no central human spiritual authority, and no overarching organisation. There may well be two or more synagogues in a single town; many more in a big city, representing different quarters of the town, or different origins of the members, or different religious ideologies. Sometimes one synagogue is technically a branch of another. In some cities or countries some or all of the synagogues may be brought together under a single communal structure. For example, in London many of the Orthodox Ashkenazi synagogues share a common organisation, the United Synagogue. In Paris both Ashkenazi and Sephardi synagogues belong to the Consistoire. The United Synagogue of America is an association of Conservative synagogues. Whatever the relationship between the synagogues, however, members are free to transfer their membership from one synagogue to another, to belong to more than one at the same time, or to worship occasionally or even regularly in a synagogue they do not formally belong to. It may even happen that members of the same family belong to different synagogues.

It is considered meritorious to help to found or run a synagogue, to attend its services and to contribute generously to its charitable funds. A special prayer is said after the reading of the Torah calling down God's blessing on

those who unite to form synagogues for prayer, and those who gather in them to pray; also those who provide lamps for lighting and wine for Kiddush and Havdalah, food for wayfarers and alms for the poor, and all who occupy themselves loyally with the needs of the community.

A synagogue is generally administered by a council and by honorary officers (chairman or president, secretary, treasurer and so forth), who are members, elected by the membership. (The right of women to vote or hold office is a matter under debate in Orthodoxy.) There may also be wardens (*gabbaim*), who supervise the smooth running of the services. It is conventional to refer to these persons collectively as the lay leadership, to distinguish them from the rabbi and his or her assistants, but it should be noted in passing that there is no foundation in Judaism for this distinction, which is borrowed from Christian usage and suggests that the religious leadership enjoys a priestly status which the lay leadership does not share. Priesthood in Judaism has a very specific meaning: it is an inherited status, implying direct descent from Aaron, the brother of Moses. A priest (*kohen*) traditionally enjoys certain privileges, a residue of the remote period when priests were responsible for the administration of the sacrificial cult in the Temple, such as the right to be called up first to the reading of the Torah in synagogue and to pronounce the priestly blessing (Numbers 6:24–6) over the congregation; and he is subject to certain restrictions, for example he may not come into contact with a corpse except a close relative, and he may not marry a divorcee. (In

Reform Judaism both the privileges and the restrictions have been abolished as having no significance and drawing unnecessary and inappropriate distinctions among Jews.) Priests exercise no authority by virtue of this hereditary status, and there is no connection whatever between the priesthood and the rabbinate: a priest may become a rabbi, in which case he is a rabbi like any other rabbi and a priest like any other priest. Besides the priests (*kohanim*) there are the Levites (*leviim*), the remaining descendants of the tribe of Levi, to which Moses and Aaron belonged. Levites are called up second in the synagogue, after a priest, and they wash the priests' hands before the priestly blessing. If the term 'layman' has any sense in Judaism it ought to refer to the ordinary 'Israelites' who are neither priests nor Levites. In fact, however, this usage has never suggested itself, presumably because the distinction is such an unimportant one in practice.

What is a rabbi, then, if he is not a priest? The title seems to have originated around the time the Temple was destroyed, to denote someone distinguished for his scholarship and powers of leadership, within the movement that we nowadays call 'rabbinic Judaism' which is the ancestor of virtually all the forms of Judaism current today. The rabbis retrospectively bestowed the rabbinic title on Moses, calling him Moshe Rabbenu, 'Moses our rabbi', presumably because they considered him to embody in a very high degree the distinguishing qualities mentioned above.

Originally there seems to have been a formal recognition or ordination of new rabbis, symbolised by a laying on of hands (*semikhah*). Only those who had been ordained in this way were able to use the rabbinic title. Eventually the practice of ordination ceased and the title was given to any teacher of Torah. Much later, in the Middle Ages, a new form of ordination was instituted among the Ashkenazim, in which a prominent scholar examined a candidate in his competence in Jewish law, and if satisfied issued him with a licence to issue decisions (*heter horaah*). It has been suggested that this system was borrowed from the nascent universities, from which Jews were excluded. Contemporary rabbinic ordination derives in part from this institution, and, particularly in the more traditional wing of Judaism, the sources of rabbinic law still play an enormous part in the rabbi's education. After the emancipation, however, new-style rabbinic seminaries were established, at first in Europe and later in the United States, which aimed to impart a much broader education in Jewish history and thought, and to train rabbis for their new role as preachers and spiritual leaders. These modern rabbis were also encouraged to obtain a university education in addition to their study at the seminary.

In the meantime an important change had occurred affecting the basic character of the rabbinate. Originally, Torah study had been an end in itself and an obligation on all Jews, and it was felt to be wrong to earn one's livelihood from it. Great rabbis like Maimonides earned their living as physicians or from some trade. From the sixteenth century, however, it became commoner for a community to employ a rabbi as its legal authority and religious leader, and in this way the rabbinate became a profession. After the emancipation in Europe the rabbinate became assimilated more and more to the model of the Christian ministry, and we even find a hierarchical system growing up, in which Chief Rabbis are recognised by the state as the spiritual heads of the Jewish community, and come to exert authority over other rabbis, a development which has no basis in Jewish law or tradition. Many rabbis are employed by synagogues to offer religious leadership and provide a wide range of services to the community.

Not all rabbis are rabbis: some of those who hold rabbinic appointments may not hold a rabbinic qualification, and some of those who are qualified as rabbis have no communal rabbinic appointment. In England for a long time there was no rabbinic ordination, and the graduates of the seminary, Jews' College, were given the title 'Rev.', which sounded attractively similar to *rav* or rabbi. Today, in a dwindling community which invests heavily in rabbinic education at both ends of the religious spectrum, there is a growing number of people entitled to call themselves 'rabbi' who do not, for a variety of reasons, choose the rabbinate as their profession.

Until recently, in keeping with the general character of Judaism at the time, the rabbinate was reserved to men. In the present century women have played an increasingly prominent role in religious leadership (particularly prominent in the British Liberal movement, where Lily Montagu was a rabbi in all but name). The Reform seminary in Berlin ordained a woman rabbi in the 1930s, but she was killed by the Nazis and after the war the impetus was lost, and it was some time before the issue came to the forefront of discussion again. With the growth of Jewish feminism in the late 1960s pressure began for the ordination of women as rabbis, at first in the Reconstructionist and Reform movements. In 1972 the Reform movement in America ordained its first woman rabbi; the British Reform movement and the American Conservative movement followed suit in 1975 and 1985 respectively. In these liberal movements the rabbinical seminaries now have more or less equal numbers of male and female students. Orthodoxy has yet to take the plunge, although the subject is under discussion at the more liberal fringe of the movement.

Sephardim have tended to prefer the title Hakham ('sage') in preference to Rabbi, but the history of the institution is similar. In the Ottoman Empire the *hakhamim* exercised communal leadership within the *millet* system regulating minorities, and there was a kind of chief rabbi, the Haham Bashı. In England the title Hakham is reserved for the leading rabbi. In recent times the Sephardi rabbinate has tended to follow the model provided by the numerically superior Ashkenazi sector, and many Sephardi rabbis have received part or all of their training in Ashkenazi seminaries or yeshivot.

Besides the rabbi, traditional Judaism evolved various parallel or subordinate offices, some of which lend themselves to confusion with the rabbinate. The first is the preacher or Maggid. In eastern Europe the town rabbi normally only preached twice a year, on the Great Sabbath before Passover and the Sabbath of Repentance between Rosh Ha-Shanah and Yom Kippur. The Maggid was often an itinerant preacher, who was rewarded for his services by each community where he preached; some larger communities maintained a permanent Maggid.

Hasidism introduced a new type of religious leader, the Tsaddik, often known as a rebbe to distinguish him from the rabbi in the normal sense (though the two words share the same etymology). Some rebbes also served as town rabbis, but they exercised a charismatic leadership over a following that was often widely scattered, in distinction to the rabbis, whose authority was strictly local. The Hasidim established a principle of hereditary succession for rebbes, which has sometimes been imitated in non-Hasidic circles. The Tsaddik or rebbe demanded complete submission from his followers, and his authority was based not on his learning but on his spiritual stature, which could sometimes border on the supernatural. Some were even said to work miracles, and holiness was thought to attach to the food they had blessed or their cast-off clothes. They are believed to have the power to intercede for their followers after their death, and some followers of the late Lubavitcher Rebbe became convinced that he was the Messiah and would return after his death. This is all far removed from the authority of the rabbi, and yet for the outside observer it is all too easy to confuse a Hasidic rebbe with a rabbi.

In eastern Europe the office of principal of the yeshivah (Talmudic academy) became detached from the town rabbinate, and with the proliferation of yeshivot attracting students from far and wide yet another religious leader came into being, the Rosh Yeshivah ('Yeshivah Head'), who was often a scholar renowned for his academic knowledge of the law. Even within modern Orthodoxy, former yeshivah students may consider their Rosh Yeshivah to be their true spiritual guide, even while recognising the practical authority of their local rabbi. A certain rivalry sometimes arises between yeshivah heads and rabbis, or even Chief Rabbis.

A synagogue service does not need to be conducted by a rabbi. Any congregant may lead the prayers (although Orthodoxy does not permit women to lead men in prayer). In keeping with the trend to transform the rabbi into a minister of religion, conducting services has come to be part of the function of a modern rabbi, at least at the more liberal end of the spectrum. In some larger synagogues this role belongs to the *hazan* or cantor, a salaried official chosen for his musical abilities as well as his good character.

THE SYNAGOGUE

The word 'synagogue', as we have already seen, comes from the Greek. The Hebrew term is Bet Kneset, 'house of assembly'. Many Ashkenazi Jews refer to it by the Yiddish term *shool*, meaning a school. This may reflect the fact that the synagogue sometimes doubled as a house of study, although that is strictly a separate institution, called in Hebrew Bet Ha-Midrash. The word *kloyz* (related to 'cloister' in English) was formerly used in central and eastern Europe for a synagogue, or for a house of study that doubled as a synagogue. Some Jewish communities use the term 'temple' in preference to 'synagogue'. This usage originated in eighteenth-century Europe, probably under the influence of French Protestantism; it gained currency in the nineteenth-century Reform movement, which was attracted by its allusion to the ancient Temple in Jerusalem. American Reform has retained the term, and it has been adopted by some Conservative congregations.

Synagogues come in all shapes and sizes, and there are no particular architectural requirements. They tend to reflect local architectural trends, sometimes flirting with church or mosque architecture and sometimes deliberately avoiding it. In the medieval period they were often small and discreetly located, so as not to attract attention to themselves. The Hasidim in Poland, barred from the synagogues, chose to worship intimately in a little room called a *shtibl*. In the course of the nineteenth century grand 'cathedral' synagogues were built in the large cities of Europe and America, reflecting the size, wealth and self-assurance of the post-emancipation communities. The favoured styles belonged to the classic European repertoire, but Gothic was deliberately avoided (presumably it was regarded as too 'churchy'), and Romanesque and the vaguely exotic Byzantine and unambiguously oriental Moorish idioms were preferred. Jews were slow to penetrate the architectural profession, and many of these grandiose synagogues were built by gentiles. In Britain the first Jewish synagogue architect was David Mocatta, a pupil of Sir John Soane and well known as a railway architect. Mocatta designed a synagogue at Ramsgate for his cousin Sir Moses Montefiore and two successive buildings for the fledgling London Reform congregation, of which he was himself a founder member and Chairman of the Council. The present handsome building of the congregation was built, with advice from Mocatta, by Henry Davis and Barrow Emanuel, who also designed other London synagogues. A similar story could be told elsewhere. The twentieth century has been marked by a more adventurous approach, and some very interesting and unusual synagogues have been built, such as Frank Lloyd Wright's synagogue at Elkins Park, near Philadelphia, or Heinz Rau's white dome for the Hebrew University in Jerusalem.

Synagogues frequently identify themselves on the outside by means of a Hebrew inscription or some Jewish symbol such as a six-pointed star of David or a seven-branched candelabrum (*menorah*). Internally, the dominant feature is the holy ark (*aron ha-kodesh*, or in Sephardi usage *heikhal* or *ekhal*), which normally occupies the middle of the wall closest to Jerusalem. The ark usually has the form of a tall cupboard with double doors opening outwards. Above it hangs a lamp known as the eternal light (*ner tamid*), and in Ashkenazi synagogues a curtain (*parokhet*) hangs in front of the ark. The only other prominent feature is a flat or sloping desk on which the scroll of the Torah is placed when it is opened for the reading. This stands on a raised dais (known as *bimah*, *almemar*, or among Sephardim *tebah*), reached by steps and often partly enclosed by railings or a balustrade.

The need to accommodate these two elements – the ark, placed against one wall, and the reading desk, which was often located in the centre of the synagogue – imposed awkward constraints on the design, particularly in terms of the seating. Traditional synagogues often have wooden pews arranged in the long axis of the hall, facing the reading desk which takes up a large part of the centre. This arrangement suits the reading of the Torah, but means that congregants must make a 90° turn when the ark is opened or when they face Jerusalem to recite the Amidah. An alternative arrangement, pioneered by the Reform movement but now found in other kinds of synagogue too, combines the ark and reading desk on a single platform at one end of the building, leaving the rest of the hall free for seating and obviating the need to turn. Traditional and Orthodox synagogues have separate seating for men and women; often the women are relegated to a gallery or separated from the men by a screen or other physical barrier (*mehitsah*), but in extreme cases they are placed in a separate room where they are completely hidden from male worshippers.

THE WORSHIP OF THE SYNAGOGUE

Like the architecture of the synagogue, the style of worship is very variable. It can be very grand and formal, with wardens in top hats and tailcoats, strict decorum and sublime organ music and choral singing; or at the other end of the spectrum, as in a Hasidic *shtibl*, it can be intimate and homespun, do-it-yourself and raucous, with congregants arriving at intervals throughout the service and chatting uninhibitedly to one another. Most services fall somewhere between the two.

Although the prayers may be led by a rabbi, they do not have to be, and often are not. In a smaller traditional synagogue the male congregants may well take it in turn to serve as *shaliah tsibbur*, literally the 'communal delegate' who leads the prayers. In larger synagogues there is often a salaried reader or cantor.

The language of prayer has been a hotly debated issue. The Talmud allows prayers to be said in any language, but throughout the Middle Ages it was universally accepted that the only language suitable for public prayer was Hebrew. Some German Reformers at the beginning of the nineteenth century promoted prayer in German, seeing in the Hebrew language an obstacle to understanding and therefore to true spirituality, and also a barrier between Jew and gentile. Even Orthodox modernists favoured a greater understanding of the prayers, and printed prayer books with facing English translations. The leading Reformer Abraham Geiger was ambivalent. He referred to Hebrew as a 'foreign dead language', and maintained that most German Jews were more affected by German prayers than by Hebrew ones; yet he had a deep love for the Hebrew language, and used it in his synagogue. The important rabbinical conference at Frankfurt in 1845, under Geiger's influence, declared that while there was no *objective legal* necessity for retaining Hebrew in the service, yet it was *subjectively* necessary to do so.[1] In a further vote it became clear that a slight majority was in favour of eventually replacing Hebrew by German or using the two languages side by side. This was not acceptable to Zacharias Frankel, the leader of the most conservative wing, and he withdrew from the conference; ever since, the attitude to Hebrew in the synagogue has been one of the issues dividing Reform from Conservative Jews. But even within the Reform movement the attitude has been by no means unambiguous or unanimous. British Reform, for example, has tended to favour a half-and-half mix, and has retained the tradition of printing its bilingual prayer books starting from the right, like Hebrew books, while Liberal Judaism in Britain at first virtually eliminated Hebrew, and its prayer books opened from the left like English books. When Isaac Mayer Wise, the great pioneer of Reform in America, issued his new prayer book *Minhag America* in 1857, it contained a totally Hebrew text opening from the right, and a separate English or German translation opening at the left. Those congregations that wished to do so could pray entirely or mainly in the vernacular, and this became increasingly common in Reform congregations. In the twentieth century, however, there was a notable return to the use of Hebrew: the Columbus Platform of 1937 included the use of Hebrew among the elements of tradition it proclaimed were required by a Jewish way of life, and the later emergence of a symbiosis between Reform and Zionism, with its strong espousal of the Hebrew language, further strengthened the place of Hebrew in Reform Judaism.

There are several different traditions of Hebrew pronunciation, most of which may be included under one of two main headings, Ashkenazi and Sephardi. While many of the differences between them are superficial and can be ascribed to the influence of Germanic and Slavic languages on the former and languages such as Spanish and Arabic on the latter, there are some very distinctive features that may go back to ancient dialects. In particular, one of the vowels pronounced *a* by Sephardim is pronounced *o* by Ashkenazim, and one of the consonants pronounced *s* by Ashkenazim is pronounced *t* by Sephardim. (Thus Ashkenazim will say *kashrus, sukkoh, sukkos, matsoh*, where the Sephardi pronunciation followed in this book has *kashrut, sukkah, sukkot, matsah*.) The Zionist movement adopted the Sephardi pronunciation, and it is the official pronunciation of Israel. For that reason it is tending to

---

[1] See Michael A. Meyer, *Response to Modernity*, pp. 96–7, 137.

encroach on the Ashkenazi pronunciation in synagogues both in Israel and abroad. The Reform movement has had a predilection for the Sephardi pronunciation from the outset.

Music was another issue dividing traditionalists and modernisers in the nineteenth century. Instrumental music was not used in the medieval synagogue, and the prayers and hymns were usually chanted to traditional melodies. The reading of the Torah and the Haftarah (prophetic reading) had their own traditions of cantillation. A greater emphasis on beautiful music is discernible from the sixteenth century on, the first known composer of synagogue music being Salamone Rossi (c. 1570–1628) of Mantua. Meanwhile the Lurianic kabbalists of Safed sang melodies to beautify the prayers and to help them concentrate on their mystical meanings. Later the Hasidim composed their own melodies or adapted current folksongs, and cultivated music enthusiastically in their quest for ecstasy. A distinctive Hasidic contribution is the wordless melody (*niggun*). All over Europe, as Jews became acquainted with the music of the world around them, the synagogue cantors (*hazzanim*) became more self-conscious and ambitious, and some combined synagogal with operatic careers. Such was the case, for example, of Meyer Leoni (1740–96), cantor at the Great Synagogue in London, who was fired for singing in a performance of Handel's *Messiah*. More recently the Polish cantor Gershon Sirota (1877–1943), 'the Jewish Caruso', was a popular performer in the concert hall. In Europe of the emancipation era a great deal of synagogue music was composed, particularly for Reform temples with their organ and choir. The best-known composers of the time, such as Salomon Sulzer (1804–90) of Vienna, Samuel Naumbourg (1815–80) of Paris and Louis Lewandowski (1821–94) of Berlin, successfully blended traditional eastern European Jewish elements with the dominant musical styles of their day. The nineteenth-century heritage still dominates synagogue music today, although twentieth-century composers have added their contributions, and many congregations have deliberately chosen to move away from art music towards more traditional styles of cantorial or congregational singing.

The congregation is made up of men, women and children. In traditional Judaism their respective roles are strictly defined. Women sit apart from men, as we have already seen, separated by a *mehitsah*, a barrier or screen. Attendance by women is not particularly encouraged, and at some services, for example on Sabbath eve, it is usual for women to stay at home and for men and male children only to go to the service. Some Orthodox synagogues remain close to this traditional model; others encourage the attendance of women and reduce the *mehitsah* to a symbolic railing, but the women are still observers who cannot lead the prayers or take any other part in the conduct of the services. In most Conservative and in Reform and Reconstructionist synagogues women and men may sit together. As for children, their attendance is encouraged (particularly in the case of boys) in traditional services, and the segregation of the sexes is not strictly applied to small children. They do not take an active part in the conduct of the service, except for one mystical hymn, the Song of Glory, which is commonly led by a small boy. Some early Reform synagogues, attempting to impose a proper decorum on the services, forbade parents to bring small children, but nowadays most Reform synagogues welcome children.

Another demand of the early Reformers was that congregants should wear clean and respectable clothes. Traditional Judaism too commends cleanliness and the wearing of fine clothes on Sabbaths and festivals, but evidently standards had slipped by the early nineteenth century, and in some traditional services today sartorial elegance does not seem to be highly prized. In fact there has been a general relaxation of dress codes in all but the most formal synagogues. Men traditionally cover their heads with a hat or skullcap and wear the *tallit*, the fringed prayer shawl. The *tallit* is not worn in the evening, except on the eve of Yom Kippur. On weekday mornings men put on *tefillin*, phylacteries, to pray. Women and children do not wear *tefillin* or *tallit*, in fact in some Ashkenazi communities men do not wear the *tallit* until they are married. Married women cover their heads. On Yom Kippur men may wear the white tunic, the *kittel*. All this is the traditional practice, which is still observed in many Orthodox congregations. With the rise of feminism, however, many women have taken to wearing the *tallit*, even in Orthodox synagogues, although it is frowned on by most of the all-male Orthodox rabbinate. In Reform Judaism, at least in its more radical manifestations, including American Reform and Liberal Judaism in England, headcovering, *tallit* and *tefillin* were all abandoned, but there has been a return to the skullcap and *tallit* recently.[2]

Congregants are seated for most of the service and for the readings, standing when the ark is open and when the scroll is elevated and to say the Amidah and certain other prayers. Traditionally the Amidah is said facing Jerusalem, and with the feet together. At four points near the beginning and end it is customary to bow. When the Torah scroll is

[2] See further Samuel Krauss, 'The Jewish Rite of Covering the Head', *Hebrew Union College Annual* 19 (1945), pp. 121–68.

carried round the synagogue the worshippers turn so that they are always facing it, and it is usual to touch it with a corner of the *tallit* which is then kissed. The same gesture is made to the open scroll when one is called up to the reading. When the scroll is elevated and displayed to the congregation, some people raise an arm towards it, holding a corner of the *tallit*. When the priests pronounce the priestly blessing they remove their shoes, cover their heads and arms with the *tallit*, and hold their fingers in a special way. Jews do not kneel, except that once a year, on Yom Kippur, they kneel and prostrate themselves. These are the only gestures normally practised in Jewish prayer, and in Reform services even these are not usually seen, with the exception of standing, but in very traditionalist circles some other gestures may be observed. Men may cover their heads with the *tallit* to say their prayers. They may sway their bodies backwards and forwards and bob their heads up and down. This ancient practice is particularly practised by Hasidim.

The prayers are meant to be said with *kavvanah*, concentration or intention. As one medieval writer, Bahya Ibn Pakuda, puts it, 'prayer without *kavvanah* is like a body without a soul'. How to achieve proper *kavvanah* is a matter of debate. It is said that the pious men of old used to meditate for an hour, then pray for an hour, then meditate for another hour. The Hasidim are particular concerned with *kavvanah*. The founder of Hasidism, the Baal Shem Tov, taught that one should say to oneself before beginning to pray that one would be willing to die through powerful concentration on the prayers. His own powers of concentration were legendary. The early Hasidim felt that a major obstacle to concentration on prayer was the requirement to pray at fixed times: they therefore did away with fixed times, and encouraged people to pray when they felt ready to do it with *kavvanah*, and for this they were severely criticised by their opponents.

The Reformers were also concerned about the times of services, but for a different reason, although in their way they were also in search of *kavvanah*. Traditional services tended to start when there was a minyan, and the principal services, on Sabbath and festival mornings, continued for several hours. The Reformers insisted that services should commence at the advertised time, and should not be too long. They pruned away many of the hymns and readings that had found their way into the liturgy over the centuries, and removed repetitions of prayers. In this way they hoped to improve worshippers' concentration and decorum, and they also made room for the new synagogue music and for the clear reading of prayers which in the traditional service had often been mumbled in an undertone. The modern Orthodox service, as in so much else, tends to represent a compromise between the style of traditional and Reform worship, while Conservative synagogues, for their part, can be situated between Orthodoxy and Reform.

The prescribed times for public worship correspond to the times when sacrifices were offered in the Temple. The morning service, Shaharit, corresponds to the daily dawn sacrifice, and on Sabbaths, New Moons and festivals it is followed by an additional service, Musaf, corresponding to the additional burnt offering on these days. The afternoon service (Minhah) corresponds to the regular evening sacrifice; it may be said at any time in the afternoon, and is sometimes held close to sunset and joined to the evening service (Maariv), which itself may take place at any time from sunset to dawn, but preferably before midnight. Maariv alone has no temple ritual corresponding to it, and for that reason there is some discussion in the literature as to whether it is strictly obligatory.

RELIGIOUS SERVICES

It is difficult to generalise about the structure and content of the regular services, because since the beginning of the great movement of prayer book reform in the early nineteenth century Jewish prayer books have come to diverge considerably from one another (and even before that time there were notable discrepancies). The divergences are particularly noticeable in comparing translations, because while the Hebrew text contained in each new prayer book represents a revision, often relatively slight, of an earlier Hebrew text, the translations are often completely new, and sometimes, for theological or aesthetic reasons, they are far from being a word-for-word rendering of the Hebrew. In what follows, I shall aim to describe the common basis of the majority of prayer books, and shall translate the Hebrew as faithfully as is consistent with the need to write fluent English. I shall point out the main differences between the different movements. I shall also point out where services for different occasions differ from each other. This is inevitably a very complex and technical area, and the reader is advised to regard this description as a very rough guide, and to refer to specific prayer books for more detailed information. By way of illustration of some of the difficulties, here are two passages from the regular prayers as they are translated in current prayer books of two modernist movements, Orthodoxy and British Reform.

The first example is taken from the second paragraph of the

Amidah, which deals with the controversial topic of the resurrection of the dead.

Singer's Prayer Book (1992) (omitting some phrases that are added on certain occasions in the year):

You, O Lord, are mighty for ever; You revive the dead; You have the power to save . . . You sustain the living with lovingkindness, You revive the dead with great mercy. You support the falling, heal the sick, set free the bound, and keep faith with those that sleep in the dust. Who is like You, O Master of mighty deeds? Who resembles You – a King who puts to death and restores to life, and causes salvation to flourish? And You are sure to revive the dead. Blessed are You – the Lord, who revives the dead.

Forms of Prayer (1977):

You, O Lord, are the endless power that renews life beyond death; You are the greatness that saves. You care for the living with love. You renew life beyond death with unending mercy. You support the falling and heal the sick. You free prisoners, and keep faith with those who sleep in the dust. Who can perform such mighty deeds, and who can compare with You – a king who brings death and life, and renews salvation. You are faithful to renew life beyond death. Blessed are You Lord, who renews life beyond death.

The second example is from the prayer called Aleynu, which comes at the end of the service. Apart from the problem of finding appropriate language to represent traditional views of the nature of the universe, this prayer in its original form makes some Jews uncomfortable by its negative and potentially offensive attitude to other religions.

Singer's Prayer Book (1992):

It is our duty to praise the Lord of all, and to ascribe greatness of the Author of Creation, who has not made us like the nations of the world, nor has placed us like other families of the earth; who has not made our portion like theirs, nor our destiny like that of all their multitude. Therefore we bend the knee, bow down, and acknowledge before the supreme King of Kings, the Holy One, blessed be He, that it is He who stretched out the heavens and founded the earth, and set His glorious throne in the heavens above, and the abode of His power in the loftiest heights. He is our God, there is no other. Truly, he is our King, there is none besides Him, as it is written in His Torah: Now be sure, and keep it in mind, the Lord alone is God, in the heavens above and on the earth below; there is no other.

Forms of Prayer (1977):

It is our duty to praise the Lord of all, to recognise the greatness of the creator of first things, who has chosen us from all people by giving us his Torah.

Therefore we bow low and submit, and give thanks before the King above the kings of kings, the Holy One, blessed be He. He extends the limits of space and makes the world firm. His glory extends through the universe beyond, and the presence of his strength into farthest space. He is our God; no other exists. Our king is truth; the rest is nothing. It is written in His Torah: 'Realise this today and take it to heart – it is the Lord who is God in the heavens above and on the earth beneath; no other exists.'

While some of the changes have clearly been made for aesthetic reasons, because of the sound of the words (and we should bear in mind that in Orthodox prayer books the translation is provided solely to help worshippers to follow the meaning of the Hebrew, while in the more liberal movements it may be read aloud, by the leader or by the congregation in unison), other changes reflect differences in understanding the facts of nature or the needs of the Jew at prayer.

The texts that make up the services may be classified under four headings

1. *Biblical texts.* First we may consider actual readings, when the text is read aloud or cantillated, and the congregants listen. Blessings are recited by the reader before and after these formal readings. The major regular readings are on the morning of Sabbaths and festival days, when passages from the Torah and the Prophets are read out. This reading constitutes the central act of the services in question, and it is accompanied with a certain amount of ceremonial. The passages from the Torah are read from a handwritten scroll, which is solemnly taken out of the ark and processed around the synagogue, and 'undressed' and held up to view by two congregants publicly named for the purpose; other congregants are honoured by being 'called up' to the reading. The prophetic passage (Haftarah) is read from a printed book. There is short reading from the Torah scroll as well on Sabbath afternoons and on Monday and Thursday mornings, as well as on certain special days which are not full festivals: New Moon, fast days, Hanukkah and Purim, and the intermediate days of Sukkot and Passover. Apart from the scroll of the Torah, there are five short books of the Bible that are known as scrolls and are read on special days of the year: Song of Songs (Sabbath of Passover week), Ruth (Shavuot), Lamentations (9th of Av), Kohelet or Ecclesiastes (Sabbath of Sukkot week), Esther (Purim). Of these only Esther is normally read from an actual scroll.

The 'reading of the Shma', although it is technically called a reading, is in a different category from the readings just mentioned. It does not have to be read from a written text (in fact some devout Jews cover their eyes when they recite the first verse, as an aid to concentration). Nor does it require the presence of a congregation, as we saw in the previous chapter. The reading is made up of three separate passages from the Torah: Deuteronomy 6:4–9, Deuteronomy 11:13–21, and Numbers 15:37–41. The Shma is a kind of profession of faith, and it is enormously important to Jews. In addition to the full reading, in the evening and morning services, the opening verse is recited on various other occasions in the services.

The biblical psalms figure prominently in the worship of the synagogue. The Book of Psalms is not read in its entirety in the services, although some pious Jews do read the whole book privately each week, or even each day. Instead, particular psalms or sequences of psalms are read at specific points in the service or on special occasions. For example, Psalms 100 and 145–150 are said in the daily morning service; Psalms 19, 34, 90, 91, 135, 136, 33, 92, 93 and 145–150 (in that order) on Sabbath and festival mornings; and in the conclusion of the morning service the 'psalm of the day' is recited, prefaced with the words 'this is the . . . day of the week, on which the Levites in the Temple used to say . . .'. On Friday evening the Sabbath is welcomed with Psalms 95–99 and 29, a custom introduced by the Safed kabbalists of the sixteenth century. Psalms 145 and 24 (on weekdays) or 29 (on Sabbaths) is sung when the scroll of the Torah is returned to the ark. A special liturgy of psalms known as Hallel is sung on festival days: it consists of Psalms 113–118, preceded and followed by a special blessing.

Other scriptural passages are included in the services. For example, 1 Chronicles 29:10–13, Nehemiah 9:6–11 and the 'Song at the Sea' (Exodus 14:30 to 15:19) are said after the main sequence of psalms in the morning service, and some congregations follow the kabbalistic custom of reciting the Song of Songs on Sabbath eve.

2. *Blessings.* Blessings or benediction (*berakhot*) play a large part in the private devotional life of the Jew as well as in the worship of the synagogue. Many of them were composed by the rabbis of the Talmud, and the Amidah, which was composed at that time, consists of a series of blessings. Liturgical blessings may be long or short, the short ones often consisting of only a few words. Blessings begin in one of two ways, 'Blessed are you, Lord, our God, King of the universe (or eternal King)' or simply 'Blessed are you, Lord.' What follows this opening may be anything from a long paean of praise to a short formula, often consisting of only two words, identifying an aspect of God's character or activity. A

curiosity of these formulae is that they are frequently worded in the third person, even though the introduction is in the second person. (For example: 'Blessed are you, Lord, who blesses His people Israel with peace'.) The formulae are best understood as being in effect titles of God, 'resurrecter of the dead', 'clother of the naked', 'blesser of his people' and so forth. If the blessing is a long one it will often conclude with a short blessing, summing up the message of the longer blessing. This short blessing is known as a 'seal' (*hatimah*). A seal is frequently found at the end of a prayer which does not begin as a blessing; in this case the whole prayer is considered to be a blessing.

3. *Other prayers.* In the course of centuries new prayers have been composed, in forms other than that of the blessing. We have already looked at one of them, the Aleynu, which is said to have been composed in the third century CE, but may well be even earlier. Traditional liturgies contain many such prayers, and contemporary liturgies have displayed considerable inventiveness in combining traditional forms of words with new ideas. One feature these prayers have in common by and large is that they are couched in the first person plural (unlike biblical prayers which are generally personal): the community expresses its needs and desires and its gratitude as a public body. With few exceptions, private prayers have no place in the synagogue. In fact Jews are encouraged to pray with the community in preference to praying alone. Maimonides argues as follows:

Communal prayer is always hearkened to and even if there are sinners among them the Holy One, blessed be He, does not reject the prayers of the many. Consequently, a man should associate himself with the community and he should not recite prayers in private when he is able to recite them together with the community.[3]

4. *Hymns.* Jews love to sing their faith and their love of God. In the home they do it in the table songs (Zemirot), and in the synagogue they do it with hymns. The power of music in the synagogue is seen at its strongest in the hymns. A firm favourite, of unknown authorship, is *Adon Olam* ('Eternal Lord'):

Eternal Lord, who reigned before any artifact was created.
When everything was made by his will he was already proclaimed King.
And when everything is ended he will still reign, alone and awesome.

[3] *Code*, Rules of Prayer 8:1, quoted from Jacobs, *Religion and the Individual*, p. 39, where the subject is discussed further.

He was, he is, and he will be in splendour.
And he is One, and there is no second to liken or join to him.
Without beginning, without ending, he has power and dominion.
He is my God, my living Redeemer, my Rock, my life-line in time of distress,
He is my banner and my refuge, my cupful when I cry out.
Into his hand I entrust my spirit whether I sleep or wake,
And with my spirit my body too: the Lord is mine, and I am not afraid.

Other popular hymns are *Ein Keloheinu* ('There is none like our God'), *Yigdal* ('Great is the living God')[4] and *Lekha Dodi* ('Come beloved to meet the bride'), the mystical welcome to the Sabbath bride composed by the Safed kabbalist Solomon Alkabets in the wake of the expulsion from Spain.

There are innumerable hymns, and their origins are diverse.[5] A great period of productivity was in Byzantine Palestine, in the fourth to seventh centuries, and a second peak was reached in Muslim Spain, in the tenth to twelfth centuries. Many hymns from both these periods grace the traditional prayer books. Some of them are complex and allusive, based on interwoven acrostics and replete with obscure allegorical allusions. The Reformers were of the opinion that they cluttered and choked the liturgy and were a major obstacle to understanding; they freely pruned them out so as to restore the classical simplicity of the prayers. Even Orthodox modernists were in favour of lightening the service in this way, though they retained many of the old favourites, particularly at Rosh Ha-Shanah and Yom Kippur, when there is less objection to long services.

These are the main types of material that make up most of a Jewish service. In addition, there are passages from other sources, for example Orthodox prayer books insert passages from the Talmud, while Reform prayer books include readings from a range of origins, including contemporary literature.

All regular services actually have the same basic structure, which is seen most simply and clearly in the weekday evening service. It consists of: 1. An invocation to prayer; 2. the Shma and its blessings; 3. the Amidah; 4. concluding prayers. Let us look at these four elements more closely.

---

[4] See below, pp. 174–5
[5] For a full account see Leon J. Weinberger, *Jewish Hymnography* (London/Portland, Oregon, 1998).

1. *An invocation to prayer.* This is the same at all services. The reader says: 'Bless the Lord who is to be blessed!' and the congregants reply: 'Blessed be the Lord who is to be blessed for ever and ever!'

2. *The Shma and its blessings.* The text of the Shma itself (see above, p. 135) is always the same. The blessings before and after it vary, however, according to the time of day. In the evening there are two blessings before the Shma. The first blesses God for making the evening: 'He causes the day to pass and brings on the night, and makes a distinction between day and night.' The second speaks of the great love of God for the Jewish people, expressed in the giving of the Torah. (Both love and Torah are themes of the Shma itself.) The blessings after the Shma acknowledge God's redemptive power, pray for shelter from the perils of the night, and look forward to the coming of God's kingdom.

3. *The Amidah.* The Amidah, always said standing, begins with an invocation from Psalm 51:17: 'O Lord, open my lips, that my mouth may declare Your praise'. The body of the Amidah consists of a series of nineteen blessings, of which the 'seals' (each of which, as observed above, identifies a facet of God's nature and activity) run as follows on weekdays:
   1. Shield of Abraham
   2. Reviver of the dead
   3. The holy God
   4. Dispenser of knowledge
   5. Desiring repentance
   6. Generously forgiving
   7. Redeemer of Israel
   8. Healer of the sick of His people Israel
   9. He who blesses the years
   10. He who gathers in the dispersed of His people Israel
   11. The king who loves righteousness and justice
   12. He who breaks enemies and humbles the arrogant
   13. The support and shelter of the righteous
   14. Who rebuilds Jerusalem
   15. Who makes the power of salvation spring up
   16. He who hears prayer
   17. He who restores His presence to Zion
   18. Goodness is Your name, and to You it is fitting to give thanks
   19. Who blesses His people Israel with peace.

Taken together, this prayer, intimately familiar to religious Jews by being repeated thrice daily, may be considered as a kind of Jewish creed. Less philosophical than the Thirteen Principles of Maimonides, it distils the essence of the biblical teachings about God, combining universal aspects with those focused on the destiny of the people of Israel. Some elements not represented in the 'seals' are woven into the body of the blessings. Thus the first blessing, 'Shield of Abraham', declares that the God of Abraham, Isaac and Jacob is also the most high God, the creator of all things, and it looks forward to the coming of the redeemer. The second blessing, 'Reviver of the dead', also mentions other aspects of God's beneficence: 'supporter of the falling, healer of the sick, liberator of captives'.

4. *Concluding prayers.* On weekday evenings these are normally very short, beginning with the Aleynu, the prayer quoted earlier insisting that the God acknowledged by the Jews is the universal and supreme God of all humankind and indeed of the whole universe. A second prayer looks forward to the coming of God's kingdom, when (in the words of Zechariah 14:9) 'the Lord shall be one and His name one'. The service is concluded by the mourner's Kaddish, which continues the theme of the kingdom of God. It is recited by mourners, the congregation responding with a series of amens.

This basic structure underlies all services, evening, morning or afternoon (with the omission of the Shma), whether on weekdays, Sabbath, or festival days. There are variations, elaborations and additions, but they do not disturb the orderly succession of these four elements. The longest service of the day is the morning service, swollen further on Sabbaths and festivals by the reading of the Torah followed by an additional Amidah. The main outlines of a service for Sabbath morning are as follows.

1. Blessings and prayers, followed by psalms and songs of praise.
2. The invocation, as above, followed by the Shma and its blessings. The blessing for the evening is replaced by a morning blessing, addressed to God 'who forms light and creates darkness, makes peace and creates all things'. There is only one blessing after the Shma, 'who has redeemed Israel'.
3. The Amidah. On Sabbath a special Amidah is recited, which has seven blessings instead of the usual nineteen. The first three and the last three are essentially the same, but instead of the thirteen

blessings in the middle there is a single blessing, with the 'seal' 'who sanctifies the Sabbath'. Festival days have their own blessing instead, naming the festival in question, and ending 'who sanctifies (the Sabbath and) Israel and the festive seasons'. It is customary for the Amidah to be said twice, the first time silently by all and the second time aloud by the reader alone. At the repetition a *kedushah* ('sanctification') is inserted in the third blessing, describing the worship of the angels who declare 'Holy, holy, holy is the Lord of Hosts, the whole world is full of His glory' (Isaiah 6:3). Later the reader also inserts the priestly blessing (Numbers 6:24–6). On festivals and semi-festive days Hallel (Psalms 113–18) is added after the Amidah.

4. The Reading of the Torah. The ark is opened and a scroll of the Torah (or two, exceptionally three, depending on the number of readings prescribed for the day) is removed. The scroll is carried in procession round the synagogue, and taken to the reading desk, where it is 'undressed', that is the silver ornaments and pointer, the velvet mantle and the binder are removed. It is then unrolled a little and held up so that the congregation can see the written words. (The Sephardi custom is to display it before the reading; Ashkenazim do it afterwards instead.) Members of the congregation are then 'called up' by their Hebrew names, beginning with a priest and a Levite if any are present. It is considered an honour to be called up. The Torah is divided up into sections (each known as a *parashah* or among Ashkenazim as a *sidrah*), and one of them is read each week, so that the whole Torah is read in the space of a year. Each section is divided into shorter readings according to the number of people to be called up. The person called up recites a blessing before and after the reading. In Reform and Liberal synagogues only a short portion of each section is read. After the conclusion of the Torah reading the scroll is rolled up and 'dressed'. A Haftarah, a short portion from the prophetic books, is read, preceded and followed by a special blessing. Unlike the Torah, the Prophets are not read in their entirety, but only in excerpts, chosen to suit the Torah readings they accompany. Special prayers are then said, for the congregation, for the state and its government, for the State of Israel, and before each month for blessings during the coming month. The scroll is then processed once more round the synagogue and replaced in the ark, with the words 'Turn us back to Yourself, Lord, and we will return; renew our days as of old.' In some congregations there is a sermon at this point.

5. Additional Amidah (Musaf). This is similar to the main Amidah. Reform liturgies have tended to omit it.

6. Concluding hymns and prayers. The Aleynu is flanked by hymns. In some congregations the Hymn of Glory, a breathtakingly anthropomorphic love-song of rare obscurity, is sung by a small child before the open ark. Various other additional psalms and readings may be inserted, and in more traditional services the mourner's Kaddish is said not once but three times.

After the conclusion of the service it is customary to recite *kiddush*, the blessing of the Sabbath, over wine and bread, and this provides an opportunity for congregants to mingle and talk to one another. People celebrating a happy event, such as a Bar Mitsvah, a wedding or some other family celebration, will often provide more substantial refreshments.

THE CYCLE OF THE YEAR

Just as in the home so too in the synagogue the regular succession of Sabbaths forms the backbone of the year, for it must be admitted that weekday attendance is generally very small and many synagogues do not even trouble to open their doors for weekday prayer. Sabbath services, then, beat out the rhythm of the year, each Sabbath taking the name of its designated Torah reading. In Orthodox synagogues the sunset Sabbath eve service is short and almost perfunctory, since Sabbath eve is considered to be a family celebration for which the most fitting place is the home, and the main emphasis falls on the morning service, with its Torah reading, its sermon and its *kiddush*. Many non-Orthodox synagogues, however, lay greater stress on Friday evening in the synagogue. It was the great American reformer I. M. Wise, in the nineteenth century, who took the step of holding a Friday evening service at a fixed time later in the evening, giving families time to eat together at home first. There being no reason to hurry this service, it may be enhanced by a Torah reading or a sermon or a lecture, and may be followed by a social get-together. But if the heart of the synagogue beats to the regular rhythm of the Sabbaths, it gives an extra leap of joy on festival days and whenever private celebrations occur.

The major festivals in the synagogue are similar to those in the home, but they are celebrated differently. The great days are the Days of Awe or High Holy Days in the autumn, Rosh Ha-Shanah (New Year) and Yom Kippur (Day of Atonement). On these days the attendance at the synagogue is swollen out of all proportion to the regular congregation. This raises an awkward problem whenever a synagogue is built: should it be built to accommodate the High Holy Day congregation, at great expense and at the risk of seeming vast and empty throughout the year, or should it be built with the normal Sabbath attendance in mind, necessitating the hiring of premises for 'overflow' services once a year? Each congregation solves the problem in its own way; many opt for a compromise: a large building divided by movable partitions, providing classrooms and meeting rooms whenever the large prayer hall is not required.

If the individual Jew needs to prepare inwardly by self-searching, penitence and prayer for the day of judgment which is Rosh Ha-Shanah, the synagogue too needs to prepare. The usual black vestments and the velvet hangings and Torah mantles are replaced with white ones. Some congregations need to hire additional readers for the overflow services, and there are many tasks that need to be allocated. The Days of Awe have their own special melodies, which readers must learn if necessary and choirs rehearse. A mood of activity and a sense of expectation infects the congregation.

The morning service for Rosh Ha-Shanah is a long one, and it is marked by a unique and unforgettable sound, the eerie and jubilant cry of the *shofar*, the ram's horn. The holiday is described in the Torah as a day of blowing the horn (*teru'ah*) (Leviticus 23:24; Numbers 29:1), and although a horn from any kosher animal may be used preference is given to a ram's horn because of the symbolism of the ram that was sacrificed in place of Isaac in Genesis 22, which is one of the readings for the festival. There is no prescribed size or shape for the *shofar*: some are short and crescent-shaped, others are long and straight with an upward turn at the end, while others spiral exuberantly. It takes a certain amount of skill to produce a fluent sound, and good *shofar*-blowers are in demand at this time of the year. Different reasons are given for the blowing of the *shofar*, some of which are alluded to in the liturgy, which cites a series of biblical verses referring to the *shofar*. Maimonides offers a striking explanation in his Code:

It seems to say: Awake, you sleepers, you who have fallen asleep in life, and reflect upon your deeds. Remember your Creator. Do not be among those who miss reality and pursue shadows instead, who waste their years seeking after vain things that neither benefit nor save them. Look well to your souls, and improve your deeds. Forsake every one of you your evil ways and thoughts.

This view is well suited to the mood of the liturgy for the festival, which lays a strong emphasis on repentance and self-improvement.

Yom Kippur is the grandest and most solemn day in the calendar of the synagogue, and this is the day when synagogues are full to overflowing. (There is a popular expression 'a Yom Kippur Jew', meaning one who attends synagogue only once a year.) In older times some Jews remained in the synagogue from the beginning of the fast until the end, twenty-five hours later. Nowadays there is a break for the night, and it is common to have a short interval in the afternoon as well.

On Yom Kippur, as at the Passover seder, some Jews still observe the old custom of wearing the *kittel*, the plain white tunic in which they will be buried. Franz Rosenzweig has this commentary on the symbolism of this practice: 'Man is utterly alone on the day of his death, when he is clothed in his shroud, and in the prayers of these days he is also alone. They too set him, lonely and naked, straight before the throne of God.'[6]

The opening service is the only really substantial evening service in the traditional synagogue, and the only one when men wear the *tallit*. It begins with a declaration known as Kol Nidrei, sung in Aramaic to a haunting melody. The effect of the Kol Nidrei is to announce that all religious vows made during the coming year are not to be considered binding. The reason for the declaration is wrapped in obscurity, and it has given rise to various misunderstandings which led to its being omitted from some Reform liturgies. However, in most synagogues it has not only held its own but stamps the services with its own unique character, indeed the eve of Yom Kippur is popularly called 'Kol Nidrei night'.

Repentance (*teshuvah*) is the keynote of the Yom Kippur liturgy, and the five services all culminate in a detailed and comprehensive public confession of sins. The prayers dwell on the awesome majesty of God, who is a judge with the power to sentence to death, yet who is also compassionate to those who sincerely repent. One of the most moving prayers is the *unetanneh tokef*, composed under the Byzantine Empire but associated by legend with a martyr rabbi named Amnon of Mainz, who after being tortured during the Crusades was carried dying into the synagogue, and expired while reciting this prayer:

We evoke the solemn holiness of this day, for it is a day of awe and terror. On it your dominion is exalted, your throne is established with love, and you sit upon it with truth. Truly you are the only judge, arbiter and all-knowing witness, you inscribe and seal, you enumerate and reckon, you recall all that is forgotten, you open the book of memorial and it recites itself, and the seal of every human hand is upon it. A great *shofar* is sounded, a still small voice is heard, the

---

[6] Franz Rosenzweig, *The Star of Redemption*, tr. W. W. Hallo (London/New York, 1970), p. 327.

angels are dismayed, seized with fear and trembling, and they say, This is the Day of Judgment: the army of heaven is to be inspected and judged. For even they cannot be justified in your judgment. As for dwellers on earth, you pass them all before you in their ranks. As a shepherd inspects his flock, passing them beneath his crook, so do you pass and count and reckon, inspecting every living soul, determining the measure of every created being, and writing down their decreed sentence.

On Rosh Ha-Shanah it is inscribed, and on the fast of Yom Kippur it is sealed: how many shall pass away and how many shall be created; who shall live and who shall die, who at his appointed time, and who before it, who by fire and who by water, who by the sword and who by the wild beast, who by hunger and who by thirst, who by earthquake and who by plague, who by strangling and who by stoning, who shall have rest and who shall roam, who shall be calm and who shall be tormented, who shall be tranquil and who shall be afflicted, who shall become poor and who shall become rich, who shall be brought low and who shall be raised up.

BUT PENITENCE, PRAYER AND CHARITY MAY AVERT THE SEVERITY OF THE SENTENCE.

Many other solemn prayers and hymns reiterate the same themes, dwelling on the power and justice of God and also on his compassion and openness to prayer. All the great hymnographers have contributed compositions to the liturgy. One of the loveliest is *Mi yitneni* ('O would that I might be . . .'), by the medieval Spanish poet Judah Hallevi, of which this is an extract:

> If in my youth I still
> Fail to perform Thy will,
> What can I hope when age shall chill my breast?
> Heal me, O Lord! with Thee is healing found–
> Cast me not off, by weight of years oprest,
> Forsake me not when age my strength has bound.
> O! would that I might be
> A servant unto Thee,
> Thou God, by all adored.
> Then, though by friends out-cast,
> Thy hand would hold me fast,
> And draw me near to Thee, my King and Lord![7]

Of all the poetic compositions few can compare with the *Keter malkhut* ('Royal crown') of Solomon Ibn Gabirol, which is printed in Sephardi prayer books, and is still recited in part in the British Reform rite, which is based on the Sephardi tradition. In North African communities it is

---

[7] Translated by Mrs Henry Lucas (Alice Lucas), *Songs of Zion by Hebrew Singers of Mediaeval Times* (London, 1894), pp. 10–11.

chanted around dawn, before the morning service begins. *Keter malkhut* is a magnificent meditation on the wonders of nature and the greatness of God, the frailty of human beings and their need for penitence, blending biblical Hebrew allusions with themes borrowed from Neoplatonist philosophy, and counts among the great Hebrew poems of all times.[8]

A unique element in the Yom Kippur liturgy is the so-called Avodah, the re-enactment of the Temple worship in the course of the Additional Service (Musaf). This was the holiest day in the year of the Temple, because on this day the High Priest, after suitable ablutions and purifications, entered the Holy of Holies and pronounced the ineffable name of God, the name that was so holy that its pronunciation eventually died out. When he said the name all the people who heard him fell on their faces, and it is still the custom in some congregations for the worshippers to kneel and prostrate themselves on this occasion. This is the only occasion when a Jew is permitted to kneel. 'And he does not kneel to confess a fault or to pray for forgiveness of sins, acts to which this festival is primarily dedicated. He kneels only in beholding the immediate nearness of God.'[9] This service also contains a martyrology, calling to mind the martyrs who perished under the Roman emperor Hadrian and at various later times, such as during the first crusade. Some modern liturgies have introduced references to the martyrs of the Nazi holocaust at this point.

The special feature of the Afternoon Service is the reading of the Book of Jonah as the Haftarah. The message of the book is that repentance averts the evil decree, even for a whole city of wrongdoers like Nineveh.

The Concluding Service (*Neilah*) is unique to this day. Its Hebrew name means 'closing of the gate', because this was the time when the gates were locked in the Temple. As the sun begins to go down the mood of the prayers changes, and a tone of confidence and hope enters the words and melodies. In the Sephardi liturgy the service begins with a beautiful hymn by Moses Ibn Ezra, *El nora 'alilah*, which is sung to a spirited, almost bouncy tune: 'O God, awesome in deeds, grant us pardon at the hour of *Neilah*.'

The climax is reached at the end of *Neilah*, as the end of the day approaches. The whole congregation proclaims in a loud voice the first sentence of the Shma: 'Hear O Israel, the Lord our God, the Lord is One!', then three times: 'Blessed be the name of His glorious reign for

[8] It is translated by Raphael Loewe in his book *Ibn Gabirol* (London, 1989) and by Bernard Lewis, *The Kingly Crown* (London, 1961). [9] Rosenzweig, *The Star of Redemption*, p. 323.

ever and ever', and finally seven times 'The Lord, He is God. The Lord, He is God.' After the regular evening service and the *havdalah*, the marking of the distinction between holy day and weekday, a single long blast is sounded on the *shofar* and people disperse to break their fast in their homes.

Only a few days later the community reassembles to celebrate Sukkot (Booths, or Tabernacles). 'Although the Feast of Booths celebrates redemption and rest, it is nevertheless the festival of wandering through the wilderness',[10] and the symbol of this wandering is the booth itself, the *sukkah*. Such a visible sign of the festival in the home, a *sukkah* is also built in the grounds of the synagogue. But the real mark of Sukkot in the synagogue is the taking of the four species. The Torah states: 'You shall take on the first day the fruit of goodly trees, branches of palm trees, boughs of thick trees, and willows of the brook, and you shall rejoice before the Lord your God for seven days' (Leviticus 23:40). The four species in question are identified as citron (*etrog*), palm, myrtle and willow, and 'taking' is understood literally as picking them up. A palm frond, three sprigs of myrtle and two of willow are bound together and held in the right hand, and the lemon-like fruit of the citron is taken in the left, and they are waved up, down, and to the four points of the compass after the recitation of an appropriate blessing. The four species are also carried in procession around the synagogue, accompanied by the singing of 'Hosannas' (*hoshanot*), petitions for salvation. On the seventh day of the festival seven circuits are made, which is why this day is known as the Great Hoshana (Hoshana Rabbah). Some Jews still observe the custom of beating a bunch of willow sprigs until the leaves come off.

The eighth day of the festival is called Shemini Atseret, usually translated as 'Eighth Day of Solemn Assembly'. This day is chosen to mark the liturgical transition from summer to winter, and in the Additional Service (Musaf) prayers for rain are recited before the open ark. The concluding words of the prayer, 'causing the wind to blow and the rain to fall', are added to every Amidah from now until Passover.

The last day of this autumn festive season is Simhat Torah, 'Rejoicing in the Torah'. In Israel and in Reform synagogues this coincides with Shemini Atseret, but other diaspora congregations celebrate it on the following day. This is the day when the annual reading of the Torah is concluded and resumes again immediately at the beginning. It is a time

[10] Ibid., p. 321.

of joyful celebration, no doubt occasioned partly by the fact that it marks the end of a very long period of solemnities and festivities, when it is natural to let off steam. All the scrolls are taken out of the ark and processed around the synagogue seven times, accompanied by singing and dancing. Members of the congregation are honoured by being called up to be the 'Bridegroom of the Torah' (*Hatan Torah*) and the 'Bridegroom of Bereshit [Genesis]' (*Hatan Bereshit*), but in some synagogues all the congregants are called up, and it is also customary to call up the children, the only day in the year when they are called up to the Torah. The children are given sweets and apples, and they process behind the Torah waving appropriately decorated flags. The two 'bridegrooms' (who in progressive congregations may be 'brides') make a party for the whole congregation.

The other festive days cannot really compete with the powerful and contrasting moods of the autumn festivals. Passover and Shavuot have special liturgies, as do all the special days of the year, and there is a custom of decorating the synagogue with greenery at Shavuot, although some rabbis have opposed it on the grounds that it seems to be an imitation of a Christian harvest festival. At Purim the scroll of Esther is read both in the evening and in the morning; those present, especially children, make a loud noise with rattles whenever the name of the wicked Haman, the persecutor of the Jews, is mentioned in the reading. On the fast day of the 9th of Av, the commemoration of the destruction of the Temple, the synagogue takes on an air of gloom. Joyful prayers are omitted; darkness reigns, and worshippers avoid sitting on chairs, like mourners. The *tallit* and *tefillin* are not put on in the morning; dirges (*kinnot*) are sung, and the book of Lamentations is chanted to a mournful melody.

MOMENTS OF LIFE

These are the special observances, solemn and lighthearted, that mark the rhythm of the synagogue's life year on year. Ceremonies of a different kind punctuate the year, beating time to the pulse of each family, and sharing with them in the joys and griefs of each member. In a small, closely knit community the boundary between synagogue and home is narrow and ill-defined. Members share each other's happiness and sorrow, gathering spontaneously for a circumcision, a burial or a Shivah. A larger congregation tends to be more impersonal, but even here the community enfolds its members in warmth and affection, as when parents come to give thanks on the birth of a child, or when a bridegroom is called up before his wedding, or when a mourner is welcomed into the synagogue and the congregation respond 'amen' as he recites the Kaddish. In many congregations the names of departed family members are read out during the memorial prayers on Yom Kippur. As we have seen, circumcision and marriage may be performed in synagogue, which may also be deemed the appropriate place for the eulogy on the death of a distinguished member.

The regular services provide an opportunity for private events to be mentioned: after a member of the congregation is called up to the Torah a blessing known as *misheberakh* is said, beginning 'May He who blessed our ancestors Abraham, Isaac and Jacob bless. . .'. (Egalitarian versions of the prayer also exist, naming matriarchs as well as patriarchs.) Such events as the birth of a child, a wedding, or even nowadays a silver or golden wedding or a seventieth or eightieth birthday, may be mentioned, and this is also a point in the service where prayers may be offered for someone who is ill. Charitable donations may be made at this point, although some synagogues discourage the practice as confusing the material and the spiritual, and encouraging unseemly and invidious displays of wealth or generosity. If the person called up has been in grave danger, during a journey or illness for example, he may say a special blessing known as *gomel*: 'Blessed are You, Lord our God, king of the universe, who bestows favours on the undeserving, for he has favoured me with such great good.'

The *gomel* may also be said by a mother coming to the synagogue for the first time after giving birth. The baby may be brought, to be blessed by the rabbi. In Reform synagogues the baby will now receive its Hebrew name.

The passage from childhood to adulthood is marked in synagogue, by what has come to be known as the Bar Mitsvah or Bat Mitsvah ceremony. This is a joyful moment for the community as well as for the family, and it is usual for the parents to invite the whole congregation to join the family for a celebration after the service. The Bar Mitsvah ceremony as we know it is not of great antiquity, and belongs to the realm of custom rather than ordinance. On reaching the age of thirteen a boy becomes technically subject to the commandments, but no particular action or observance is laid down in this connection. It was apparently in medieval Germany that it was decided to mark the occasion by calling him up to the Torah, and having a party at which he made a speech, displaying such learning as he had mastered. This is the basis of the present practice. The boy attends synagogue with his parents, and chants or reads a portion from the Torah and the Haftarah. There is a special blessing to be pronounced by his father: 'Blessed be He who has freed me from the responsibility of this [child].' The idea is that hitherto he was responsible for any wrongdoing committed by his son, who from now on will take responsibility for his own actions. The rabbi will address the boy, exhorting him to be a loyal and steadfast Jew. It is usual for the Bar Mitsvah to take place on Sabbath; it may also occur on a Monday or Thursday (the other days when the Torah is read), in which case the boy will put on *tefillin* for the first time.

Since in traditional synagogues girls were not called up to the Torah, and indeed played no part in the life of the synagogue, no such ceremony was devised for them, and some Orthodox rabbis today object to any kind of Bat Mitsvah ceremony on the grounds that it is untraditional. Some Orthodox congregations have a special weekday service at which a number of girls who have reached the legal age of twelve recite biblical texts and prayers; others permit a Bat Mitsvah to deliver an address during the Sabbath service. In Conservative and Reform synagogues girls read from the Torah just as boys do.

The Bar Mitsvah ceremony has been under attack for a long time, because thirteen seems a very early age for a boy to become a man, and indeed many boys at this age hardly seem mature enough to appreciate the responsibilities they are supposed to be undertaking. Only rarely do Bar Mitsvah boys have sufficient Jewish education to be aware of a respectable number of the 613 commandments of the Torah, and those who do may very well not have much general ethical and religious education. By the beginning of the nineteenth century in Germany a confirmation ceremony had been introduced, at which the rabbi asked the boy to give well-rehearsed answers to questions about such subjects as belief in God, and then to recite Maimonides' Thirteen Principles. Large numbers of Jewish catechisms were published, both in Hebrew and in German, and the emphasis was on general rather than specifically Jewish principles. The influence of the Christian environment is obvious, and this new ceremony was objected to by some who felt it went too far towards imitating the Church, and pointed out that Judaism does not have a creed, so that catechising is not strictly appropriate. Nevertheless, confirmation became an established feature of Reform Judaism, being made available to girls as well as boys, and spreading to America, where it gradually replaced the Bar Mitsvah. The age of confirmation also rose, from thirteen to fifteen or sixteen. This was connected to a notable emphasis on Jewish education in American Reform Judaism in the years between the two World Wars. Confirmation at a later age meant that young people were better prepared, in terms both of knowledge and of religious and moral maturity. It also provided an answer to one of the other worrying features of early Bar Mitsvah: in the absence of any subsequent educational goals, teenagers tend to abandon their Jewish education and indeed to drift away from the synagogue. Meanwhile, all denominations of Judaism have tried to remedy the educational problems associated with Bar Mitsvah by insisting on a certain level of synagogue attendance and educational attainment beforehand, and by trying to encourage commitment afterwards in various ways.

OTHER COMMUNAL INSTITUTIONS

We cannot take leave of the Jewish community before taking a look at some of its other institutions besides the synagogue. In the days of the ghetto each community maintained a number of individuals and teams of people and various buildings set aside for specific functions: schools; kosher butchers; a bakery making bread, and *hallah* for Sabbaths and festivals; a *matsah* bakery for Passover; a *mikveh* (bath-house); a *mohel* (circumciser), and a *sofer* (scribe) to write *mezuzot* and *tefillin* as well as Torah scrolls and other texts.

Little survives now from all of this, except in the larger traditional Jewish communities. There are still kosher butchers, but many kosher products are mass-produced, and most *matsot* come from a few large factories. One has to look quite hard to find a *mohel* or a *sofer*. *Mikvaot* are few and far between, although they have undergone a certain revival in some places recently. On the other hand there has been a proliferation of youth groups, attached to synagogues or to national or international youth organisations.

The one area which still attracts a large investment of effort and money is education, whether for children or for adults. Jewish education is no longer an orderly progression from elementary schooling for children to advanced studies for adults. So neglected was religious education during the emancipation period, and so disrupted was it by pogroms and migrations, that many otherwise well-educated adult Jews feel that in terms of Jewish knowledge they are infants. Education fights therefore on two fronts. Children are taught in Sunday schools, evening classes, and increasingly also in day schools. (The age of the Jewish boarding school seems to be past.) Adults can choose from a range of evening classes and other educational options, including residential courses and Jewish options in universities and colleges. Rabbinic seminaries tend to offer courses for the wider public, and are blurring the distinction between seminary and university. The content of all these classes ranges from traditional options such as biblical and Talmudic study to historical and social studies and languages (not only Hebrew, but Yiddish and Judaeo-Spanish too).

The training of rabbis takes place in a rabbinic seminary, or (for the traditional sector) in a yeshivah. Graduating rabbis are employed by synagogues, or serve the community in some other capacity. Some will become teachers. And some will end up sitting on a Bet Din, a rabbinical court. The full range of activities of a Bet Din embrace dispensing justice according to the code of rabbinic law in all its aspects, as well as supervising the rules of holiness and purity. (It is the Bet Din that stamps kosher foodstuffs with its seal of approval and licences kosher butchers, caterers and restaurants.) Since in practice, however, outside Israel the Jewish courts have very limited jurisdiction, in practice most their work is concerned with matters of personal status, such as divorce and conversion. A Bet Din consists of three rabbis; a rabbi acting as a judge is termed a *dayyan*. Formerly *dayyanim*, like rabbis, were always males, but now that the Conservative and Reform movements have women rabbis, they have women judges too.

One institution of the medieval community still plays the same role as it always has done: the cemetery. Jewish cemeteries are set apart by a wall or hedge, and are treated with great respect. In the matter of tombstones Sephardi and Ashkenazi practice differs sharply: Ashkenazi graves have a standing headstone while Sephardi graves are covered with a stone lying flat. The stones carry an inscription in Hebrew or the vernacular, or both. Occasionally one will see a grave marked 'genizah': this is where discarded holy books are buried. Jewish gravestones are normally simple, without elaborate carvings. Flowers are not placed on the coffin or on graves; people who visit a grave will often place a small stone on it to mark their visit.

Jewish tradition teaches that the dead must be buried as soon as possible, usually within twenty-four hours, unless death has taken place on the eve of Sabbath or a festival, or if there is a particular reason to postpone the burial, for example to wait for relatives and friends to arrive from far away, or if suitable shrouds or a coffin are not available. Traditionally, Jews buried their dead, and did not countenance cremation. Cremation became popular in the late nineteenth century, and Reform Judaism has no strong objection to it, but it is frowned on in Conservative Judaism and forbidden in Orthodoxy. In Britain the Orthodox authorities permit the ashes of someone who has been cremated to be buried in a Jewish cemetery, provided the ashes are placed in a normal coffin. Elsewhere some Orthodox rabbis do not even permit this.

Before the body is placed in the coffin it is cleaned and ritually washed. This is often done by members of a special society, the Hevrah Kadisha ('Holy Society'). To assist in the burial of the dead is a valuable service and a sacred duty, and it is considered an honour to belong to a Hevrah Kadisha. Separate teams attend to male and female corpses, out of respect for the deceased, and throughout the washing great care is taken to maintain due respect. The body remains covered at all times. After the body has been carefully washed the 'purification' (*taharah*) is performed, by pouring a quantity of water over it. The body is then dried and dressed in a special set of clothes (*takhrikhim*), which are the same for everybody, without distinction of wealth, status or learning. They are made of white muslin, cotton or linen, and are made and put on without any knots. If a man has his own *kittel*, the tunic which is sometimes worn on Yom Kippur and at the Passover seder, it forms part of the *takhrikhim*, and a man is also wrapped in his *tallit* (prayer shawl), which has had the tassels (*tsitsit*) removed. A little earth from the Holy Land is sprinkled on the body, and it is placed in a plain coffin which is then sealed: it is not the custom to display the body to view, nor is the application of cosmetics allowed.

The funeral is known as *levayah*, 'accompanying'. It is considered a duty to accompany the dead, and a mark of respect which is all the more commendable as the recipient is unable to reciprocate. Prayers are said at home before proceeding to the cemetery, where further prayers are said in a hall or chapel, and a eulogy praising the deceased's virtues and accomplishments may be delivered. Nowadays a rabbi often officiates at a funeral, but there is no requirement to have a rabbi present: like officiating at marriages, this development is an example of the adaptation of the functions of a rabbi to those of a Christian minister or priest. Pallbearers, or relatives and friends, carry the coffin from the chapel to the grave, pausing seven times on the way. The coffin is lowered into the grave, and immediate relatives, followed by the rest of those present, shovel some earth onto it. Worn-out Bibles, prayer books and other texts containing the divine name may be buried in the grave, or they may be placed in a grave of their own, since they too are to be disposed of respectfully and not simply jettisoned.

After burial the mourners recite the prayer known as Kaddish. This prayer contains no mention of death or of grief, but is a glorification of God and a prayer for the coming of his reign on earth. The recitation of this prayer by mourners, both at the cemetery and subsequently, represents an act of submission to the divine will on the part of mourners, and is popularly thought to bring merit to the soul of the departed. This is one of the practices (like attendance at the Passover seder and Yom Kippur services) that are observed by large numbers of Jews who do not otherwise observe many religious rituals.

Before the mourners leave the cemetery, they are greeted with these words of condolence: 'May God comfort you together with all those who mourn for Zion and Jerusalem.' It is customary to wash the hands before leaving the cemetery.

The consecration of the tombstone generally takes place either a month or a year after burial, depending on local custom, with a simple ceremony. Thereafter it is customary for relatives to visit the grave on the anniversary of the death, during the month before Rosh Ha-Shanah, or at any other time they choose.

In some countries there is a custom, going back to the Middle Ages, of visiting the tombs of individuals reputed for their piety or learning as a sign of respect or to offer up prayers. This custom is particularly strongly established in Morocco and other parts of North Africa, where it is not confined to Jews: in fact Jews, Muslims and Christians visit each others' shrines. In Poland the Hasidim developed the custom of visiting the tombs of their rebbes on the anniversary of their deaths. In the Middle East, particularly in Israel, Iraq and Iran, the tombs of biblical patriarchs and prophets attract pilgrims, and the kabbalists of Safed identified tombs of famous ancient rabbis all over Galilee. All these sites are visited by pilgrims, particularly kabbalists and Hasidim. The annual pilgrimage to the supposed tomb of Simeon bar Yohai at Meron has already been mentioned, and a new pilgrimage has been introduced, to the tomb of a modern North African saint called Baba Sali at Netivot. Such observances, however, are completely unknown in the West.

Besides the specific responsibilities of children towards their parents, the whole community has a responsibility towards those of its members who are in distress, whether through poverty, ill-health, mental anguish or old age. Every congregation has charities that administer funds for the benefit of the poor, the sick and the elderly, and there are generally panels of members who share in visiting the sick. It is now common in western countries for the Jewish community to make its contribution also to charities benefiting the wider community.

In these various ways the Jewish communities, even in places where they constitute a tiny minority, proudly and loyally maintain their individual identity and their ancient traditions.

CHAPTER SEVEN

God and the Jewish people

THE JEWS AND GOD

The relationship of the Jews to God is a very special one. In theory it is a relationship of mutual love, and a mutual commitment formally embodied in a binding legal agreement, known as 'the covenant'. In other words, it is very much like a human marriage, and in fact the language of marriage pervades the biblical passages which touch on the relationship.

The most vivid of these, and the only one where the sexual urge comes openly to the fore, is the short book known as the Song of Songs, which is understood as a dialogue of love between God and the people of Israel. 'Oh, that he would kiss me with the kisses of his mouth: your love is better than wine . . .' Small wonder that in congregations under kabbalistic influence the Song is sung on Friday night, when the male and female principles are united in the Sabbath, bringing a foretaste of the future reconciliation. The mood of longing and expectation that infuses this poetic work helps to account for its appeal even at times in history when the relationship might seem to have broken down. After falling from favour in the rationalism of the nineteenth century, this interpretation of the Song has come to the fore again in the twentieth, more open at once to mystical allegory and to physicality, and seeking language to express the relationship between God and humanity. 'The voice of my beloved, there he is, he is coming, bounding over mountains, leaping over hills': no obstacle can stand in the way of the lover's exultant return.

The relationship in practice has not been an easy one, and the marriage has often been threatened with breakdown. In the Bible the blame is placed on the fickleness and infidelity of the Jews. God is a jealous husband, and the people are constantly being seduced by other gods. The result is not only national catastrophe, destruction and exile, but natural disasters too. They are linked in the words of the Shma: 'Take good care that your heart is not seduced, so that you are distracted and serve other gods, and worship them. Then the Lord's anger will blaze up against you: he will shut up the sky so there is no rain, and the soil will not yield its produce, and soon you will all perish from the good land which the Lord is giving you' (Deuteronomy 11:16–17). The book of the prophet Hosea is a long meditation on this theme. Israel is unfaithful to God, flirting with lovers and pursuing prostitutes, and God's response seems to waver between fierce anger and pleading with the people to return, because his love is constant and overcomes all obstacles. He looks forward to the day when she will 'respond as she did when she was young, when she came up out of the land of Egypt', when she will call him 'my husband' and forget the names of the false gods. Then all war and destruction will be wiped out, and even the animals will lose their fear. 'I shall betroth you to me for ever. I shall betroth you to me with fairness and justice, with tenderness and love. I shall betroth you to me with faithfulness, and you will know the Lord' (Hosea 2:19–20).

Passages like this one reveal a deep yearning for the renewal of the ancient, lost days when, it is supposed, the relationship between God and the Jewish people was a close and harmonious one. 'Turn us back to You, Lord, and we shall return; renew our days as of old.' These words (from Lamentations 5:21) are sung in synagogue as the scroll of the Torah is returned to the ark and the doors are closed, and they express a powerful sense of a rift that must be healed, whether at the level of the individual, or of the people, or of the whole human race. Nostalgia, dissatisfaction, and a longing for restoration and healing are emotions that are strongly represented within Judaism, side by side with confidence, love and pride.

The presence of so many conflicting emotions and unresolved contradictions makes it impossible to present a concise picture of the Jewish relationship with God. The problem is exacerbated further by the lack of an official creed. In the case of a religion like Christianity it is possible to list the official beliefs, while perhaps pointing to areas where the different denominations disagree or where popular opinion diverges. This is not possible in the case of Judaism. It is difficult to know what to make of any generalisation about Jewish belief, including the often-heard statement that 'Judaism stands or falls on the belief in the existence of God.' On the one hand, it is no doubt true that within the accepted canon of Jewish theological writing the existence of God is such a fundamental assumption that even to state it has sometimes been interpreted as too daring, because it somehow implies that the contrary is thinkable. And yet there are many Jews, not only Marxists, for whom the non-existence of God is equally axiomatic.

What to say about God in an age of so much unbelief? In an age when many Jews who would like to believe in God feel betrayed and abandoned by him? This is certainly not the first period in history when this feeling has existed, but in the aftermath of the Holocaust it does seem to be particularly widespread and vocal. At the same time there are large numbers of Jews, especially but not exclusively in Israel, who relegate all talk of God to an earlier, less scientific, more credulous period of history. Is there anything that would authorise us to dismiss such voices as not really Jewish?

One possible starting point is the observation that virtually all Jews, including Orthodox rabbis, would agree in principle that a Jew who rejects belief in God is still a Jew. Indeed many maintain that technically even a Jew who converts to Christianity remains a Jew. In this case, it would be easy to dismiss the theological beliefs of such a person as not really representative of Jewish belief, since they coincide with those of another faith (although this argument is not as straightforward as it may at first sight appear). The out-and-out Jewish atheist might be dismissed by believers in the same way: it could be argued that atheism is by definition un-Jewish.

However, atheism can easily shade into agnosticism, and agnosticism into religious scepticism and debates about what precisely, according to theists, we can truly know and say about God. Even some Orthodox rabbis would probably agree with the many Jewish thinkers down the centuries who have argued that God is essentially unknowable, and that any human statement about God is imperfect and open to question.

The knowability of God was debated particularly by the medieval philosophers. Joseph Albo, in the fifteenth century, remarked, 'If I knew God I would be God', and there is a general trend to insist that anything we say about God is liable to be false and misleading. All the attributes people attribute to him are extrapolated from human experience, which is by its nature fundamentally and categorically different from God,

> The secret of whose strength doth quite exceed
> Our thought, as Thou transcendest our frail plane.
> All might is thine, swathed in a mystic shawl,
> The fundament of all:
> Hid from philosophers thy name . . .[1]

[1] Solomon Ibn Gabirol, *The Kingly Crown*, I, tr. Loewe, *Ibn Gabirol*, p. 119.

Neoplatonist and Aristotelian philosophers agreed that we can neither know nor say anything about God's essence. Only his actions can be known, and even these, Maimonides famously insisted, only tell us what God is not like, not what he is like.

The kabbalists go even further along the negative way. The philosophers, having established the impossibility of saying anything meaningful and true about God, somehow manage to end up saying a good deal about him. The kabbalists make an explicit separation between God as he can be known and God as he is in himself. The latter they call the Infinite (En Sof in Hebrew). The En Sof is utterly unknowable. Even the Sefirot, which are contained, as it were, within God, do not have knowledge of the En Sof. The En Sof plays no part in creation or revelation, is not an object of contemplation, study or prayer. These can only reach the Sefirot.

This debate about the knowledge of God arose out of, and in turn encouraged, a widespread interest in the nature of God. As to the existence of God, however, both the philosophers and the kabbalists entertained no doubts at all. Of course they lived in an age when God's existence was taken for granted by virtually everybody, Jew or non-Jew, with whom they would have come in contact. One wonders how they would have responded to the current situation, in which atheism and agnosticism are so widespread, and when even religious Jews express serious doubts about God's power to act in the world.

Yet although the prevalence of atheism coupled with a habit of questioning all received orthodoxy makes our age different from earlier periods, it would be mistaken to imagine that the radical nature of contemporary disagreements is totally novel. Let us take the key question of whether events – on the personal level or on the stage of world history – are under the control of human or divine power, whether the world is guided by divine providence or whether people have control over their own actions. Josephus, writing about Israel in the time of the Hasmonean wars of the second century BCE, divides the Jews of the time into three 'philosophical schools', and sums up their differences as follows:

At that time there were three schools among the Jews, the Pharisees, the Sadducees and the Essenes, and they all held different views about human behaviour. The Pharisees hold that some, but not all, events are the work of Fate: in some cases it is for us to decide whether they should happen or not. The Essenes claim that Fate is mistress of everything, and nothing befalls people except by its decision. Meanwhile the Sadducees rule Fate out altogether, considering that it counts for nothing and has no effect on human actions, but that everything is up to us: we ourselves are responsible for the good things that happen to us, while the bad things happen because of our poor planning.[2]

'Fate' here does not mean blind chance but divine intervention, and the debate about the extent of God's interference in human affairs has a strangely modern ring, particularly reminiscent of arguments in Israel today. While it would not be entirely accurate to liken contemporary secularists to the ancient Sadducees, who did not deny the existence of God but, on the contrary, were concerned to distance him from any contact with evil, there is something similar between their views in practice. The Essene position on this issue is close to the view of those who refuse to recognise Israel as a Jewish state, arguing that God will send the redemption when he wills it, and it is wrong for humans to try to 'hasten the end'. Moderate religious opinion would correspond, then, to the standpoint of the Pharisees, that all choices involve both God and man.

Here we can glimpse one possible reason for the eclipse of Jewish theology in our time. The secularists see no point in discussing God. Even to talk about him is a major concession to those who claim that he exists or has any power in the world. As for the Orthodox, their argument is a closed circle, which is not up for discussion: everything we know about God and the demands he makes on mankind comes from the Torah, which He himself revealed. The traditional teachings can only be questioned by casting doubt on the doctrine of revelation; but if that is impugned the whole edifice may collapse. Theology can only be pursued by those in the middle, who cannot bring themselves to accept either atheism on the one hand or the idea that God literally dictated the whole of the Torah (including the teachings of the Talmud) to Moses on the other. And they in their turn are attacked by both wings, who in Israel at least constitute a majority of the Jews.

In the Diaspora the situation is rather different, particularly because the secularists are not as organised or vocal as they are in Israel, and consequently they are not the main target of attacks from the 'revelationists', who seem more concerned to combat the progressive religious sector (which in Israel is new and tiny). Hence what Jewish theology there is comes out of the Diaspora, and particularly today from America. And it flourishes very largely within the ranks of Progressive Judaism.

Another reason for a lack of theological reflection is the impact of the

---

[2] Josephus, *Jewish Antiquities* 13. 171–3. Cf. *Jewish War* 2. 162–5.

Shoah, which has raised again in an acute form and on a massive scale the most intractable conundrum in classical theology: how can a good and all-powerful God preside over a world in which such evil acts are committed?[3] The enormity of the evil blocks attempts to think about it. As Arthur Cohen has put it: 'The death camps are a reality which, by their very nature, obliterate thought and the human programme of thinking.'[4]

It is not that the Holocaust put an end to belief in God for those who lived through it. On the contrary, an investigation conducted among survivors revealed not only that many had come through with their faith in God unimpaired, but that for some their faith was strengthened, while a significant minority who had previously been atheists found God in the camps.[5] However, survivors and theologians alike have found it impossible to solve the riddle 'How could a God who is good and omnipotent let the Holocaust happen'? With this crisis Jewish theology seems to have blown a fuse. It has been pointed out that there is nothing inherently unique about the Nazi Holocaust: the same questions about God are raised by every single case of suffering. The biblical book of Job deals precisely with this issue. Nevertheless, perhaps because of the hugeness of its scale, or perhaps for some other reason, the Holocaust seems to have cut short a very fertile period of Jewish theologising that began in the early nineteenth century in Germany. Some theologians have indeed addressed the theological questions raised by the Holocaust, and we shall consider their arguments later in this chapter, but they are very few in number, and they have tended to be tentative, unadventurous and even apologetic, and do not approach the best level of Jewish theology in times gone by.

SOURCES OF JEWISH THEOLOGY

What are the textual materials on which today's theologians have to base themselves, and what are the earlier writings with which they have to wrestle? What weight do these texts carry, and what do they have to say about the character and activity of God? To answer these questions fully would require a whole book, but some summary, however brief, is necessary here.

---

[3] On this question see Oliver Leaman, *Evil and Suffering in Jewish Philosophy* (Cambridge, 1995).
[4] Arthur Cohen, *The Tremendum* (New York, 1981), p. 1.
[5] R. R. Brenner, *The Faith and Doubt of Holocaust Survivors* (New York/London, 1980), especially chapter 3.

The Bible

First and foremost among the sources is the Bible, for several reasons. Even if many Jews can no longer accept that the Bible is literally revealed or inspired by God, it is held in such a high regard by most Jews that no other written text can approach it. Reference to biblical quotations provides, in effect, common ground to Jews who might disagree on virtually everything else.

The Bible, however, does not present a single, coherent view of God, and if certain generalisations are permissible that seems due more to chance than to a concerted programme.

There is very little that can be called philosophical discourse, in the Greek sense, in the Bible. The biblical God may be superhuman, but he is definitely a person, an actor in a drama that encompasses the destiny of individuals and nations and indeed ultimately the whole of the universe.

This personal God is often described in language that is so personal that it has proved an embarrassment to thinkers schooled in Greek thought. He is called a judge, a king, a shepherd, a man of war. He has emotions which are all too human: he is said to be jealous, and angry, and he sometimes changes his mind and feels regret. Nor does biblical language hesitate to speak of God's activity as though he had a human body: he is described as sitting in the sky with his feet resting on the earth as on a footstool; his hand is raised up, his forearm is outstretched, his right arm is powerful; his mouth speaks, he roars aloud, and he has 'long nostrils' (meaning that he is patient and slow to lose his temper). No doubt this language can be explained as metaphorical or as poetic licence, but it is so common in the text that it inevitably colours the personality of God.

And yet at the same time the Bible is insistent that God is not visible. It is true that occasionally people see God (e.g. Exodus 24:9, Isaiah 6:1), but such passages are rare, and the general idea seems to be that normal, living people cannot see God. Even Moses was not allowed to see God, 'for no man can see me while living' (Exodus 33:20). The Israelites are reminded that

when God spoke to you on Horeb out of the fire you saw no form; so take care not to relapse and make yourselves any idol in representational form, a carving whether male or female; a carving of any animal on the ground or of any winged bird that flies in the sky; a carving of anything that creeps on the ground or of any fish in the water underground; and not to look upwards to the sky and see the sun and moon and stars like an army in the sky, and abase yourselves and worship and serve them. (Deuteronomy 4:15–19, alluding to Exodus 20:3–5, cf. Deuteronomy 5:7–9)

Worship of such images is acceptable for the other nations, but God's own people are forbidden to follow suit.

The polemic against worshipping God in a visible form is closely connected to the polemic against worshipping a multiplicity of Gods. If there is any theological principle that is asserted repeatedly and consistently in the Bible it is the unity of God. The slogan 'the Lord is one' (*Adonai ehad*), proclaimed in the first line of the Shma (Deuteronomy 6:4), is repeated by the prophet Zechariah in his vision of a day when 'the Lord shall be king of all the world, when the Lord shall be one and his name one' (Zechariah 14:9). This unity is not only numerical, meaning that God is singular and not, as some falsely claim, dual or plural; it also means that God is unique: because he is the one true God he is different in kind from all other gods men worship.

Another frequently stressed attribute of God is his eternity. He has always existed, and he always will exist; he is the First and the Last (Isaiah 44:6, cf. Psalm 90:2, 146:10). As we might say, he is outside time. He is also outside space. He is beyond the world and yet he is everywhere within it.

> Where could I go to escape from your spirit?
> Where could I flee from your presence?
> If I were to soar into the sky you would be there.
> If I were to sink into the underworld you would be there.
> If I rose on wings of dawn, made my home on the furthermost seashore,
> even there your hand would guide me, your right hand hold me.
> (Psalm 139:7–10)

God in the Bible knows everything and can do anything he pleases: nothing is beyond his ability (Genesis 18:14, cf. Jeremiah 32:27). In other words, from the Bible's often poetic language we gain an impression of someone whose vantage-point is so high that he can see everything that happens on earth, however secret, including what has not yet happened, and his strength is so great that nothing can thwart his will. Fortunately, although he can be stern and a stickler for justice and fair play, he is goodness personified and is loving and beneficent. Sometimes his patience is tried too far by human selfishness and rebelliousness, and then he can strike ruthlessly. But such events are rare and always justified. More often he is loving and forgiving.

The Bible tells a story, and in that human story God is intimately implicated from the very first moment. It was God who made the world out of chaos, and created the human race 'in his own image and form'. Later he chose Abraham, Isaac and Jacob and their descendants, the people of Israel, and made a covenant with them. When they became slaves of the Egyptians he rescued them, fed them in the desert, and at Mount Sinai he gave them the Torah. Then he led them to the promised land and helped them to conquer it from its inhabitants, and eventually he took up residence in the Temple built by King Solomon in his capital city, Jerusalem. After Solomon the kingdom was divided into two, and as a punishment for bad behaviour the northern kingdom was destroyed by the Assyrians and the southern kingdom was later attacked by the king of Babylon, Nebuchadnezzar, who razed the Temple and led the people away as captives. After seventy years of exile the victorious Persian king Cyrus gave permission for them to return and rebuild the Temple. One day God will bring this cycle of history to an end with an ultimate intervention, which will leave Israel ruling the world from Jerusalem under God's kingship, and all the other nations acknowledging his rule.

Since the rise of critical biblical study in the nineteenth century the Bible is no longer read either as a sufficient and reliable guide to ancient history or as an infallible account of God's character and activity. Research may have confirmed some of the details, but it has disproved so much else that the authority of the whole has been fatally undermined for all but those who choose to put their trust in the Bible and suppose that it is the scholars who are in error.

That is not to say that Jews have cast off the Bible as a worn-out vessel that has served its purpose. It still has the power to fascinate and even compel new generations, and modern scholarship has served to enrich understanding. In Israel even godless Jews read it and bandy quotations in support of their views. Nevertheless it is fair to say that the power of the Bible has declined, for a number of reasons besides the abandonment of the old doctrine of divine revelation. For all the immediacy and poetry of its language (and the revival of Hebrew has made this language accessible to a much wider audience), the Bible speaks of very remote times. The way of life it advocates has noble elements, some of which may have been in advance of their times, but in other ways it strikes readers as archaic and even primitive. Even Orthodox Jews have expressed perplexity at the complex regulations for animal sacrifices, for example, and one does not have to be a feminist to feel that the biblical assumptions about the respective roles of men and women can no longer serve as the basis for Jewish society. Many of the Bible's teachings are too vague or inconsistent to be put into practice, and a great deal is simply irrelevant to contemporary life.

Midrash and Haggadah

The classical texts of rabbinic Judaism, the Talmud and Midrash, contain many observations about God, although they are not presented in a systematic way. Sometimes they reiterate biblical statements, sometimes they go beyond them, adapt them, or implicitly contradict them, but almost always the rabbis attach their remarks to a quotation from the Bible. This is the way of Midrash: to reread the Bible as a contemporary document.

A few examples will illustrate the matter.

Psalm 65 begins with the obscure statement 'To you, God, silence is praise in Zion, and to you a vow will be repaid.' Often, though not always, it is such obscurities in the Bible that attract midrashic interest. A rabbinic explanation connects this verse with the negative way of theology: no human language can do justice to the nature of God. 'It can be compared to a jewel without price: however high you appraise it, you still undervalue it.'[6]

' "May the Lord make his fact to shine towards you" (Numbers 6:25): Rabbi Nathan says, This is the light of the Shekhinah, as it says (Isaiah 60:1): "Arise, shine, for your light has come, and the glory of the Lord has risen upon you." '[7]

' "I, even I, am He, and there is no god beside me; it is I who kill, and it is I who make alive; I wound and I heal" (Deuteronomy 32:39). This verse is a reply to [three categories of Jews]: those who say that there is no power in heaven, those who say there are two powers in heaven, and those who say there is no power who can make alive or kill, do evil or good.'[8]

---

[6] Palestinian Talmud, *Berakhot* 9:1; Midrash to Psalm 19:2. For the connection between this Midrash and the *via negativa* see Louis Jacobs, *A Jewish Theology* (London/New York, 1973), pp. 47–8. As Jacobs observes, Maimonides quotes this verse of the Psalms in support of his negative theology. For a fine modern meditation on this theme see A. J. Heschel, *Man's Quest for God* (New York, 1954), pp. 41–4.

[7] *Sifre Numbers*, 41. This interpretation, stressing the indwelling presence of God among his people, is offered to contradict another view, that the light in question is that of the Torah, implying a more remote and intellectual relationship between God and Israel. See below.

[8] *Sifre Deuteronomy*, 329.

In the absence of a systematic exposition of theological beliefs, we can gain a sense of rabbinic theology from the themes to which they return again and again. The unity of God is one of these, evidently asserted in the face of a range of alternative theologies: not only pagan polytheism, but Christian trinitarianism, Persian dualism, in which this world is a battleground between the forces of good and evil, and another kind of dualism in which the supreme God had an assistant, a sort of lesser god, in creating and administering the world. The rabbis insist adamantly that God is utterly alone and unique, and has no helper.

Building on biblical foundations, the rabbis continue to combine the idea of God's transcendence with his presence in the world, for which they have a special name, Shekhinah. The concept of Shekhinah preserves the idea of a loving personal God in the face of philosophical speculation that stresses his perfection and remoteness. The rabbis can even speak of the Shekhinah as sharing human suffering, or going into exile with the people of Israel. In the context of the strong insistence on divine unity, these two logically conflicting understandings of God are somehow superimposed, in the manner of the Bible, without the need to analyse or resolve the inconsistencies. It is rather similar with the twin images of God as ruthless judge and as loving parent. On the face of it these roles may seem irreconcilable, but in the rabbinic view of God they are held in balance:

There was once a king who had some fragile goblets. He said, 'If I put hot water in them, they will shatter; if I put cold water in them, they will crack.' So the king mixed cold and hot water together and poured it in, and they were not damaged. Similarly God said, 'If I create the world with the attribute of mercy, sin will multiply; if I create it with the attribute of justice, how can it endure? I shall create it with both together, then it will endure.'[9]

Many Jews who do not have direct knowledge of the rabbinic texts are familiar with their theology from the prayer book. The rabbinic Haggadah also furnishes endless material for sermons; indeed, much of it is drawn from sermons in the first place, as its frequent parables and exhortations remind us. The method of the rabbinic argument is unsatisfying if one wants philosophical answers to questions about God, and the clarity of logical reasoning. But in the immediacy and intuitiveness of its apprehensions and the way it extracts multiple and often surprising answers from a close reading of texts it often seems remarkably modern.

---

[9] *Genesis Rabba* 12:15.

The philosophers

The first Jewish philosopher was Philo of Alexandria, who lived in the first half of the first century CE. He was a prolific author, many of whose works have survived. Yet it appears that he had little or no impact on the living Jewish tradition, and his writings have only survived because they were copied by Christian scribes. The impetus to write philosophy seems to have come to Philo from the encounter that took place within the Judaism of his day between biblically based Judaism and Greek thought based mainly on Plato. Many of his books try to reconcile the two by interpreting the Bible as a kind of textbook of Platonism.

After Philo Jewish philosophy was silent for several centuries, until it surfaced again in the context of the Muslim *kalam* (scholastic theology) in the ninth century. The outstanding figure of this revival is Saadya (882–942), Gaon (principal) of the Jewish academy of Sura in Iraq. The aim of *kalam*, largely apologetic, was to justify religious beliefs by rational arguments, and the Jewish thinkers of this early period, both Rabbanite and Karaite, shared these aims, with the difference that for the Jews the source of revealed truth was the Hebrew Bible, not the Qur'an. The age of the Jewish *kalam* was short-lived, and it was soon superseded by a more fully fledged philosophical tradition which rested on Greek foundations, mediated through Arabic translations.

Aristotelian philosophy dominates the medieval Jewish intellectual tradition, but there is also an important Neoplatonist strand, of which the prime representative was Solomon Ibn Gabirol (1020–57?), who was also one of the most sublime Hebrew poets of all times. His greatest poem is the *Kingly Crown* (*Keter malkhut*), which has already been mentioned, and his most important philosophical work is the *Fountain of Life*. The best-known Jewish Aristotelian is Maimonides, a prolific author whose ideas about God are found not only in his philosophical masterwork, the *Guide of the Perplexed*, but scattered throughout his other writings such as his commentary on the Mishnah and his code of Jewish practice, the *Mishneh Torah*. In fact the last-mentioned work opens with a classical statement of God's existence, combining and reconciling biblical and Aristotelian elements:

It is the basis of all foundations and the pillar on which all wisdom rests to know that there is a Prime Being who brought into being everything that exists and that all creatures in heaven and earth and between them only enjoy existence by virtue of His existence. If it could be imagined that He did not exist, then nothing else could have existed. But if it could be imagined that all beings other than He did not exist, He alone would still exist and He would not suffer cessation in their cessation. For all things need Him but He, blessed be He, needs not a single one of them. It follows that His true nature is unlike the nature of any of them. (*Foundations of Torah*, 1:1–3)

Of God's attributes little can be truly said, according to Maimonides, because of his utter otherness and the incapacity of our minds to grasp his nature. It is possible to describe his activity, as opposed to his essence, by analogy with human behaviour. When we say of his actions that they are good, we mean that we would have judged them good if they had been performed by humans. When on the other hand we say that he is one, we are not saying anything positive, but merely ruling out the opposite. This is what is termed Negative Theology. It is an influential approach, but has also had its critics, such as Hasdai Crescas (d. 1412), who insisted that the divine attributes really are to be understood positively.

If the medieval Jewish philosophers worked against the background of Arabic thought, the thinkers of the Enlightenment period were writing in a German milieu, and the pressures imposed by emancipation. A Jew like Maimonides was certain of his place in society, with fewer privileges than a Muslim, but enjoying a stable and clearly defined status, and able to engage confidently on that basis with Muslim thinkers, whose intellectual background he shared and who had no desire to convert him to Islam. If no similar Jewish philosophy emerged in medieval Christendom, no doubt it was because it offered no such basis for a confident Jewish participation in intellectual life. As late as the end of the nineteenth century brilliant young thinkers like Edmund Husserl and Henri Bergson, who might have made a great contribution to Jewish religious thought, succumbed to the pressure to convert to Christianity. Others turned their backs on religious philosophy and engaged in 'neutral' currents of thought opened up by the Enlightenment, where their Jewish identity would be no handicap. And those Jewish thinkers who remained faithful to Judaism felt the need to engage in apologetics, justifying Jewish values in the face of Christian or German ones.

Moses Mendelssohn (1729–86), a contemporary of Kant and friend of Lessing, represents these dilemmas in an acute form. A champion of political emancipation of the Jews, he found his career blocked by his refusal to be baptised, and constantly felt called to defend the teachings of Judaism from Christian attacks. Mendelssohn embraced the principles of the Enlightenment wholeheartedly while remaining faithful, as he saw it, to Judaism. In his book *Jerusalem* (1783) he distanced Judaism from Christianity by proclaiming that whereas Christianity was a revealed religion, Judaism had no dogmas that were not accessible to the reasoning of any human being. Its only distinctive, divinely given heritage was its law.

This somewhat artificial dichotomy between universal reason and particularist law, which reflects the dichotomy between Mendelssohn the Enlightenment man and Mendelssohn the traditional Jew, determined in a sense the destiny of Jewish religious philosophy throughout the nineteenth century. On the one hand, a succession of idealists (such as Salomon Formstecher, Ludwig Steinheim and Samuel Hirsch) pursued the theme of the religion of reason, describing Judaism in terms drawn from contemporary German philosophy; on the other, the partisans of 'divine legislation' (Samuel David Luzzatto, Samson Raphael Hirsch, Elia Benamozegh, Moritz Lazarus) focused on the realm of practice. Important though some of their insights were in other fields, none of these men made any original or permanent contribution to the Jewish doctrine of God. We can find some indication of this in the fact that although their names are well known, hardly any of their works have been translated into English, which has been the main, in fact virtually the only, language of Jewish theology since the middle of the twentieth century. A sole exception is S. R. Hirsch, who is remembered as the founding father of Modern Orthodoxy; perhaps for that reason, his main works, *Horeb* and *The Nineteen Letters of Ben Uziel*, have been translated.[10]

Hermann Cohen (1842–1918), straddling the threshold of a new century, marks a new beginning in Jewish religious philosophy. A distinguished academic philosopher, founder of the Marburg Neo-Kantian school, Cohen stands in the line of German Jewish idealists, and in his nineteenth-century writings God serves only as an idea that supports the structure of his philosophy of ethics. In the last part of his life, however, Cohen changed tack, and began to address the God of faith. Rejecting Kant's view that Judaism was obsolete, Cohen declared it to be true religion, and in his book *Religion of Reason out of the Sources of Judaism* he completed, as it were, the project initiated by Mendelssohn.

Taking the Jewish philosophical tradition as a whole, we must admit

---

[10] *Nineteen Letters*, tr. Bernard Drachman (New York, 1942); *Horeb*, tr. I. Grunfeld (London, 1962); abridged translation of the *Commentary on the Pentateuch* by Isaac Levy (London, 1958–62); I. Grunfeld, ed., *Selected Essays from the Writings of S. R. Hirsch* (London, 1956); *Collected Writings of Rabbi Samson Raphael Hirsch* (New York, 1985–8). See also Z. H. Rosenbloom, *Tradition in an Age of Reform: The Religious Philosophy of Samson Raphael Hirsch* (Philadelphia, 1976).

that its impact has been enormous, both within Judaism and outside it (both Philo and Maimonides had an influence on Christian philosophy). And yet this impact has not been at all straightforward. Philo was a dead end, in the Jewish tradition. Maimonides was opposed in his lifetime and after his death his books were burned, as his opponents considered that philosophy was inimical to faith.

Mystical approaches

When we speak of 'Jewish mysticism' we mean not so much the individual's private quest for union with God as a quest for knowledge of the divine pursued by groups, who committed their ideas to writing. The modern study of the subject was pioneered by Gershom Scholem,[11] who laboured untiringly on kabbalistic and other texts, analysing the ideas they contain and tracing their history and their relationship with traditions outside Judaism. What these texts testify to is really a gnosis, that is esoteric knowledge reserved for the members of a group, and by means of which they believed they had direct access to knowledge of God not available to those who toiled in the mainstream texts such as the Talmud. It is a learned tradition, which tends to take on the outward form of classical Jewish scholarship (for example the *Zohar* is made to look like a rabbinic Midrash). Many of the authors were scholars with a reputation in another field: they include Joseph Caro (1488–1575), the author of two major legal codes, and Moses Hayyim Luzzatto (1707–47),[12] who also wrote Hebrew dramas in a classical Italian style.

In the wake of Scholem's work there has been a good deal of scholarly interest in the various mystical schools, such as the Descenders of the Chariot (*Yordei Merkavah*) and the German Pietists (*Hasidei Ashkenaz*), as well as the classical kabbalists of the Middle Ages and the Safed school of the sixteenth century. It is the kabbalists who offer the richest material concerning the nature of God.

We have already seen that the kabbalists draw a sharp distinction between God as he is in himself (the unknowable En Sof) and as he manifests himself, through a process of emanation, by means of ten Sefirot, which are powers within the Godhead. Unlike the Neoplatonist theory of emanations, which constitute a graduated bridge between the totally abstract God and the totally concrete earth, the Sefirot are all within

---

[11] See David Biale, *Gershom Scholem: Kabbalah and Counter History* (Cambridge, MA, 1982).
[12] See M. H. Luzzatto, *Mesillat Yesharim: the Path of the Upright*, tr. and ed. Mordecai M. Kaplan (Philadelphia, 1936).

God; nevertheless they do function as a bridge between the perfection of the En Sof and the imperfection of our world, and they are an answer to the same intellectual problem.[13]

The three highest Sefirot are beyond all human understanding. *Keter*, 'Crown', the first emanation from the En Sof, represents the first inchoate stirring of a will to create the universe, but as yet it is a preliminary stage, which only becomes, as it were, a will to create in *Hokhmah*, 'Wisdom', in which all the creative processes are potentially contained, to be understood in their details in *Binah*, 'Understanding'. *Hesed*, 'Love', and *Gevurah*, 'Might', are a pair: *Hesed* represents unadulterated love, which would enfold and overwhelm the world if it were not held in check by *Gevurah*, representing judgment, which is in turn softened by love. It is *Tiferet*, 'Beauty', which holds the two in balance. Beauty in turn is supported by another pair, *Netsah*, 'Victory' and *Hod*, 'Splendour', and all these eight merge in *Yesod*, 'Foundation', which brings the power of the other Sefirot into *Malkhut*, 'Sovereignty', which represents God's rule over the created world and is identified with the Shekhinah.

The Sefirot are sometimes represented in the form of a human body. The Crown is above the head. Wisdom is the brain and Understanding the heart. Love and Might are the right and left arms, Beauty the torso and Victory and Splendour the right and left legs. Foundation, the generative principle, is the sexual organ, and Sovereignty is the mouth. The body in question is a male body, but the Sefirot themselves are divided into male and female. Those on the right are male and represent divine love, while those on the left are female and represent divine judgment. The ones in the middle represent the harmonisation of the two opposing principles. Beauty, known as 'Holy One, blessed be He', is male, but sovereignty, the Shekhinah, is female. In addition to these holy Sefirot there are Sefirot belonging to the Sitra Ahra, the 'Other Side'.

This system of the classical Kabbalah, incorporated in the *Zohar* and other works, was fundamentally modified by Isaac Luria in the sixteenth century. Before the Sefirot, and ultimately the universe, can be created, the En Sof must, as it were, make room by withdrawing into itself. This withdrawal (*tsimtsum*) leaves a kind of empty space into which a ray of divine light was projected in the form of the Primordial Man (*Adam kadmon*), and from this the Sefirot emanated. The process of emanation is achieved through further streams of divine light which, issuing from the Primordial Man, produce the vessels into which the Sefirot will

---

[13] See further F. Lachower and I. Tishby, *The Wisdom of the Zohar*, tr. D. Goldstein (Oxford, 1989).

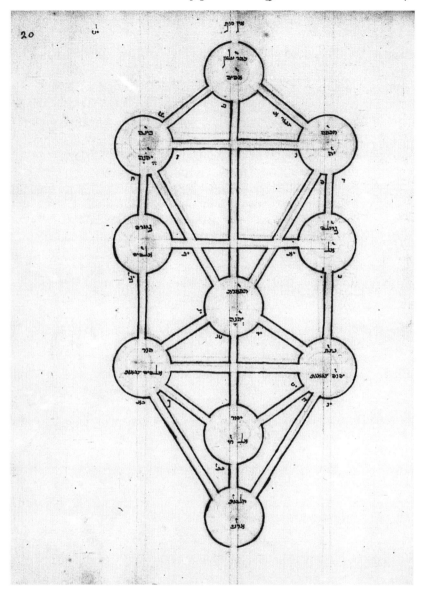

5. The ten Sefirot (a diagram from a Hebrew manuscript written in Italy in 1577). The names of the Sefirot are accompanied here by the divine names that correspond to them, and lines show their connections to each other. At the top, above the first Sefirah, is En Sof, the Infinite One from which the Sefirot emanate. From *D'une main forte: manuscripts hébreux des collections françaises*, plate 122 [hébreu 64, folio 19v–20], by Michel Garel, 1991, Bibliothèque Nationale de France.

emerge. The Sefirot themselves are produced by a further radiation from the eyes of the Primordial Man. At this point an unplanned disaster takes place: this additional light is too powerful for the vessels of the lower Sefirot, and they collapse. Because of the breaking of the vessels nothing is quite as it should have been, so that the cosmos is flawed even before its creation. The Sefirot, now incapable of containing the divine light, are rearranged in 'configurations' (*partsufim*) in which they support and strengthen one another. The idea of the breaking of the vessels has been associated with an acute sense of disruption following the catastrophe of the expulsion from Spain in 1492. In the Lurianic system there is a need for 'Repair' (*tikkun*), in which humankind can play a part.

Kabbalah continued to attract adherents after the time of Luria and his circle, and it enjoyed a tremendous resurgence in the form of Hasidism. Hasidism does not put forward a single theology; in fact it very soon became fragmented into a number of schools, all of which share a vivid sense of the presence of the divine energy within everything. This idea is pushed to its limit in the most intellectual branch of Hasidism, the Lithuanian or Habad branch. *Tsimtsum*, which in the Lurianic system preserves the Infinite from being directly implicated in the creation, does not really take place. Everything is in God, and from God's point of view the created universe does not really exist. This amounts to an extreme assertion of the unity of God, for all multiplicity is a kind of illusion.[14] This 'panentheism' was strongly attacked by opponents of Hasidism.

After being perhaps unduly neglected and even vilified in the high period of rationalism in the nineteenth century, the mystical tradition has now been brought out into the light of scholarly research. Yet although some of its hymns have entered the synagogue service and have even experienced a revival in Reform liturgies, it is doubtful whether its theological ideas exert much real influence today, outside strictly kabbalistic and Hasidic circles.

The liturgy as a source of theology

Perhaps the most influential source of theological beliefs today is the liturgy. The reason is obvious. A Jew does not need to make the effort to decide on a course of reading and carry it through, with the need to decide between different approaches or schools. The liturgy is ready-

---

[14] See Jacobs, *A Jewish Theology*, pp. 34–6.

6. *Tefillin* (phylacteries) are worn during morning prayers on weekdays. There are two leather cases, placed on the forehead and upper arm respectively, and they contain tiny parchment scrolls on which four passages from the Torah are written by hand. These four passages (Exodus 13:1–10 and 11–16; Deuteronomy 6:4–9 and 11:13–21) all ordain that the words of the Lord should be bound for a sign on the arm and for a symbol or reminder on the forehead. Photograph by Emmanuel de Lange.

made and very widely accepted, and it is sufficient to attend the synagogue week by week to absorb, almost without being aware of it, a large dose of theology.

But what are the theological beliefs of the liturgy? Here it is necessary to draw a distinction between traditional liturgies, which have grown up over a very long period by a kind of sedimentary process without the active intervention of an editor, and modern liturgies, edited by individuals or more often by panels of rabbis, concerned to purge the text of theological ideas that have been discarded and to incorporate others that have been adopted.

The traditional liturgies do not reject the biblical view of God. On the contrary, they take it very seriously and frequently quote from the Bible. They are fond of quoting from the three parts of the Bible, the Torah, Prophets and Writings, as though to stress their underlying unity. But they modify and even subvert the biblical view by juxtaposing with it beliefs from other sources, often of a philosophical or mystical character. Sometimes the result is faithful to the Bible, but at other times it is rather different from the image of God derived from a simple reading of the Bible.

An example of interference is found in the morning prayer, the *yotser*, which makes use of the words of God in Isaiah 45:7: 'Forming light and creating darkness, making peace and creating evil, I the Lord am the maker of all these.' The theological idea behind these words is God's uniqueness: those who claim that there is one source of light and good and another of darkness and evil are mistaken, because there is only one God. However, the statement that God is the creator of evil must have seemed too direct and shocking at some point, because in all liturgies the prayer reads: 'Forming light and creating darkness, making peace and creating all things.'

This change is evidence of a sensitivity to theological issues, and a similar concern is found throughout the liturgy. The main beliefs identified by the philosophers are all put forward in the form of prayers, and hymns combined in various ways and adorned with biblical allusions and proof texts, so that the worshipper comes to learn the principles themselves but also to think about them in depth. Some examples have already been given in the previous chapter, and perhaps the most striking illustration of the use of a hymn to convey theological teachings is the versified form of the Thirteen Principles of Maimonides known as the Yigdal:

Great is the living God and to be praised:
existing and unlimited by time.

Unique in his uniqueness he is One,
concealed in his infinite unity.

He has no body, no substance or form,
no image can define his holiness.

Preceding all created things, the First,
with no beginning to his primacy.

Eternal Lord is he, and all the world
declares his greatness and his majesty.

To men he chose to glorify his name
he gave abundant gifts of prophecy.

No prophet has there been in Israel
like Moses, who beheld him face to face.

Through him, the prophet 'faithful in his house',
God gave his people the one true Torah.

Nor will he ever abrogate his law
or substitute another in its place.

He sees into the secrets of our hearts
and knows the end of all things in advance.

For all good deeds he grants a due reward,
but punishes the sinner for his sin.

Finally our Anointed will he send
to save those who await the glorious end.

The dead our loving God to life will raise:
for ever be his name adored with praise![15]

GOD IN THE TWENTIETH CENTURY

Hermann Cohen and his legacy

Hermann Cohen, as we have already remarked, introduces not only a new century but a new era in Jewish reflection on God. He seems to draw a line under a period that was rich in publications but ultimately sterile, because its main concern was to demonstrate the congruence of

[15] The translation is mine. See Jacob J. Petuchowsky, *Theology and Poetry* (London, 1978), pp. 20–30.

Jewish with German culture. In Cohen's late writings we can witness, as it were, the Jew breaking through and demanding to be heard. One feature of Cohen's writing about God points clearly towards Jewish theology as it was to develop in the twentieth century: his principle of correlation.[16] God cannot be properly thought of without man, and man cannot properly be thought of without God. Consequently, despite the huge gulf that divides them, man and God are related to each other. God creates, and man is created; God reveals, and man receives the revelation; God redeems, man is redeemed. None of these events has any meaning if one of the two terms is removed.

Cohen served as a model and an inspiration to a younger generation of German Jews. Among the German Jewish theologians of the twentieth century three names stand out: Leo Baeck (1873–1956), Franz Rosenzweig (1886–1929) and Martin Buber (1878–1965).

Leo Baeck is remembered particularly for his heroic and inspirational rabbinic leadership when he was imprisoned by the Nazis in the concentration camp of Terezín (Theresienstadt), but in his day he was known also for his books, particularly *The Essence of Judaism* and *This People Israel*.[17]

There is a strong apologetic tendency in Baeck, as there is also in Rosenzweig and Buber. All three try to demonstrate that Judaism is not either the monster or the ghost that it was often portrayed as. Unlike their nineteenth-century predecessors, they are not content to defend, but carry the war, as it were, into the enemy's camp.[18] The title of his book *The Essence of Judaism* echoes that of an earlier book by the well-known Christian theologian Adolf von Harnack,[19] and is intended as a Jewish response to Harnack, although he does not mention him by name. Baeck begins with the distinction made explicit by Mendelssohn: 'Judaism has no dogmas and therefore no orthodoxy, as religious orthodoxy is usually understood' (p. 12). In Judaism, 'man's function is described by the commandments: to do what is good; that is the begin-

---

[16] See Arthur Cohen, *The Natural and Supernatural Jew* (London, 1967), p. 98.

[17] *The Essence of Judaism*, tr. V. Grubenweiser and L. Pearl, revised by Irving Howe (New York, 1948); *This People Israel*, tr. A. H. Friedlander (London, 1965). See also A. H. Friedlander, *Leo Baeck, Teacher of Theresienstadt* (London, 1973).

[18] 'Leo Baeck was the first contemporary Jewish thinker to see the problem of Judaism as existence before the face of Christendom' (Cohen, *The Natural and Supernatural Jew*, p. 106). In addition to Baeck's *Essence of Judaism*, see his collection of essays *Judaism and Christianity*, tr. Walter Kaufmann (Philadelphia, 1958).

[19] Adolf von Harnack, *What Is Christianity?*, tr. Thomas Bailey Saunders (London, 1901). The original title was *Das Wesen des Christentums*, 'The Essence of Christianity', and Baeck entitled his book *Das Wesen des Judentums*.

ning of wisdom' (p. 14). We glimpse the lapse of time that separates the Liberal Jew Baeck from his eighteenth-century predecessor in the next sentence: 'Man's duty toward man comes before his knowledge of God, and the knowledge of him is a process of seeking and enquiring rather than an act of possession.' It is through understanding one's own spiritual needs and those of other people that one comes to understand and have faith in God. This approach places Baeck firmly in his own century. In keeping with the tenets of Liberal Judaism, Baeck interprets the 'commandments' as basically the moral law, and following the philosophical tradition to which he is heir, he sees God as being that which gives continuing meaning and value to man's moral behaviour. In this respect he is close to Hermann Cohen. Baeck seems to strive to go further than Cohen when he speaks, as he often does, of God as 'mystery': he was, after all, a rabbi and preacher, whereas Cohen was a professor of philosophy. The characteristic feature of Judaism, Baeck says, is the relation of man to God, and specifically the uniquely Jewish sense of being created. 'Though he is unfathomable and inscrutable, yet we emanate from him' (*Essence*, p. 99). The stress, in the midst of encounter, on the unknowability of God is characteristic of Baeck. The very centrality of encounter links him to Rosenzweig, Buber and later to Heschel. But Baeck's theology remains always tentative and provisional, in keeping with his original insistence on the absence of dogma in Judaism.

Franz Rosenzweig, like Baeck, was concerned with situating Judaism vis-à-vis Christianity, and his great book *The Star of Redemption*[20] is largely taken up with this question. But it is also about the encounter with God. God breaks into the world of man at three points, which we call creation, revelation and redemption. The means by which he operates in all three is by speech. God addresses man speech, like a lover addressing his beloved. The words of the lover are not 'mere' words: they are a vehicle for his love:

Death, the conqueror of all, and the netherworld that zealously imprisons all the deceased, collapse before the strength of love and the hardness of its zeal. Its glowing embers, its divine flames warm the stone-cold past from its rigor mortis. The living soul, loved by God, triumphs over all that is mortal, and that is all that can be said about it.[21]

Rosenzweig writes in a mixture of scientific prose and mystical poetry. In putting God, the lover of the Song of Songs, back into Jewish

[20] *The Star of Redemption*, tr. W. W. Hallo (London, 1971). Original title *Der Stern der Erlösung* (1921).
[21] *Star*, p. 202.

theology he is consciously breaking with the sterile philosophising of the previous century. Philosophy cannot cure man's fear of death, which is central to his very being.

Rosenzweig died in 1929, at the age of 43, of a disease which had left him almost totally paralysed for several years. Yet his short life was extraordinarily productive. Once he had realised how little German Jews of his generation really knew about Judaism he opened an adult study centre in Frankfurt (the Freies Jüdisches Lehrhaus) where others could join him in the quest for an authentic Judaism, mediated by what he called 'the new thinking'. Martin Buber became one of the lecturers at the Lehrhaus, which he directed after Rosenzweig's death.

Martin Buber is best known now as the author of *I and You*,[22] one of the most original and influential Jewish books of the twentieth century. He was, however, a prolific author; among his more important publications, apart from the translation of the Bible begun with Rosenzweig, are several books on Hasidism.[23] He also wrote on Zionism: he settled in Israel and campaigned for a humane version of Jewish nationalism in which the Arab inhabitants of the land would be equal partners.[24]

The term 'I and You' can be traced back to Hermann Cohen, who wrote in a study published in 1908: 'The ethical self must be engaged in action. For this self, there exists no I without a You.'[25] The argument of Buber's *I and You* is by now well known. So far as God is concerned what it boils down to is that God is not to be studied, he is only to be encountered. Just as Rosenzweig uses the language of lovers to illuminate the relationship between God and mankind, so Buber uses the analogy of a close relationship between two people (who may but need not be lovers). The speaker who says 'you' is also an 'I'; within the I–you relationship the two terms, although they do not merge to the point of losing their identity, do not have an independent existence. The relationship is recip-

---

[22] Also known as *I and Thou*, tr. R. Gregor Smith (2nd edn New York/Edinburgh, 1958); tr. Walter Kaufmann (New York, 1970, Edinburgh, 1971). Pamela Vermes has described this English title as 'one of the most obvious examples of the misinterpretation that can ensue from lax translation' (*Buber on God and the Perfect Man*, 1994 edn, xviii). The remote and archaic pronoun 'Thou', which is almost a title of God, is at odds with the argument of Buber's book. Vermes herself uses *I and You*, and one has to agree that this is a better rendering of the German title.

[23] There is a useful select bibliography of works by and about Buber in Vermes, *Buber on God and the Perfect Man*. Vermes's *Buber* (London, 1988), in the Jewish Thinkers series, is the best short introduction.

[24] See Martin Buber, *On Zion: The History of an Idea*, tr. S. Goodman (Edinburgh, 1985); Paul Mendes-Flohr, *A Land of Two Peoples* (New York, 1983).

[25] See Eva Jospe, ed. and tr., *Reason and Hope: Selections from the Jewish Writings of Hermann Cohen* (New York, 1971), pp. 29, 218. Cf. also Rosenzweig, *Star*, pp. 173–6, 198–204.

rocal. Behind each 'you' whom we address, we catch a glimpse of the unique everlasting You, whom we call God.

Buber was once asked if he believed in God. After a slight hesitation he said he did. Later he wondered if he had been truthful, and he drew this distinction: 'If belief in God means being able to speak *of* him in the third person, I do not believe in God. If belief in him means being able to speak *to* him, I do believe in God.'[26] Nothing could encapsulate more succinctly the gap that separates Buber from his nineteenth-century forebears.

With Buber we seem to leap across the centuries of philosophising to the biblical God who is not studied but encountered, albeit anthropomorphically. A key biblical text in Buber's account is the story of the first meeting between God and Moses, at the burning bush. God introduces himself as 'your fathers' God, the God of Abraham, the God of Yitzhak, the God of Yaacov' and gives Moses the task of leading the Israelites out of Egypt. Moses says: 'When I go to the Israelites and say to them, "The God of your fathers has sent me to you", they will answer, "What is his name?" What shall I say to them?' God gives the mysterious reply: 'I shall be what I shall be (*ehyeh asher ehyeh*). Tell the Israelites: I shall be has sent me to you' (Exodus 3:6–14). Hermann Cohen had interpreted this name philosophically as 'Being-as-such'. Buber's interpretation is light-years away. The verb *ehyeh* here, and in the divine name *yhvh*, denotes not *existence* but *presence*. This interpretation, arising out of a long dialogue between Buber and Rosenzweig,[27] is central to Buber's theology. The crucial point about God, in the Bible, throughout Jewish history, and in the lives of men and women today, is not that he exists in the abstract but that he is present in the life of the individual and the people.

AMERICAN JEWISH THEOLOGY

Since the middle of the nineteenth century the centre of gravity of the Jewish world had been gradually shifting to the English-speaking countries, and with the Nazi inferno in Europe that movement became complete, although a vitally important secondary centre was already developing in the ancient Holy Land. The ideas that had been matured

---

[26] Quoted by Vermes, *Buber on God and the Perfect Man*, p. 137.

[27] See Vermes, *Buber on God and the Perfect Man*, pp. 90–100. Everett Fox, in his translation (*The Five Books of Moses*, New York/London, 1995), which is heavily influenced by the Buber–Rozenzweig German version, writes: 'God said to Moshe: EHYE ASHER EHYE/I will be-there howsoever I will be-there. And he said: Thus shall you say to the Children of Israel: EHYE/ I-WILL-BE-THERE sends me to you.'

in Germany were translated into the language of America by men like Solomon Schechter, 'the theologian of the historical school',[28] and the giants of Reform Judaism, Kaufmann Kohler and Emil G. Hirsch.[29] Kohler's monumental book *Jewish Theology* has been described as 'a summing up and defence of nineteenth-century Reform Judaism viewed through the history of its component elements'.[30] While Kohler, who in his youth had been a pupil of the Orthodox leader Samson Raphael Hirsch, retained an attachment to the ideals and rituals of Jewish tradition, his brother-in-law Emil Hirsch, whose father was the Liberal German thinker Samuel Hirsch, was an out-and-out rationalist. The Pittsburgh conference of Reform rabbis (1885) was dominated by Kohler, and the statement it issued, the celebrated Pittsburgh Platform, begins with a statement about what it calls, in unashamedly philosophical jargon, the 'God-idea':

We recognize in every religion an attempt to grasp the Infinite, and in every mode, source or book of revelation, held sacred in any religious system, the consciousness of the indwelling of God in man. We hold that Judaism presents the highest conception of the God-idea as taught in our Holy Scriptures and developed and spiritualized by the Jewish teachers, in accordance with the moral and philosophical progress of their respective ages. We maintain that Judaism preserved and defended, midst continual struggles and trials and under enforced isolation, this God-idea as the central religious truth for the human race.

While this statement is more concerned with asserting the place of Judaism alongside the other religions in a pluralistic society, it does also convey a certain position about the God of the Jews, which is actually intended to distance the Reform movement from two opposing extremes, ethical humanism on the one hand and Jewish particularism on the other. At the same time it contains a strong hint that God is not so much a real supernatural person as an idea that all sensitive humans share and to which Jews are open to an outstandingly high degree. Universalism rubs shoulders with pride in the Jewish heritage; philosophical theism marks a compromise between full-blooded faith and secularism tending to atheism.

A straight line leads from this approach to the fully fledged natural-

---

[28] Louis Ginzberg, 'Solomon Schechter', in his *Students, Scholars and Saints* (Philadelphia, 1928), pp. 241–51 (here p. 248).

[29] See Meyer, *Response to Modernity*, pp. 271–6.

[30] Ibid., p. 276. *Jewish Theology* was published in New York in 1918 and reissued in 1968. It was originally published in German in 1910. It remained the only systematic account of its subject until the appearance of Samuel Cohon's *Jewish Theology* in 1971 and Louis Jacobs's *A Jewish Theology* in 1973.

ism of Mordecai Kaplan (1881–1983). Born in Lithuania, Kaplan graduated from the Conservative Jewish Theological Seminary before serving as rabbi of an Orthodox congregation in New York. Gradually he became aware that he did not share the congregation's faith in a personal, supernatural god and he resigned his rabbinic position, despite reassurances that the congregation did not object to his beliefs provided he kept them to himself. He taught at the Seminary, and founded a new movement, Reconstructionism, which was intended to transcend the divisions between Orthodox, Conservative and Reform Judaism.

Mordecai Kaplan's view of Judaism is best set out in his book *Judaism as a Civilization*, published in 1934. Kaplan analyses Reform and what he calls Neo-Orthodoxy (the modernist wing of Orthodoxy) and subjects both to withering criticism. Conservative Judaism he does not regard as an authentic third way but rather as an uneasy coalition between the centrist tendencies in the other two. He calls for a reorientation to the problem of religion, in the light of modern conditions and particularly the pluralism which has become a fundamental and permanent feature of Jewish existence. Study of Jewish history shows (1) the perennial and central importance of the 'God-idea' and (2) the changing character of that idea in different times and places. What really matters is not how God is thought of, but how the idea is translated into action. Supernaturalism, Kaplan argues, has no place in modern religion; it is unproductive today to imagine God as a person or being outside and beyond the universe, and better to see it as our name for a power that makes for righteousness. Kaplan offers a programme for reinvigorating Jewish society and Jewish civilisation, with the aim of helping each individual Jew to lead a more fulfilled life.

Depending how one cares to look at it, Kaplan either put religion back into Jewish nationalism or cleansed Jewish religion of its outmoded supernaturalism. His distinction is to have wedded the best insights of the atheistic voices of Jewish peoplehood and civilisation (men like Ahad Ha-am and Simon Dubnow) to the synagogue-based society of the Diaspora. In fact Kaplan's conception of the synagogue as a kind of Jewish civic centre where secular and social activities have their place side by side with religious ones corresponds closely to the reality in western countries. Although the movement he founded has remained relatively small, his views are probably shared by many Jews who do not belong to it, who indeed may never have heard of it.

Milton Steinberg (1903–50) was a disciple of Mordecai Kaplan who became one of the pillars of the Reconstructionist movement. Like

Kaplan he was a rationalist deeply concerned with the dilemmas of
Jewish survival and open to current intellectual trends. However, he
diverged radically from his teacher in refusing to relegate God to an
aspect of nature or a figment of the human mind. He wanted Jews to
take God seriously, and shortly before his early death he launched a
demand for a return to Jewish theology.[31] In 1949, in the immediate
aftermath of the Nazi genocide and the creation of a Jewish state this
was a remarkable and almost prophetic appeal. While fully aware of the
limitations of the medieval philosophers, Steinberg expressed
confidence in the power of reason to address questions of faith, and in
the power of faith to transcend facile intellectualisation. 'Religious faith
is a hypothesis interpreting reality and posited on the same grounds as
any valid hypothesis.'

Of the many remarkable American Jewish theologians of twentieth-
century America it is hard to think of anyone who can rival Abraham
Joshua Heschel (1907–72). Born into a Hasidic dynasty in Poland,
Heschel studied philosophy in Berlin, and eventually ended up teaching
at the Jewish Theological Seminary in New York. He was far from being
a cloistered academic, however. He reached out to thousands in his
books, and became something of an icon when photographed on a civil
rights march arm in arm with Martin Luther King.

Heschel's understanding of God is diametrically opposed to that of
naturalists like Kaplan. God is not merely a power or function, but a
living reality, and it is a great shortcoming of religions to have lost the
sense of immediacy and wonder at God's power and the sense of
urgency concerning the demands he makes on human individuals and
societies. Heschel's God is unlike the God of the classical philosophers
in that he has emotions and needs. God suffers together with his
suffering creatures and is angry at their moral failures; and in particular
he needs man as much as man needs him.

God and the Shoah

There is general agreement that the Nazi Holocaust gave a terrible jolt
to Jewish beliefs about God. Indeed, according to some it rang his death
knell. Why this should be so is a puzzling question. The basic issues
raised by the Holocaust were hardly new ones. As a manifestation of the

---

[31] Cohen, *Natural and Supernatural*, p. 232. For more on Steinberg see Cohen's introduction to
Anatomy of Faith (New York, 1960), which Cohen edited after Steinberg's death, and which contains the latter's most important thought on religion.

human capacity for evil it has many predecessors, the echoes of which can be traced in Jewish literature going right back to the Bible. The same can be said about the theological problems raised by the existence of evil in the world. In the area of the Covenant, the idea of a special relationship between God and the Jewish people, one could cite the classical biblical challenge of the destruction of the Temple by the Babylonians, followed by the later destruction by the Romans and a whole series of events, culminating in the Russian pogroms, which caused terrible shock waves in the Jewish world which were still in living memory at the time the Nazis came to power.

The reasons are probably to be sought in other areas than theology: in the unprecedented enormousness of the destruction and its extraordinary brutality, and in the traumatic betrayal of the aspirations of those who had put their faith in moral progress and in the values of German civilisation. Nevertheless, the impact on theology has been profound, and after an initial phase of relative silence, from the 1960s on there has been a seemingly inexhaustible stream of publications addressing the issues raised for Jewish belief by the Shoah. The dominant tone of the overwhelming majority has been one of bewilderment.

Given the general eclipse of philosophical theology in the first part of the twentieth century, it is surprising how many writers focused on the classic philosophical problem of theodicy, or justification of God: how can one reconcile such evil with the philosophers' portrait of a god who is both all-powerful and the embodiment of all goodness? Clearly the simple answer is that one cannot. Yet however damning this crudely mechanical statement of the puzzle might be when applied to medieval philosophy, it hardly seems relevant to Jewish philosophy as it had developed in the nineteenth century and the early part of the twentieth. In the thought of Hermann Cohen and Leo Baeck there is not much that humans can assert positively about God as ultimate reality, and there is little point in speculating about divine omnipotence and its possible limits: what we can talk about is human ethics and responsibility. In the more explicit naturalism of Kaplan there is even less reason to speculate about divine responsibility. Evil is not a philosophical problem for Kaplan, and in so far as he mentions it at all it is as an aspect of human behaviour. The effect of the airing of the conundrum of theodicy in the context of the Holocaust is to hammer the last nail into the coffin of classical philosophical Judaism.

We could phrase the same question in biblical terms: why does the almighty God, who is the lord of creation and history and the source of goodness and love, send or tolerate evil on such a scale? The Bible is perfectly familiar with this question, and it gives one consistent answer: God is all-good, indeed he is a generous and patient ruler who is astonishingly forbearing, but ultimately he must act to punish wrongdoing. He did not shrink from inundating the world and drowning the whole human race, with the exception of a few individuals, on account of the evil that had infected society. Some traditionally minded writers attempted to apply this logic to the Holocaust, but the results were partial and unsatisfactory, and were received with nothing but outrage. It seemed that modern sensibility, even when schooled on biblical stories like Noah's flood, could not tolerate the judgment involved in applying the biblical logic to the Holocaust: how could one possibly claim that a million and a half babies and small children were brutally killed because of their sins, or indeed because of the sins of their parents? And how can one compare the possible sins of the Jewish victims with those of the non-Jewish perpetrators? Even the most biblical of post-Holocaust theologians, Ignaz Maybaum, who in one sermon went so far as to speak of God sending Hitler as his agent just as he sent the Babylonian king Nebuchadnezzar to destroy Jerusalem,[32] drew the line at blaming the Holocaust on the sins of the victims. In the wake of the Shoah, it seems that this crudely mechanical biblical theology is dead. Yet surely it was already dead long before among sophisticated and sensitive readers?

Some theologians took refuge in silence, or in the shelter of divine inscrutability. Heschel, for example, studiously ignores the subject of the Holocaust in his writing, even though his own life was disrupted by it and many members of his own family were among the victims.[33] A number of writers, like Eliezer Berkovits,[34] have appealed to the doctrine of *Hester Panim* ('concealing of the Face'): at certain times God removes himself from human affairs, so as to give human beings full opportunity to experience their own power to act, for good or ill. In part this is an application of the philosophical gambit known as the 'free-will defence': the gift of free will necessitates a voluntary limitation of divine power. It has not won wide favour from theists because it tends to harm the conception of divine providence: how can you say that God cares for us if he refuses to step in when we need him most? As for Martin Buber,

[32] Ignaz Maybaum, *The Face of God After Auschwitz* (Amsterdam, 1965), p. 67.
[33] Eugene Borowitz, *Renewing the Covenant* (Philadelphia, 1991), p. 28, speculates that Heschel 'believed that whatever could be given utterance had already been said in his discussion of the universal problem of theodicy – and the vastly greater suffering we had so recently experienced, to which words must ever remain inadequate, required silence.'
[34] *Faith After the Holocaust* (New York, 1973), pp. 94ff.

whose conception of God as 'everlasting You' had completely done away with earlier theology, since any discussion of God's attributes would transform him from a 'you' to an 'it', even he was forced to adapt his views: how could the God whose name is 'I shall be there' have been so notably absent? He began to speak of an eclipse of God. Hard as it is for us to accept the absence of loving parents when we need them, it is even harder for us to accept the absence of God. Our task is not to explain it but to learn to overcome it, to maintain our relationship with God despite what seems like a betrayal of that relationship.

So far no radical new theology has emerged from the Shoah to compare in its daring and its impact to the ideas of the biblical prophets that followed the catastrophe of the Babylonian exile, or those of the rabbis following the Roman destruction, or the Lurianic Kabbalah that followed the reconquest of Spain. No doubt more time is needed. The resounding message of the writers of the first post-Holocaust generations is one of consolation, and a call to remain true to Jewish values. The powerful nostalgia of Abraham Joshua Heschel's *The Earth Is the Lord's*, the confidence of Ignaz Maybaum's *The Jewish Home*, Emil Fackenheim's talk of the commanding voice from Auschwitz telling Jews to survive, all in their different ways represent a refusal, as Fackenheim memorably put it, 'to hand Hitler posthumous victories'.[35] One or two early attempts are being made to break through the impasse of post-Holocaust theology, but real progress is still awaited.

New issues

In the absence of real progress on the central issues of Jewish theology, there are many developments currently among special interest groups; some of these developments are attracting a great deal of interest, and will eventually feed into the mainstream.

This has already begun to happen with feminist theology, which began in earnest in the 1970s, as part of a campaign to draw attention to and to remedy the subordinate status of women within Judaism. The main focus of discussion was the representation of God in the liturgy as father, king and judge. As often happens in theology, once the basic questions were articulated it became clear that the problems were far deeper and wider than had been imagined, and the debate now concerns not only the gender of God but the whole of God's nature and activity when

---

[35] *God's Presence in History: Jewish Affirmations and Philosophical Reflections* (New York, 1970), p. 84.

seen from a feminist perspective. It has taken a while to clear away some
of the misleading undergrowth so as to lay bare some well-established
theological points, such as the purely metaphorical and symbolic character of biblical and liturgical images (though they may be none the less
hurtful for that), or the multiplicity of ways of relating to the one God.
Feminists have reclaimed some long-established images of God as
mother and nourisher, and have dwelt on the feminine gender of the
Shekhinah.[36]

Ecology is another area that has attracted interest lately, and where
older materials that had been forgotten or treated as marginal have been
put under the limelight. The idea of God as creator and sustainer of the
world is of course fundamental to classical theology, and there are many
Talmudic and later rabbinic teachings on the subject of the proper
human treatment of nature, but it is only recently that they have been
brought together into a coherent argument in the framework of a wider
concern with ecology.[37]

It would be misleading to end with the impression that theological discussion is at all widespread among Jews at the present time. To judge by
the Jewish press, it is accorded a very low priority. The reasons for this
neglect are probably manifold, and include not only the apparent pre-
dominance of secular and materialistic values and the continuing bewilderment resulting from the Holocaust, but also uncertainty arising from
the pluralism which has become such a pronounced feature of contemporary Jewry. It is hard for the diverse religious denominations to find a
common basis on which to begin to air their theological disagreements
in a constructive spirit, and even harder for religious and secular Jews to
approach each other in sophisticated debate about the place of God in
Jewish life. If this analysis is correct, it is not the lack of topics for discussion that is the obstacle, but that lack of a common language.

---

[36] On this subject see the useful collection of essays in Susannah Heschel, ed., *On Being a Jewish
Feminist: A Reader* (New York, 1983), and Judith Plaskow's important book *Standing Again at Sinai:
Judaism from a Feminist Perspective* (San Francisco, 1990).

[37] See Aubrey Rose, ed., *Judaism and Ecology* (London, 1992); Robert Gordis, 'Ecology and the
Jewish Tradition', in *Contemporary Jewish Ethics and Morality*, ed. E. N. Dorff and L. E. Newman
(New York/Oxford, 1995), pp. 327–35.

CHAPTER EIGHT

Objectives

In this chapter we approach the question 'How can one be a good Jew, and what is the ultimate purpose of it?' Simple answers are available, but none holds the field. Consequently our search must be wide ranging, and we shall begin by looking at some biblical answers, and at the ways they have been interpreted and applied in subsequent tradition. What is the characteristic that a Jew should aim to embody, above all others, in his or her life?

HOLINESS

'Now if you listen to my voice and keep to my covenant you will become my special possession out of all the peoples, because the whole world is mine. You shall be mine, a kingdom of priests and a holy nation' (Exodus 19:5–6). These words, spoken through Moses to the people Israel at Mount Sinai, indicate a key meaning of holiness: Israel is separated from the other peoples and dedicated to the service of God, just as priests are separated from other people and dedicated to his service. 'Holy' in Hebrew is *kadosh*; 'holiness' is *kedushah*: the words combine the twin concepts of separation and dedication. The English word that most closely combines these two meanings is 'special', although 'special' will not usually do as a translation of *kadosh*. The 'sanctification' or dedication of the people is mentioned very often in the prayers.

At Sinai the holiness of Israel is linked to obedience to God's commands ('to listen' also means 'to obey') and loyalty to his covenant. Later it is linked to the holiness of God himself: 'You shall be holy as I the Lord your God am holy' (Leviticus 19:2). These words are followed by a series of regulations, beginning 'You shall each revere your mother and father, and keep my Sabbaths: I am the Lord your God.' And a little later it says: 'You shall keep my commands and carry them out: I am the Lord. You shall not profane my holy name, but I shall be made holy

among the children of Israel: I am the Lord who makes you holy'
(Leviticus 22:31–2). Profanity and profanation (*hol, hillul*) are the opposite of holiness and sanctification (*kodesh, kiddush*). By observing God's
commands the people Israel preserve God's sanctity; by breaking them
they profane it. 'Sanctification of the [divine] name' (*kiddush ha-shem*) is
the Hebrew equivalent of martyrdom, while its opposite, 'profanation
of the name' (*hillul ha-shem*), means blasphemy, bringing God's name
into disrepute.

The holiness of God is a difficult concept to grasp. It hints at his
uniqueness, his being absolutely separate and different from all other
beings. The prophet Isaiah had a vision of the Lord sitting on an
exalted throne, surrounded by winged seraphim who called to one
another: 'Holy, holy, holy is the Lord of Armies: the whole world is full
of his glory' (Isaiah 6:3). 'The holy God' is one of the seals of the blessings in the Amidah, and when the prayers are repeated in a congregation the prayer called 'Holiness' (Kedushah) is added, recalling Isaiah's
vision:

We will sanctify your name in the world just as it is sanctified in the highest
heaven, as it is written by your prophet: And they called to one another
  Holy, holy, holy is the Lord of Armies: the whole world is full of his glory.

The holiness of God is mentioned on several other occasions in the
prayers, most notably in the prayer called the Kaddish ('Sanctification'),
which begins: 'Magnified and sanctified be his great name in the world
which he created according to his will . . .'

In the Bible the priests, the descendants of Aaron, were 'holy to the
Lord', and these words were inscribed on the high priest's headdress, just
above his forehead (Exodus 28:36). They ministered in the Temple,
which was known as the sanctuary or holy place (*mikdash*). The inner
shrine was the Holiest of Holies, but the whole city of Jerusalem where
the Temple stood was called the holy city. It is hard for us today to appreciate the sense of holiness that attached to the Temple, and few hints of
it remain in the synagogue or in Jewish home life. A synagogue is not a
sanctified building, and none of its contents or fittings are regarded as
holy, although the ark where the scrolls are kept is called *aron ha-kodesh*,
'holy ark'. Although there are still hereditary priests, they are people like
everyone else: the last vestiges of their earlier status are that they may
not come in contact with a corpse unless it is that of a close relation
(Leviticus 21:1–4) or marry a divorcee (Leviticus 21:7). The Hebrew language is still sometimes referred to as 'the holy tongue' (or 'language of

the sanctuary' – *lashon ha-kodesh*), because it was the language used in the Temple.

One area where the concept of sanctity is still very much alive is in the Sabbaths and festivals. The Bible speaks of the Sabbath as a day sanctified by God (e.g. Genesis 2:3, Exodus 20:8–11), and these verses are quoted (respectively in the evening and the morning) in the special blessing for the Sabbath, pronounced over a goblet of wine and known as Kiddush, 'Sanctification'. The blessing runs as follows:

Blessed are you, Lord our God, king of the universe, who has sanctified us by his commandments and taken pleasure in us, and has lovingly and willingly given us his holy Sabbath as an inheritance, a reminder of the story of Genesis. It is also the first of the holy festivals, in memory of the exodus from Egypt. Out of all of the peoples you chose and sanctified us, and you have lovingly and willingly given us his holy Sabbath as an inheritance. Blessed are you, Lord, who make the Sabbath holy.

Thus the special status of the Sabbath is linked to the special status of Israel. This idea is made even more explicit in the Amidah for Sabbaths:

O Lord our God, you did not give it to the other nations of the lands, nor did you make it the inheritance of idolators, nor are the uncircumcised at home in its rest, but you have lovingly given it to your people Israel, to the descendants of Jacob whom you chose. The people who sanctify the seventh day will all receive ample sustenance and delight from your goodness. You took pleasure in the seventh day and made it holy, calling it the most desirable of days, a memorial of the story of Genesis.

The other days of the week, from which the Sabbath is differentiated by its holiness, are called *hol*, 'profane', and the Sabbath ends with the blessing called Havdalah, 'differentiation':

Blessed are you, Lord our God, king of the universe, who make a distinction between sacred and profane, between light and darkness, between Israel and the other nations, between the seventh day and the six working days. Blessed are you, Lord, who makes a distinction between sacred and profane.

Another area where the language of sanctification comes to the fore is in marriage. The bridegroom, as we have seen, betrothes the bride with a ring, pronouncing these words: 'See, you are sanctified to me by this ring according to the laws of Moses and Israel.' The married couple are separated from other people and dedicated to each other alone: adultery is a profanation of this solemn bond.

Judaism has generally remained close to the biblical concept of holiness as obedience to the divine commands, and it has not been greatly influenced by the Christian usage, in which the term carries a connotation of spiritual elevation.[1] However, Moses Nahmanides, the thirteenth-century Spanish kabbalist, in commenting on Leviticus 19:2 observes that while the Torah forbids certain things it permits others, such as sexual acts within marriage or eating and drinking, without specifying a legitimate degree. Anyone who indulges in them to excess is 'a villain with the full sanction of Torah'. In commanding holiness, the Torah is advising us to separate ourselves from what is unnecessary. Nahmanides' commendation of a life of self-restraint, denying oneself legitimate pleasures, has found some followers, particularly among kabbalistically minded Jews, some of whom have conceived of holiness as an ideal only available to a select few. It must be stressed, however, that asceticism is not characteristic of Judaism, and some rabbis have warned that 'in times to come we shall be called to account not only for the sins we committed but for the legitimate pleasures we denied ourselves'.

OBEDIENCE

Abraham in the biblical story is told to offer his son to God as a burnt sacrifice. He unhesitatingly obeys; it turns out to be only a test. The outcome? 'All the nations of the world will be blessed by your descendants because you listened to my voice' (Genesis 22:18).

In Hebrew, as mentioned earlier, the same verb means 'to listen' and 'to obey'. Abraham was rewarded for his obedience. So the opening word of the Shma, 'Listen, Israel' (Deuteronomy 6:4), could be translated 'Jew – be obedient.' When Moses told the people all the laws he had received from God at Sinai they said: 'Everything that the Lord has said we will do and obey' (Exodus 24:7).

The reward of obedience is spelt out in Deuteronomy 11:13–15:

If you are truly obedient to the commands I am giving you today, to love the Lord your God, and to serve him with all your hearts and souls, I shall send the rain of your land at the right time, early rain and late rain, and you shall gather in your corn, new wine and oil, and I shall put grass in your meadows for your cattle, and you will eat your fill.

---

[1] 'Homo religiosus ascends to God; God, however, descends to halakhic man . . . Transcendence becomes embodied in man's deeds, deeds that are shaped by the lawful physical order of which man is a part . . . Holiness, according to the outlook of Halakhah, denotes the appearance of a mysterious transcendence in the midst of our concrete world, the "descent" of God, whom no thought can grasp, onto Mount Sinai.' J. B. Soloveitchik, *Halakhic Man*, tr. Lawrence Kaplan (Philadelphia, 1983), pp. 45–6.

This passage forms part of the Shma, and like many other passages in the Torah it draws a very close connection between obedience and prosperity. The reward for obeying the commands is a long life, and the punishment for disobedience is death. Nowhere is this stated more clearly than in Deuteronomy 30:15–18:

See, I am setting before you today life and good and death and evil, in that I am commanding you today to love the Lord your God, to walk in his paths and to keep his commands and rules and laws, so that you will live and be numerous, and the Lord your God will bless you in the land which you are entering to take possession of it. But if your heart is diverted and you are disobedient, and you let yourself be distracted and worship other gods and serve them, I tell you today that you will perish, you will not live a long life on the land you are crossing the Jordan to take possession of.

This whole structure of obedience to commands, rewarded by health and prosperity, is built on the foundation of an anthropomorphic conception of God. God as supreme authority is modelled on a human ruler or father, who gives orders and demands obedience. Later tradition, particularly in its more philosophical strands, expresses unhappiness about this conception, which seems inappropriately concrete. To put it at its most crudely, how can God speak if he has no mouth or vocal cords? When the Bible speaks of God's mouth, God's voice, this language has to be understood as metaphorical, but what is the reality that underlies the metaphor? Can the divine spirit inspire humans in such a way as to command a certain way of life or course of action? And in that case can we be certain that the command has been correctly understood? Does it not all boil down effectively to individual humans usurping the role of God and telling other humans what they must or must not do?

Such speculation, however, was confined to an intellectual elite until the nineteenth century, when, as we have seen, it became widespread among the Jewish leadership in the German-speaking countries. Until then, rabbinic Judaism had taught that the commands (as interpreted and modified by the rabbis) had to be observed scrupulously because they were the word of God. Since the growth of critical biblical study this approach has become difficult to sustain intellectually, but it should be noted that it is still maintained by Orthodoxy as a matter of faith.

Concern was also expressed about another aspect of the structure: the rewards and punishments. Experience does not consistently bear out the validity of the assurance that obedience will be rewarded with long life and freedom from want and anxiety. Indeed the Bible itself recognised the problem, and it is a major theme of the books of Job and

Ecclesiastes. The ancient rabbis were also aware of the problem, but they concluded that it is beyond human comprehension: 'It is not in our power to explain the prosperity of the wicked or the suffering of the righteous.'[2] The grace after food includes this quotation from King David (Psalm 37:25): 'I was young and now I am old, and I have never seen a righteous man abandoned or his descendants begging for bread.' In some homes these words are not said aloud, for fear of giving offence to a poor guest, or simply because they are contrary to experience.

Despite these various concerns and suspicions, the idea of obedience to the divine command is still accepted by virtually the whole of the traditional and Orthodox sector of Jewry, and receives limited assent from many others. Even in Liberal synagogues the old biblical and liturgical texts are read out unchanged, affirming that the Torah was given by God and that its rules are binding on the congregation of Jacob.

The technical term for a rule of Judaism understood as a divine command is *mitsvah*, a biblical term which is familiar in the phrase Bar or Bat Mitsvah. (In popular usage the term is often applied to an act of charity or generosity which may well go beyond what is strictly believed to be 'commanded'.) The whole body of *mitsvot* is known collectively as the *halakhah*. We have already seen that this term is applied to the teachings of the Bible and the Talmud which have practical applications, as opposed to narrative or speculative portions, which are called Haggadah. In speaking of 'the *halakhah*' Jews indicate a notional body of rules, roughly comparable to the English phrase 'the law'. One can say, for example, 'What does the *halakhah* say about . . . ?' or 'That would be against the *halakhah*'. (In the latter sense it is possible also to use the equivalent expression 'the Din': the word *din* means 'law', as in Bet Din, a court of law.)

According to a widely accepted ancient rabbinic statement there are no fewer than 613 *mitsvot*, of which 248 are positive injunctions and 365 are prohibitions. In practice the term *mitsvah* tends to be reserved for the former; the technical term for the latter is *averah*, 'transgression'.

The rabbis maintained firmly that all the rules of the *halakhah*, whether specifically mentioned in the Torah or deduced by the rabbis themselves and mentioned in the Talmud, and even the further ramifications derived later from these, all originated with God at Sinai and are to be observed. At the same time, they strongly defended the doctrine of human free will. Every human person is a battleground of

[2] Mishnah, *Avot* 4:15.

two conflicting forces, the evil urge (*yetser ha-ra*) and its opposite, the good urge (*yetser tov*), roughly equivalent to what we call the conscience. Much has been written on the subject of the evil urge, its origin (how did something evil come from a God who is all good?), its nature, and the way it operates. It is up to each person to recognise the evil urge and to subdue it (with God's help) or channel it into positive and beneficial actions.

Some Jews today place *halakhah* at the centre of their Judaism, and others place it differently within their conception of what Judaism is about, but all refer to the same *halakhah*.[3] That *halakhah* is not found in the Bible, but in the so-called Oral Law of the Talmud and its commentaries.[4] Specialised students of *halakhah* need to be familiar with these sources, and also with the various codes and published responsa. Non-specialists may rely on various compendia; in case of doubt they may address a question to a rabbi, who may refer it to a reputed authority, whose reply could end up being published and thus contributing to the *halakhah*, which is an organic process.

One of the most celebrated philosophers of *halakhah* in recent times was J. B. Soloveitchik (1903–93), who was a leading figure in American Orthodoxy from the 1950s until his death.[5] In his beautiful essay *Halakhic Man* he explains and illustrates with examples some of the complexities and antitheses involved in living one's life according to *halakhah*. He explains that halakhic man has something in common with both the religious and the cognitive or scientific type, and yet is different from both. In particular, unlike the cognitive type of man he has a sense of the transcendent and longs for it, but unlike the religious man he does not aspire to ascend to it, but brings it down to earth into the 'four ells' of the *Halakhah*.

Similar in some ways to the approach of Soloveitchik is Yeshayahu Leibowitz (1903–94), an Israeli scientist who wrote and lectured extensively on religious matters. However, Leibowitz goes further when he

---

[3] Solomon B. Freehof, an American Reform rabbi who has published two collections of 'Reform Responsa', might seem to be an exception, and he is indeed an exception in American Reform Judaism, which has rejected the whole concept of sacred law; but as a halakhist he works with the content and methodology of the traditional *halakhah*, even if his conclusions are often far removed from those of Orthodox or Conservative halakhists.

[4] 'Current attempts to identify Judaism with the Hebrew Bible . . . are unrelated to the Halakhah and are independent of it. This kind of bibliolatry is Lutheran, not Jewish. Historically, Israel never lived or intended to live by Scripture, nor was it ever intended so to live religiously. Israel conducted its life in accordance with the Halakhah as propounded in the Oral Law.' Yeshayahu Leibowitz, *Judaism, Human Values and the Jewish State*, ed. E. Goldman (Cambridge, MA, 1992), p. 11.   [5] Also known as J. D. Soloveitchik.

insists that the only purpose of obeying the commands is to serve God, and the only way to serve God is by obeying the commands.

'You shall love your neighbour as yourself' without the continuation 'I am God' is the great rule of the atheist Kant. So long as a person's religiosity expresses only his personal awareness, his conscience, his morality, or his values, the religious act is merely for himself and, as such, is an act of rebellion against the Kingdom of Heaven.[6]

This is an extreme view, and many observant Jews would have more sympathy with Soloveitchik's openness to the religious dimension, and would feel that if man's only role in the scheme of things is to obey blindly something is being missed both of the complexity of the human person and the richness of the human sense of God.

RIGHTEOUSNESS

Israel is commanded to pursue righteousness (*tsedek* or *tsedakah*) (Deuteronomy 16:20), a word which can be a synonym of justice. Righteousness goes beyond strict justice in connoting a concern for the well-being of all members of society, including those who are disadvantaged but who have no particular claim to justice. In current use the term *tsedakah* has only one meaning: almsgiving.

The demand for righteousness in this sense is an important element in the commands of the Torah (e.g. Exodus 22:21–7; Leviticus 19:9–18; Deuteronomy 24:10–15). It is even more important in the prophets, because it is set against a hypocritical façade of false justice and religiosity:

Tell my people their transgression and the House of Jacob their sins:
They consult me every day and seek to know my ways,
Like a nation that acts righteously and has not rejected the justice of its God,
They ask me for righteous laws, seeking to be close to God.
'Why have you not seen our fasting, or noticed our self-affliction?' . . .
Is this what you call a fast, a day acceptable to the Lord?
This is the fast of my choosing:
To loosen the fetters of injustice, to untie the knots of the yoke,
To set free the downtrodden and snap every yoke,
To share your bread with the hungry and take the poor and homeless into
　　your house,
To cover anyone you see naked, and not ignore your own flesh and blood.
　　　　　　　　　　　　　　　　　　　　　(Isaiah 58:2–7)

---

[6] Leibowitz, *Judaism*, pp. 19–20.

Or again the prophet Micah, replying to a questioner asking what sacrifices he should bring to God, offering thousands of rams or ten thousand rivers of oil, or even his eldest son:

> He has told you, man, what is good, and what the Lord demands of you:
> Only to act justly and love kindness, and walk modestly [or humbly] with
> your God. (Micah 6:8)

Passages such as these appealed to the nineteenth-century Reformers because they suggest that social action and sensitivity to injustice is a substitute for formal religion, or at least (since neither the prophets nor the Reformers wished to see religion disappear) an essential concomitant. The Zionists, too, quoted them with approval, and the declaration of the State of Israel in 1948 says that the state 'will be based on the precepts of liberty, justice and peace taught by the Hebrew prophets'.

Of particular interest in this context is the Musar movement, founded in Lithuania by Israel Salanter (1810–83). 'Musar' is the name given to a type of literature beginning in the Middle Ages which went beyond the letter of the law in promoting religiously sensitive behaviour. The Musar movement collected and studied these texts. Salanter addressed himself at first particularly to businessmen: he explained that some Jews who observed the ritual requirements of Judaism meticulously could still be unscrupulous in their business dealings or their treatment of their employees. Later the movement gained a wider appeal, and strongly influenced the Lithuanian yeshivot.[7]

The Hasidim, who were opposed to the Musar movement, gave their own interpretation to righteousness when they applied the term Tsaddik, 'righteous one', to their own charismatic leaders.[8] The qualities of the Tsaddik are extraordinary saintliness and almost superhuman gifts. While such a figure has some antecedents in classical Judaism, for example in the wonder-working prophets like Elijah or Elisha, in its Hasidic form it is a new development, and has little to do with the traditional concept of righteousness.

The relationship between righteousness and the *halakhah* is obviously a delicate one, because while traditional Judaism insists that the *halakhah* embodies God's will for the Jewish people and therefore by definition represents the highest standards of morality, the idea of righteousness implies that there is a higher standard. The *halakhah* itself acknowledges

[7] See Immanuel Etkes, 'Rabbi Israel Salanter and His Psychology of Mussar', in Arthur Green, ed., *Jewish Spirituality: from the Sixteenth-Century Revival to the Present* (London, 1987), pp. 206–44.

[8] See Samuel H. Dresner, *The Zaddik* (New York, 1960); Arthur Green, 'Typologies of Leadership and the Hasidic Zaddiq', in Green, *Jewish Spirituality*, pp. 127–56.

a category of actions which fall 'inside the [strict] line of the law' (*lifnim mi-shurat ha-din*). An example of such behaviour which is actually quoted in the Talmud is restoring lost property to its owner even in circumstances where the law does not require it. Most people would instinctively feel that such an action was meritorious.

FAITH

One characteristic of the righteous in the Bible is faith (*emunah*) (Habakkuk 2:4). The model of faith is the patriarch Abraham (Genesis 15:6), who had such faith that he could undertake to offer his own son as a sacrifice to God. To have faith is therefore a prime goal of any Jew.

For the medieval philosophers faith came to mean belief. So Maimonides' Thirteen Principles were much later reformulated as a creed, in which each clause begins with the words 'I believe with perfect faith . . .', and in this form they entered Jewish prayer books, in many of which they are still found today. However in the Bible and the rabbinic writings the meaning of *emunah* is confidence or trust: not belief *that* but belief *in*. (*Emunah* is related to the word *amen*, the response spoken on hearing a blessing.) Modern thinkers have returned to this conception of faith, following in the footsteps of Moses Mendelssohn, who preferred to translate the opening words of Maimonides' creed as 'I am firmly convinced . . .', since he himself believed that Judaism had no dogmas, and therefore no creed.[9]

One modern thinker who has written a good deal about faith is Ignaz Maybaum (1897–1976). While insisting that *emunah* means belief in the sense of 'confidence', he draws a distinction between belief and trust, which in Hebrew is *bitahon*. The Bible says, 'Blessed is the man who trusts in the Lord, and whose trust the Lord is' (Jeremiah 17:7). Unlike trust, belief implies unbelief. If I say 'I believe you', I may be hinting 'despite some doubts'. If I say 'I trust you', I have no doubts. Also, if I say 'I believe you', I am referring to a single statement; if I say, 'I trust you', I mean I shall believe your future statements too. That does not mean that trust has to be completely blind. 'Judaism is trust in God, and this trust in God is in our hearts without renouncing reason, common sense or everyday experience.'[10] But trust means an attitude of complete confidence, like the trust a child has in caring parents. This trust is the faith of Abraham, and it is also the characteristic of the true Jew.[11]

---

[9] For a clear account of Jewish views of faith see Louis Jacobs, *Faith* (London, 1968).
[10] Ignaz Maybaum, *The Faith of the Jewish Diaspora* (London, 1962), p. 16.   [11] Ibid., pp. 22–4.

FEAR

In the story of the testing of Abraham, known as the *akedah*, Abraham, on the point of slaughtering his son, is told: 'Do not harm the child or hurt him, because now I know that you are a God-fearer' (Genesis 22:12). To be a God-fearer is another important goal. The fear of God is described as the beginning of knowledge (Proverbs 1:7), and the book of Ecclesiastes concludes with these words: 'Finally, when everything has been heard, fear God and keep his commands, for this is the whole of the human condition: God judges every deed, even secret ones, to see if it is good or bad' (Ecclesiastes 12:13–14).

The medieval philosophers, however, while agreeing that the fear of God is of central importance, are at pains to stress that it should not be founded on fear of punishment. They distinguish two kinds of fear, a lower type which is fear of pain, and a higher type which is what we would call reverence or awe: the feeling one has about someone who is incomparably more elevated than oneself.[12]

Related to the fear of God is the fear of sin, which in rabbinic writings is often the equivalent of a moral sense: the person who fears sin naturally avoids it, not because of the fear of punishment, but, as the kabbalists in particular emphasise, out of reverence for God, because sin offends against God's grandeur and creates a barrier between the sinner and God.

Among modern writers on Judaism the great prophet of fear or reverence is Abraham Joshua Heschel (1907–72). In his writings Heschel brings to the philosophy of religion something of the passion of the biblical prophets and the powerful Hasidic sense of the presence of God in the natural world. His influential book *Man Is Not Alone* begins with an encomium of what he calls 'wonder or radical amazement', which he argues is the first step towards understanding the world and God. Knowledge begins not in doubt and ratiocination but in wonder or reverence before the grandeur of the ultimate reality of the world we inhabit. Wonder goes beyond knowledge. Reverence is an innate human attitude:

Reverence is one of man's answers to the presence of the mystery. The meaning of things we revere is overwhelming and beyond the grasp of our understanding. To the spirit of man his own spirit is a reliable witness that the mystery is not an absurdity, that, on the contrary, things known and perceptible are charged with its heart-stripping, galvanizing meaning.[13]

---

[12] On the topic of fear of God see Jacobs, *A Jewish Theology*, pp. 174–82.
[13] *Man Is Not Alone* (New York, 1951), pp. 26–8.

The immediate and unquestionable feeling of awe that we feel before the grandeur of the stars in the sky or a dramatic sunset is the first step towards appreciating the reality of the transcendent and the demands that God makes of us:

The beginning of faith is not a feeling for the mystery of living or a sense of awe, wonder or fear. The root of religion is the question what to do with the feeling for the mystery of living, what to do with awe, wonder or fear. Religion, the end of isolation, begins with a consciousness that something is asked of us. It is in that tense, eternal asking in which the soul is caught and in which man's answer is elicited.[14]

Heschel's philosophy of Judaism embraces and affirms the radical wonder which has been a living stream within Judaism since the Psalmist's 'The heavens declare the glory of God', but it did not lead him into introspective withdrawal from the world of human action: on the contrary, he became famous as a political activist, against the American war in Vietnam and in favour of the civil rights movement. By putting awe and mystery back into the heart of Judaism he touched a chord in Jews who felt alienated from the rather arid rationalism associated with Reform Judaism at the time and the materialism of Jewish life in America, but who had no sympathy with the folkloric exoticism of neo-Hasidism.

LOVE

A number of Jewish thinkers have stressed that without fear of God there can be no true love of God. To love God is actually commanded in the Shma: 'You shall love the Lord your God with all your heart, soul and being.' It may be asked, how is it possible to command love? The rabbis understand that what is intended is obedience to God's commands, although they do admit that one can feel a deep emotional attachment to and longing for God, such as is spoken of in some of the Psalms and elsewhere in the Bible. The medieval authors, on the other hand, whether they are mystically or rationally inclined, tend to emphasise the emotional aspects. One of the main writers on the subject is Bahya Ibn Pakuda, in the eleventh century, whose book *The Duties of the Heart*[15] culminates in the love of God. This is the ultimate aim of the religious person, when, emptying itself of the love for any material thing, the believer's heart is filled with the love of God. He has perfect faith and

---

[14] Ibid., pp. 68–9.   [15] Translated by Menahem Mansoor (London, 1973).

trust in God, and everything he does is in accordance with God's will. This love is completely disinterested and unselfish, and it occupies true lovers of God totally, to the exclusion of every other concern.

Bahya represents a rare extreme among the thinkers of his day, though he has had some followers, particularly among the kabbalists and Hasidim. Even more sober philosophers like Maimonides, however, insist on the elevated status of the love of God, and uses the analogy of erotic passion (which is commonly employed by the kabbalists) to indicate the intensity of the love of God.[16]

We cannot leave the topic of the love of God without sparing a few words for two related topics, God's love for humanity and the love of people for one another.

The biblical God is sometimes severe and even angry, but he is more often kind, generous and forgiving. The Psalms in particular speak of his generosity and love, and as we have seen the Song of Songs is understood as a dialogue of love between God and the Jewish people. The prayers of the liturgy often speak of this love, in particular in connection with the gift of the Sabbath and more broadly with all the commands of the Torah: in both cases the loving gift is associated with the choice of Israel as God's special people. The theme is expressed particularly clearly in the prayer spoken before the evening Shma (a similar prayer is said in the morning):

With everlasting love you love your people the house of Israel; you have taught us Torah and commands, rules and laws. Therefore, Lord our God, when we lie down and when we rise up we shall speak of your rules and rejoice in the words of your Torah and your commands for ever, for they are our life and the length of our days, and we shall meditate on them day and night. Never remove your love from us. Blessed are you, Lord, who loves his people Israel.

So strong is the sense of God's love that we even find some sources explaining suffering, particularly the suffering of the righteous, as 'chastisements of love'. Just as a loving parent sometimes chastises a child, so God sometimes chastises those he loves (Proverbs 3:12). Others however do not agree with this view, which conflicts with the idea of God's justice and with our sense of healthy behaviour for a lover.

Among the commands of the Torah one of the most precious ones is 'You shall love your neighbour like yourself' (Leviticus 19:18). This has been variously explained as meaning 'You shall love your neighbour as much as you love yourself' or 'because he is like yourself'. Maimonides

---

[16] On love of God see further Jacobs, *A Jewish Theology*, pp. 152–73.

adopts the first view: one must have as much regard for another's money
or honour as one would for one's own, and he goes so far as to comment:
'Anyone who gains honour for himself by bringing dishonour to his
neighbour has no share in the Coming Age.' Others stress that the neighbour has the same feelings as you do, and before doing anything that
might harm him you should put yourself in his place. In a famous rabbinic story, a pagan asked one of the greatest of the teachers of the
period before the destruction of the second Temple, Hillel, to sum up
the whole Torah in a single maxim. He replied: 'Do not do to another
what you would not wish him to do to you.'

In recent times the love of one person for another has been put to
good use by Martin Buber in explaining his conception of the I–You
relationship. The You does not have to be a fellow human, but can be an
animal or even an inanimate object, but it is in the relationship of two
humans that the relationship can be seen most clearly. 'He is not a character to be described and experienced, a loose bundle of named idiosyn-
crasies. Distinct and all of a piece, he is you and he fills the heavens. Not
as though nothing exists apart from him, but all else lives in his light.'[17]
The loving relationship between two people becomes a model for the
relationship between people and God, for Buber as it was also, in a
different way, for Rosenzweig.

We have singled out a few of the ways in which a Jew can aim to be a
good Jew, which generally boils down to having the right relation to God.
All are deeply rooted in the tradition of Judaism, and there are others as
well which have not been mentioned, belonging to the more mystical tradition: concepts such as the piety of the Hasid or the devotion of the
mystic. The range of possibilities is bewildering, and the relationship
between them is far from clear. Perhaps the best approach is to see them
as possible models which exist, and which the individual Jew may choose
for himself or herself, separately or in combination.

So far we have been looking at states or attitudes that may be cultivated.
It remains to consider one or two of the answers that have been given to
the question 'What is the purpose of being a good Jew?' We shall not
examine answers that are framed in terms of the individual, such as
satisfying oneself as a human being, or acquiring knowledge, or achieving union with God, as these are not distinctively Jewish goals (though
they may be pursued in terms of distinctively Jewish activities, such as

[17] Quoted from Vermes, *Buber on God and the Perfect Man*, p. 202, where the subject is discussed
further, and see also p. 240.

obeying the commands of the Torah or studying Hebrew texts), nor are they characteristic of Jewish teaching.

A small but vocal and probably growing number of Jews maintain that the purpose of Jewish life is to 'bring the Messiah'. The *Jewish Catalog*, a kind of self-help guide to Judaism addressed to a wide readership and published by a respected Jewish publisher in 1973, contains a chapter headed 'How to bring Mashiah' which includes the following advice (among others):

Plant a tree in Vietnam in a defoliated former forest. Plant a tree in Brooklyn where the asphalt has buried the forest.

Read Torah with some friends and talk about it [on Sabbath]; walk on grass barefoot; look very carefully at a flower without picking it; give somebody something precious and beautiful without asking him to pay you; give love.

If you're a man, practice having a baby…

If you're a woman, surround the nearest warrior type with a ring of laughing, singing women. But more important, whether you're a man or a woman let the female *within you* encompass the warrior *within you* . . .[18]

To understand this idea it is necessary to consider its historical background.

The doctrine of the Messiah is one of the most distinctive ideas of classical Judaism. Hermann Cohen called it 'the most significant and original product of the Jewish spirit'. The roots of the idea are found in the Bible, together with the term *mashiah*, which means 'anointed with oil', and can refer to an office holder, such as a king or high priest, who is anointed at his installation. The prophets look forward to a time when the people Israel will be freed from subjection to other nations, and when justice and righteousness will be established in the world under the rule of God, and some of the prophets (Isaiah, Jeremiah, Micah, Zechariah) associate this transformation of history with an exceptionally exalted human leader. Others envisage a 'day of the Lord' when the dynasty of David will rule but there will be no special leader. These ideas are developed in the post-biblical literature, and the rabbinic writings are full of references to the idea of a Messiah who will rescue Israel from its historical predicament and inaugurate a golden age of peace and harmony.

---

[18] *The Jewish Catalog. A Do-it-yourself Kit* compiled by Richard Siegel, Michael Strassfeld, Sharon Strassfeld (Philadelphia, 1973), pp. 250–1.

However, the concept is not developed with clarity, and many conflicting opinions are recorded. One rabbi, for example, states that it is vain to hope for a future Messiah, because the Messiah mentioned in the Bible came in the time of Hezekiah, at the beginning of the seventh century BCE. There is a widespread assumption that the Messianic Age is not a supernatural disturbance in history but rather, as the third-century Babylonian teacher Samuel puts it, 'is no different from the present except that Israel will no longer be in subjection to the kingdoms of the world'.[19] At the same time many rabbis insist that it is wrong to calculate when the redemption will come about, and still worse to take action to hasten it. In other words they were generally opposed to the occasional outbreaks of messianic fervour that arose particularly under Roman rule. Even this hostility, however, is not unanimous, and some rabbis, including the outstanding leader Akiva, recognised the rebel Bar Kochba as the Messiah.

Several blessings embodying rabbinic Messianism have been included in the Amidah, where they help to keep the ideas alive, with phrases such as:

Sound the great horn for our liberation, and raise a banner to gather our scattered ones, and gather us together from the four corners of the earth

Restore our judges as they were and our counsellors as at the beginning; remove from us sorrow and sighing and rule over us yourself alone

Speedily uproot and crush, cast down and humble the rule of arrogance

Return to your city, Jerusalem, in mercy, and make it your home as you have promised; rebuild it soon to last eternally, and set up the throne of David within it

Cause the shoot of your servant David to sprout forth, and exalt his horn with your salvation, for we wait all day long for your salvation

Restore the service to the shrine of your house, and willingly and lovingly accept the fire-offerings of Israel and their prayer

May the remembrance of the Messiah, the son of your servant David and of Jerusalem your holy city . . . rise up before you.

During the Middle Ages there was unanimity concerning the belief in a personal Messiah, but there was disagreement about whether the Messianic Age would be a natural or a supernatural event. Maimonides insists that it is wrong to imagine that the course of nature will change

---

[19] Babylonian Talmud, *Berakhot* 34b.

with the coming of the Messiah. The King Messiah will restore the kingdom of David to its former glory, restore the Temple and the sacrificial worship, and gather in the dispersed Israelites. He will be a wise ruler who will study the rules of the Torah and compel all Israel to observe them. At the same time, he points out that the Talmudic rabbis had no detailed tradition on this subject, but tried to interpret the biblical teachings.

The purpose of the Messianic Age, according to Maimonides, is not that the redeemed Israelites should lord it over the other nations, but simply that they should be free to study the Torah, so as to prepare themselves for the Coming Age or 'World to Come' (*olam ha-ba*).

Isaac Luria gave a new direction to Messianism by claiming that it is up to each individual either to impede or hasten the messianic redemption by performing good or evil deeds. Previously the dominant belief was that God would intervene to bring the Messianic Age at a moment of his deciding, and that it was useless for humans to try to influence him. Luria, living as he did in the century following the epoch-making event of the completion of the Christian reconquest of Spain, when many Jews had been forced to become Christians and many others had become exiles, was deeply troubled by the urgent need for messianic redemption. It seems that he considered himself to be the prophet Elijah, the harbinger of the Messiah, or the Messiah of the tribe of Joseph who would prepare the way for the Messiah, son of David. As we have seen in an earlier chapter, Luria devised a complex new kabbalistic theory to explain the fundamental defects in the world, and the same theory also pointed the way to redemption. In the Lurianic kabbalah, after the breaking of the vessels sparks of divine light became trapped within broken fragments. Some sparks are imprisoned in the *klipot* or husks, demonic forces in our world. Human beings, by performing good actions and refraining from evil ones, can release the sparks. When all the sparks have been freed the Messiah will come.

Shabbetai Tsvi (1626–76), the most famous among a series of messianic pretenders, gathered an enormous following at a time of intense millenarian expectation among Jews and Christians. He was profoundly influenced by the ideas of the Lurianic kabbalah, but he administered a new twist to them by teaching that the holy sparks may be released through the performance of sinful acts. Even when he eventually accepted conversion to Islam as the price of his life many of his adherents continued to believe in him, claiming that he had apostasised so as to release the holy sparks trapped in the domain of impurity. They continued secretly to perform 'holy sins' to bring his work to completion.[20]

Hasidim too gives prominence to the idea of the holy sparks and develops it still further. Sparks are trapped within food, drink and other mundane things, and therefore the Hasid must be fully involved with worldly matters in order to release them. In addition, each individual has the task of freeing not only his own sparks but others, which may in some cases only be reached after a long journey, and which only he and no one else can release.[21]

There is no clear or unanimous understanding today about the Messiah or the Messianic Age. Orthodoxy maintains the belief in a personal Messiah who will come in God's good time to restore the sacrificial worship and lead all mankind back to God. Many of the nineteenth-century Reformers wanted to do away with the whole idea of the Messiah, but eventually the concept of a Messianic Age was incorporated into Reform thought, not in a sense of the restoration of a Jewish state, which they rejected, but in the moral and political advances of the time. As the Pittsburgh Platform put it: 'We recognize in the modern era of universal culture of heart and intellect the approaching of the realization of Israel's great Messianic hope for the establishment of the kingdom of truth, justice and peace among all men.'

This somewhat bland interpretation of a powerful doctrine has not satisfied everyone, and there has been a revival of interest recently in the kabbalistic and Hasidic approaches. Among neo-kabbalistic and neo-Hasidic groups the bringing of the Messiah occupies a high priority. Some are content with the straightforward idea of cultivating the good life and keeping the commands of the *halakhah*. An old saying is quoted with approval: If all Jews observed two successive Sabbaths properly the Messiah would come. Others pursue the liberation of the trapped sparks through meditation and by other means.

Messianism can also take more concrete forms. Zionism, although essentially a secular movement, makes use of some of the ideas and language of Messianism. As we have already seen, the proclamation of the State of Israel in 1948 spoke of the ingathering of the dispersed and of the prophetic vision of liberty, justice and peace. The Zionist enterprise has united religious Jews with secular Jews some of whom have been mil-

---

[20] The oustanding study is Gershom Scholem, *Sabbatai Sevi, The Mystical Messiah*, tr. R. J. Zwi Werblowsky (Princeton, NJ/London, 1973).

[21] See further Louis Jacobs, 'The Uplifting of Sparks in Later Jewish Mysticism', in Green, *Jewish Spirituality*, pp. 99–126.

itantly anti-religious. The alliance has been an uneasy one, with the secularists prevailing both numerically and in terms of power and influence. The leading theoretician of religious Zionism, Abraham Isaac Kook (1865–1935), who served as Ashkenazi chief rabbi of Palestine under British rule, maintained that despite its secularist impetus, the Zionist movement represented 'the beginnings of the messianic age', quoting a Talmudic dictum that 'in the footsteps of the Messiah insolence will increase'. He was convinced that the holiness of the land of Israel would penetrate the souls of the atheists, releasing their trapped sparks and bringing redemption in the very near future. Since the creation of the State, and particularly since the Six Day War of 1967, some religious Zionists have taken to speaking of the creation of the State of Israel as the 'beginning of redemption', not as being itself the future restored kingdom, of which it lacks too many features, but at least an indication that the redemption is on its way. The Gush Emunim movement has gone further, and seen the State itself as sharing in the character of the Messianic kingdom, so that it is actually a first step towards the final goal of redemption. All Zionists are fond of a song that says: 'David King of Israel lives, lives and exists!'

We have seen that down the centuries there have been many examples of people who either claimed to be the Messiah or had the claim advanced on their behalf by their followers. While there has been no outstanding claimant in recent times, some Jews have claimed particular political or spiritual leaders to be the Messiah. Leaving aside self-styled 'messianic Jews' – converts to Christianity who accept the Christian claims about Jesus and the Christian understanding of the Messiah as a supernatural, spiritual figure who is the son of God and part of a divine 'trinity' – the most striking example was the seventh Lubavitcher Rebbe, Menahem Mendel Schneerson. Many of his followers hailed him as the Messiah, and gathered in public places singing 'We want the Messiah now!', and even the Rebbe's death in 1994 did not put an end to their Messianic enthusiasm.

Messianism seems to correspond to a deeply rooted yearning for redemption arising from a profound dissatisfaction with the real world when judged against religious teachings about the perfection and power of God. This perennial yearning, reinforced by the vivid words of the liturgy, has kept the messianic idea on the Jewish agenda, but at the same time the doctrine has remained vague in the extreme, as we have seen, and only rarely has messianic fervour infected a large part of the Jewish people. Today it is confined to very small numbers, except in the attenuated and largely secularised form of Zionism. Closely related to Messianism is another idea, which is expressed in the slogan 'repairing the world'.

One of the concluding prayers in the synagogue prays for the day when God will be king over all the world, and everyone will call on his name. It uses the phrase 'to set the world right under the kingship of Shaddai (God)', and this idea of *tikkun*, repair, becomes very important in the Lurianic kabbalah.

In the Lurianic system the term is applied to the reparation of the disruption caused by the breaking of the vessels. Reparation is achieved through the *partsufim* or configurations, which are different arrangements of the ten Sefirot. The same process has to be applied within a series of four interlinked worlds, the World of Emanation, the World of Creation, the World of Formation and the World of Action. The original breaking of the vessels was a cosmic event occurring (as it were) within the godhead long before the creation of our world, and Adam, the father of the whole human race, was intended to achieve the reclamation of the holy sparks and so restore the world to harmony. However, Adam by his disobedience not only failed to fulfil this task but precipitated a further disaster, a second breaking of the vessels. Adam's soul shattered, and a spark of it is trapped within each of his descendants. A third catastrophe occurred during the giving of the Torah at Mount Sinai, which was potentially a further opportunity to set the realm of the Sefirot to rights, when the people rebelliously worshipped a golden calf (Exodus 32–3). After this new disruption there is no other opportunity to restore harmony in a single act, but *tikkun* is a matter of piecemeal, step-by-step restoration which will only be completed in the Messianic Age.

Every individual Jew now has the personal task of sharing in the task of restoring cosmic harmony by avoiding evil and doing good, and so releasing the holy sparks from the demonic realm of the *klipot* and enabling them to fly upwards to share in the reparation of the Sefirotic realm. In addition, since the second disaster each human being has its own soul, a fragment of the soul of Adam, which needs to be perfected and reclaimed. A burden of active responsibility thus falls upon the individual.

The early Hasidim seized on the Lurianic concept of *tikkun* and made it even more the responsibility of the individual by shifting the focus from the cosmos to the soul of each person. 'Breaking' and 'repair' can become psychological concepts, and in the thought of some Hasidic masters the repair is considered so valuable that it is possible to say that the breaking only happened for the sake of the repair.[22] Hasidism attaches a very high value to ethical and pious behaviour, through which the Hasid can raise up his own sparks, and achieve closeness to God.[23] There is also, however, a strong tendency in Hasidism for the individual to improve himself not so much through study and knowledge as through contact with and imitation of a charismatic leader, the Tsaddik, without whose mediation other individuals are unable to lift up the sparks. Hasidim thus represents a radical and unique development of the concepts of the Lurianic kabbalah, which, in their revised form, reached a huge new Jewish public and indeed are still influential in some circles today.

Tikkun, mending the world, has now become part of the vocabulary of younger Jews who have probably never heard of Isaac Luria. It can be applied to anything from tree-planting and respect for ecology to programmes of social action. The conjunction of ecological and social awareness is not haphazard. It is characteristic of Judaism to place greater stress on this world than on the transcendent, and so even a sublimely transcendent concept like *tikkun* can be popularised in a this-worldly form. Both ecological and social reformers, in taking action to repair real damage, seem to be embodying a certain religious ideal in a practical way that can be attractive to young Jews to whom talk of the realms of the Sefirot and the Primeval Man might seem mere mumbo jumbo. (At the same time other young Jews are attracted precisely to the kabbalistic speculation.)

The Israeli author Amos Oz (born 1939) has captured something of this practical, this-worldly interpretation of *tikkun olam* in his short story of that name,[24] in which Hasidic vocabulary is applied in the context of kibbutz socialism. It is a profoundly ambiguous and somewhat pessimistic vision. The story concerns a solitary, morose member of a kibbutz, who believes that only he is true to the world-reforming ideals of the founders of socialism, Zionism and the kibbutz movement, and observes with loathing the degeneracy of those around him. He spends his days

---

[22] See, for example, Rivka Schatz Uffenheimer, *Hasidism as Mysticism*, tr. Jonathan Chipman (Princeton, NJ/Jerusalem, 1933), p. 209.

[23] Known as *devekut*. See G. Scholem, 'Devekut, or Communion with God', in his *The Messianic Idea in Judaism* (New York, 1971), pp. 203–26.

[24] 'Setting the World to Rights', tr. Nicholas de Lange, *Ariel* 41 (1976), pp. 104–18.

repairing broken machinery: this is his own contribution to *tikkun*. In the end his hatred, despair and loneliness get the better of him, and he takes his own life. Oz returns to the idea of *tikkun* in his novel *Touch the Water Touch the Wind*,[25] which begins in wartime Poland and ends in Israel during the 1967 war. The Jews are represented as watchmakers, both literally and figuratively. They can repair broken clocks, and they can also set right time that is out of joint. There is a metaphysical element here which borrows from Luria, while giving it a contemporary twist.

The philosopher Emil Fackenheim (born 1916) projects a different this-worldly image of *tikkun* in his post-Holocaust reflections entitled *To Mend The World*[26] (the title itself is a translation of *tikkun olam*). The Holocaust disrupts and challenges our understanding of God and of history, yet somehow demands what may seem impossible:

> A Tikkun, *here and now, is mandatory for a Tikkun, there and then, was actual.* It is true that because a *Tikkun* of *that* rupture is impossible we cannot live, after the Holocaust, as men and women have lived before. However, if the impossible *Tikkun* were not also necessary, and hence possible, we could not live at all.[27]

Fackenheim rejects the possibility of applying to the post-Holocaust world the kabbalistic concept of repair by means of obedience to the *mitsvot*. The Nazis killed the kabbalists, and their *tikkun* died with them. After the Holocaust a new point of departure is needed, and Fackenheim finds it in the State of Israel, a miraculous rebirth which offers new hope in the midst of total chaos. There is little if anything left of the transcendent element in Fackenheim's version of *tikkun*.

The same is true of the sense in which the term *tikkun* is commonly used in Jewish youth movements today, where it refers to concrete ecological objectives, recycling, planting trees, using renewable forms of energy. This is a purely this-worldy vision of *tikkun* which totally ignores its kabbalistic history.

MAKING PEACE

Hillel said: Be of the disciples of Aaron, loving peace and pursuing peace, loving people and bringing them to the Torah.[28]

Shalom, 'peace', or *shalom aleikhem*, 'peace be with you', is an old Jewish form of greeting, indeed the most common everyday greeting in Israel

---

[25] Tr. Nicholas de Lange (New York, 1974, London, 1975).
[26] New York 1982, 2nd edn 1989.   [27] Ibid., p. 254.   [28] Mishnah, *Avot* 1:12.

today. The absence of peace in the world, peace within the family, peace between neighbours, between sections of society, and between nations, is a source of constant disappointment to prophets, rabbis and political leaders alike. Many rabbinic sermons sing the praises of peace, as in these typical specimens:

Rabbi Simeon bar Yohai said: Great is peace, for all blessings are contained in it, as it says, 'The Lord will bless his people with peace' (Psalm 29:11). Bar Kappara said: Great is peace, for if it is needed by the beings above, who know neither jealousy nor hatred nor contention nor wrangling nor quarreling nor strife nor envy, as it says, 'He creates peace in his high places' (Job 25:2), how much more is it needed by those below. Rabbi Yudan ben Rabbi Yose said: Great is peace, for God's name is peace, as it says, 'And he called the Lord Peace' (Judges 6:24).[29]

The liturgy resounds with prayers for peace, of which the most prominent are the benediction which concludes the Amidah (which exists in two different versions) and the closing paragraph of the Kaddish. All three of these prayers have become songs which are sung with gusto in Jewish youth groups:

Shalom rav . . . 'Grant abundant peace to your people Israel for ever, for you are the king and lord of all peace.'

Sim shalom . . . 'Grant peace, favour, blessing, grace, kindness and mercy to us and to all your people Israel.'

Oseh shalom . . . 'May he who makes peace in his high places make peace for us and for all Israel.'

The reference to Israel in these prayers should not be understood in too narrow a sense. The sources make it plain that peace is indivisible, and cannot be confined to one people alone. It is in line with this thought that some reformed liturgies have amended the words of the prayers, removing the word Israel or replacing it by 'all the world' or 'all humankind'.

AFTER LIFE

We have considered various theories which place the goal of life within the life of the individual or at some future stage in history. It remains to consider those which look beyond death. The Lurianic concept of *tikkun* effectively carries us outside the framework of nature and history, although it was convenient to describe it together with some this-worldly adaptations of it.

---

[29] See Montefiore and Loewe, *Rabbinic Anthology*, p. 533, and for other examples pp. 530–7.

In discussing the biblical promise that obedience to the commands is rewarded in this life we noted the objection that experience does not always bear this out. Some texts suggest that people may be rewarded or punished for the behaviour of their ancestors, but while this may overcome some of the objections it seems inherently unjust, and was roundly rejected by the prophet Ezekiel (Ezekiel 18).

It remained for post-biblical Jews to develop the answer that rewards and punishments are meted out after death. This view could not be introduced, naturally, until Jews had adopted the idea of the survival of the soul after the death of the body. This idea seems to have been borrowed from Greek thought. At any rate it is not found before the period of Greek influence, but it is taken for granted by Greek Jewish writers such as Philo and the author of the Wisdom of Solomon (see especially Wisdom 3:1–4). The Talmudic rabbis speak of the repose of the souls of the righteous departed in the Garden of Eden, and this idea is mentioned in the memorial prayer for the dead, the *El male rahamim*:

O God full of compassion, who dwell on high, grant perfect peace under the wings of the Shekhinah, in the ranks of the holy and pure ones who shine like the splendour of the firmament, to the soul of N son/daughter of N who has gone to his/her eternity, may he/she rest in the Garden of Eden. Master of mercy, please conceal him/her in the secret of your wings for all eternity, and bind his/her soul in the bundle of life. The Lord is his/her inheritance, and may (s)he rest in peace upon his/her couch, and let us say Amen.

It seems from such texts as though the fortunate souls who have passed an initial examination live on forever in tranquillity, while, we are told, the souls of the wicked go down to Gehinnom, where, according to some views, they suffer torments.

It is hard, however, in studying Talmudic views on the subject, to separate the fate of the soul from another idea, that of resurrection. Originally these two ideas were separate, and perhaps even contradictory (or at least alternative) versions of what happens after death. In the rabbinic literature, however, they are somehow amalgamated, although the details are not worked out systematically. One idea seems to be that the souls of the dead wait in the Garden of Eden until a general resurrection of the dead takes place at some point after the coming of the Messiah, when they will be reunited with their bodies. This will be followed by a great judgment day, to be followed in turn by the Coming Age (*olam ha-ba*).

The idea of the Coming Age also goes back to the ancient rabbis, and like those of the doctrine of the Messiah its details are highly unclear. In general it seems that whereas the Messianic Age is a new phase of history, the Coming Age refers to a new order. Those who have led a good life will be rewarded in the Coming Age, but in what the reward consists is not clear. According to one rabbi, Rav: 'In the Coming Age there is no eating or drinking or reproduction or business activity or envy or hatred or competition, but the righteous sit with crowns on their heads feasting on the radiance of the Shekhinah.'[30]

In medieval and later thought the uncertainty persisted, and various attempts were made to reconcile the vague and conflicting accounts of the rabbis. Some thinkers (such as Maimonides, followed later by the Hasidim and the Musar school) envisaged the Coming Age as a condition of the soul after death, relying on rabbinic passages like the one just quoted. Only the soul, according to Maimonides, can enjoy immortality; the resurrected body will eventually die again. Maimonides was criticised in his lifetime for apparently not believing in bodily resurrection, although he does make it one of his Thirteen Principles.

More modern thinkers have tended to shy away from the subject of the hereafter, or have followed Maimonides in stressing the immortality of the soul rather than the resurrection. Moses Mendelssohn wrote a well-known treatise on the immortality of the soul, naming it *Phaedo* after a Platonic dialogue. He does not seem to accept the idea of bodily resurrection. Reform has followed a similar line, and tends to remove references to resurrection from the prayers, or interpret them as referring to the immortality of the soul. Some Orthodox writers have taken a similar view; others take refuge in obscurity. Very few insist on taking the idea of bodily resurrection literally, even though the Orthodox refusal to countenance cremation is based on it. Many religious Jews today, if pressed, would probably agree with secularists that there is no survival after the death and decomposition of the body, and stress instead that Judaism is an essentially this-worldly religion. Even Orthodox Jews would probably agree that given the inherent difficulties of the subject, the lack of clear guidance in the sources, and the absence of empirical evidence, it is difficult if not impossible for the finite human mind to find a clear path among the various possibilities.

The kabbalists accept the idea of reincarnation, i.e. that a soul can pass from one body to another. This notion is not known in Jewish sources before the eighth century, when it began to find favour among Karaites, possibly because it offered another explanation of the suffering

---

[30] Babylonian Talmud, *Berakhot* 17a.

of infants: they could be presumed to have sinned in a previous existence. The whole idea is strongly condemned by Saadya, but pervades the *Zohar* and subsequent kabbalistic writings, and was taken up by the Hasidim.

The whole area of rewards and punishments after death reveals Judaism at its most credulous and its most hard-headed. The confusions and complexities of the various interwoven beliefs, existing side by side (apparently irreconcilably) in the thought of a single group or occasionally even a single individual, testify to an unwillingness to abandon any element in the tradition that may have an element of truth in it, yet at the same time the almost universal refusal to codify any of the beliefs as dogmas or articles of faith displays a resolute pragmatism. What is remarkable is the adoption by virtually all schools of the idea that actions are rewarded and punished after death or in some future existence rather than in this life, in blatant contradiction of the repeated claims of the Bible. It is one indication among many that the role of the Bible in Judaism is not as central and absolute as is sometimes supposed.

CHAPTER NINE

Judaism and the future

It would be rash at this point in time to predict how Judaism will evolve over the coming years and decades. Prediction is always hazardous, and Judaism has changed astonishingly and sometimes dramatically in the past, and particularly after moments of national catastrophe. After the Babylonian destruction it went from being a local Judaean cult to an embryonic world religion with a universal vocation. After the Roman destruction, following an initial period of upheavals, rabbinic Judaism emerged from the ruins of the priestly temple worship, replacing animal sacrifice with study and prayer. The period of the Christian destruction, beginning with the first crusade and culminating in the reconquest of Spain in 1492, gave birth to mystical Judaism, from the German pietists through the classical Kabbalah of Spain to the Lurianic Kabbalah of Safed. European antisemitism, manifested at the end of the nineteenth century in the Dreyfus trial and the Russian pogroms, led to Zionism. It remains to be seen whether the most recent destruction, wrought by the Nazi Germans, will give rise to some comparably creative and original development.

At the same time, as we look back over the history of Judaism, we can see how fruitful has been the encounter with other civilisations. The Judaism of the Bible would be impossible without the contribution of the surrounding Near Eastern civilisations. The encounter with the Greeks produced extraordinarily rich results (including both Christianity and the western philosophical tradition). Islamic civilisation, too, has made a vital contribution to Judaism, and even Christianity, the sworn enemy of Judaism, has influenced it in innumerable ways. I have tried to show in this Introduction how the encounter with modern European civilisation has changed Judaism: the effect of the changes is still being felt, and already postmodernism is at hand, with its inbuilt incoherence and uncertainty, to challenge modern Judaism and suggest new lines of development. From this viewpoint, too, it is difficult to predict what changes are in store.

Nevertheless there are certain hints in the present situation which may point the way into the future. In this final chapter I shall take stock of the present condition of Judaism and venture some tentative predictions.

EXTERNAL PRESSURES

A hundred years ago Jews were subject to two great and not unrelated pressures: the pressure of antisemitism and the pressure to conform. Antisemitism, an irrational, pathological form of group hatred arising out of political developments in nineteenth-century Europe and nourished by the hostile language of the Christian Church, was actually opposed to the integration of the Jews into the nation-state. It targeted with special vehemence assimilated Jews, who dressed and behaved like the ruling elite. The French army officer Alfred Dreyfus is a good example of such a Jew, and so for that matter is the Austrian journalist Theodor Herzl. The press of the time is full of caricatures of prominent Jews, their facial and bodily features distorted to make them appear alien. While a few antisemites, like the English humorist Hilaire Belloc, argued in favour of ending the 'Jewish problem' (a 'problem' invented by the antisemites themselves) by assimilating the Jews into the wider society, on the grounds that it was more effective as well as more humane than expelling or exterminating them, most preferred the latter alternatives. The Nazi Germans, by taking antisemitism to its logical conclusion, made it unacceptable. Along with other forms of group hatred it is now condemned and disowned (at least publicly) by most governments and political parties, and 'antisemite' in many social circles has become virtually a term of abuse. Naturally it would be rash to assume that it has been disarmed for ever (we may recall Herzl's misplaced confidence that no civilised power would put the antisemitic political programme into practice), but the situation today is vastly different from what it was a century ago.

Reacting to the pressure of antisemitism, and to the new horizons opened up by political emancipation, many Jews in Europe and elsewhere adapted their way of life to that of their surroundings so well that they seemed almost indistinguishable from gentiles (except to the trained eye of the antisemites). When the immigrants from Russia at the end of the nineteenth century came off the boats in England and America they were welcomed by assimilated local Jews, among them clean-shaven rabbis wearing clerical collars: the newcomers were unable to believe that these were Jews, and viewed them with deep suspicion. This process of adaptation had its effect, as we have seen, on Jewish religion in the West. The synagogue became more like a church, the rabbi more like a Christian minister. Nor was the adaptation only on the outside: it affected the ways Jews thought as well. Today this pressure to conform, while it has not vanished, has become enfeebled, both because of the weakening of antisemitism, and because western society itself has changed and become more tolerant of difference. Jews in most countries no longer need feel compelled to pretend to be what they are not. An outward token of the change is the large number of young male Jews who wear a skullcap in public, as a sign of Jewish identity.

It is not easy for Jews to adjust to these changes. Old habits die hard, and there are still many Jews around who grew up under the old regime. The instinct to conform still exists. Jews are still sensitive to any hint of antisemitism, and react accordingly. Nevertheless it may be expected that if both these pressures continue to be enfeebled, as time passes Jews, as individuals and also collectively, will gain the confidence to be them-selves and act as they feel is right, without fear of contempt, discrimina-tion or attack. Some signs that have already appeared lend some support to this prediction. American Reform and British Liberal Judaism, which had adopted a very assimilated form of worship, with organ music and choirs, bareheaded rabbis and congregants, and little or no use of Hebrew, have evolved towards a much more recognisably Jewish service. Orthodox worship too, has changed and become more 'folksy' and exotic, and in the latest prayer books prayers that had been revised with the aim of avoiding giving offence to non-Jews have been restored to their original wording. There are hints, too, that a new toughness is creeping into the dialogue with Christianity: the Jewish participants are becoming less apologetic and more assertive. All these trends may be expected to continue and become stronger.

DEMOGRAPHIC TRENDS

As we saw in chapter 1, the world Jewish population has not recovered from the Nazi genocide, and numbers are generally in decline. People are living longer, which masks the low birthrate that prevails in all but the most traditional sectors: the Jewish population is steadily ageing. Since there is no growth overall, population increase in one place, due to migration, is balanced by a decrease elsewhere. The trend in popula-tion movement is away from smaller centres towards larger ones. The one exception to this rule is movement from the United States to Israel, but this is balanced by emigration from Israel to the United States. If the general trend continues, all Jewish communities, with the possible exception of Israel, will continue to decline in numbers, and as people grow older they will place strains on communal resources. Small communities will tend to disappear. Already in many countries there are more disused synagogues than active ones.

Various factors could influence this general trend. A rise in the birthrate relative to the deathrate is unlikely. More likely is a change in the attitude to mixed families. At present the halakhic definition of Jewish identity serves to differentiate Jews from non-Jews within a single family. Children of a Jewish father and non-Jewish mother are not considered by the Orthodox rabbinate to be Jews; they and their children are lost to Judaism. The Orthodox rabbinate has state-backed power in Israel and, to a lesser extent, in France, and considerable influence in other countries, such as Britain, where Orthodox synagogues are in the majority.

What alternative approaches are available? In Israel the state registers all the non-Jewish family members as Jews, although this does not affect their status in the eyes of the rabbinate. The result is a double system which will inevitably lead to confusion and conflict. In the United States the Reform movement recognises the children as Jews provided they are brought up to regard themselves as Jews. This bold step accentuates the rift between the Reform movement and the other sectors of Jewry, although the idea seems to be gathering some support in the Conservative sector. Another possibility would be to facilitate and encourage conversion, for the non-Jewish parent and particularly for the children, in cases where the family declares a commitment to Judaism.

The result of such a step, could the relevant religious authorities agree to it, would be to turn what is currently a serious seepage into a numerical gain, as well as putting an end to confusion and unhappiness on the personal level. However, on a global scale it would probably not have a significant impact on the world Jewish population, at least in the short term.

Another possibility would be to address the question of missions. In the past Judaism has grown considerably through conversion, sometimes embracing large numbers. (The ruling houses of Adiabene, in the Middle East, and Khazaria, on the northern shores of the Black and Caspian Seas, were converted in the first and eighth centuries respectively; it is likely that many Jews today are descended from them and their subjects. The Berber-speaking Jews of North Africa are often thought to be of proselyte origin. The Mishnah speaks of 'proselyte stock' as a category of Jews, and further back still the Bible refers to a 'mixed multitude' that accompanied the Israelites in the Exodus from Egypt and became part of the people.) Under Christian rule it was illegal for Jews to convert Christians (although some cases are recorded), and similarly under Muslim rule it was forbidden to convert Muslims. This long history, combined with the uneasy position of the Jews in the period of emancipation, has given rise to a general feeling against proselytising missions. If, however, remedying the bleak demographic prospects was considered a priority, there seems to be no reason why such missions could not be launched.

To be realistic, it must be admitted that neither of these two solutions is likely to receive widespread support in a Jewish community which currently seems content to ignore the statistics or speak in biblical language of a 'faithful remnant'. Those rabbis who do address the issue tend to focus their efforts on encouraging Jews to marry Jews, which, in demographic terms, may actually exacerbate the problem.

POLITICAL ASPECTS

The age of emancipation is virtually over. Were it not for the period of Nazi rule in the 1930s, with its temporary return to the medieval system of segregation and subjugation, we would say that it ended with the abolition of the restrictive legislation in Russia in 1917. Today the countries which deny full civil rights to Jews are few and far between, and the legislation in question applies not only to Jews but to all minorities which do not share the ruling religion. (Apart from Britain the examples are mainly in the Muslim world.) Virtually everywhere where Jews live they are, whether they like it or not, subject to the constitution, the law and the fiscal system on the same basis as other citizens. Generally they are also free to express their distinctive identity if they wish, and in many countries special legislation or ad hoc provisions protect their religious requirements. While it is not uncommon, particularly in the United States, to speculate about a 'Jewish vote', there are no Jewish political parties.

The glaring exception to all this is Israel. In this country alone, with its Jewish majority, the problems of religion and state are far from being solved, and Jewish identity and religious observance are at the forefront of the political agenda. As we have seen, there are Jewish political parties, enjoying small but significant support, and Jewish issues not unfrequently lead to violent clashes. In addition, the issues in question have a direct bearing on the rights of the non-Jewish minorities and on relations between Jews and non-Jews, as well as the status of the progressive Jewish movements.

The present volatile situation cannot survive indefinitely, but it is impossible at the present time to predict in which direction the tensions will be resolved. What can be predicted is that if not addressed these tensions will become more severe. Already there are very pronounced inequalities between different categories of citizens, which cannot be tolerated in a secular democratic state. The existence of two different official definitions of Jewish identity (that of the state and that of the rabbinate) leads to considerable personal hardship, particularly but not only in relation to marriage and burial. The powers vested in the rabbinate under a system inherited from the Ottoman Empire are clearly not appropriate for the twenty-first century. The polarisation between entrenched religious conservatism and militantly antireligious secularism, which is one of the two main sources of conflict in Israeli society, is the direct consequence of the present mixed constitution, in which the secular and democratic character of the state is deliberately limited with a view to protecting the position of the religious sector.

Until recently the Jewish Diaspora (with the exception of the small ultra-traditional religious factor, which is in any case ambivalent or hostile to the state) has held back from becoming embroiled in these internal Jewish affairs. Increasingly since the 1970s, however, as progressive (including Conservative) Jewish organisations in the West have taken Israel more seriously (setting up headquarters, rabbinical schools, congregations and even kibbutzim), they have been drawn into the debate about political frameworks which severely disadvantage them, and at the same time democratic political factions in Israel have appealed directly for diaspora support. The ensuing debates embrace not only the specific questions of religion and the state but more general questions of civil rights, including those of women and non-Jews. The problems of Israel are now the problems of the whole Jewish world. Whether this development will encourage or impede a solution remains to be seen.

Meanwhile there are wider questions concerning Israel that remain to be resolved. They focus on the central question of the nature of a 'Jewish state'. This phrase, which originally in Zionist parlance meant a state for the Jews, can also be understood to refer back to an old halakhic and philosophical discussion about the character of a state run on Jewish principles. Both the religious and the secular sources have a good deal to say about the kind of virtues that an ideal state would embody.

As we have seen, Ahad Ha-Am and the 'cultural Zionists' envisaged the state as first and foremost a source of ethical and cultural enrichment for an impoverished Jewish world, and indeed a beacon of light to the world as a whole. Is it possible for Israel to live up to this optimistic vision? Many would like it to. Israel has many natural advantages, and its impact on Jewish visitors from around the world is immense; but it is hard for it to speak out with moral persuasiveness so long as it harbours inequalities and injustices which would not be tolerated by these visitors in their own countries. Moreover, visitors can hardly avoid noticing the low regard in which Jewish religion is held by a large part of the population, in contrast with the conditions with which they are familiar back home. Perhaps when the domestic problems have been tackled, Israel will be in a position to become 'a light to the nations'.

SOCIAL ASPECTS

Jewish life, as we explained in chapters 5 and 6, has traditionally been structured around the family and the community or synagogue. Both those institutions have been changing, and the changes may be interrelated. Traditionally on marrying a couple joined a synagogue, either that of the parents of the bride or bridegroom, or another synagogue if they were moving to a new area. Couples tend to marry at a later age then in the past, often after a period of living together. Some couples choose not to marry in a synagogue but only civilly; others do not marry at all. Often they do not join a synagogue until such a time as they have children. They may well be attracted, however, by a *havurah* (fellowship) or other kind of informal Jewish group. Such groups are also attractive to single people and to homosexual couples. Synagogues tend (often unintentionally) not to be very hospitable to people who do not conform to the traditional family pattern. Some synagogues are making an effort to remedy this situation, and in doing so they tend to alter their own character.

These changes have hardly begun to have an effect, but they will become more pronounced with the passage of the years. There may also be an attempt by the establishment to close ranks around the traditional family, whose demise may appear threatening to some. Such a rearguard action is unlikely to prove very effective. The leaders and organisers of Jewish communities will have to recognise that individuals have come to expect and demand satisfaction of their needs as individuals, which will often be supplied only at the cost of the traditional family or community structure. Far from receding, these expectations and demands have already begun to spread from feminists and gays, who have been in the forefront of this movement, to young people generally, and will probably make inroads also among older men and women.

As patterns of identity and of intergroup relations change, synagogues are beginning to learn to accommodate mixed (Jewish and non-Jewish) families and increasing numbers of proselytes, including some who take an interest in Judaism for its own sake and not with a view to marriage. Synagogues are also becoming better integrated into the wider community, joining up with local churches and other religious institutions not only for purposes of dialogue and encounter but in pursuit of a wide range of social, educational and other aims.

RELIGIOUS PLURALISM

It is clear that pluralism is once again a fact of Jewish life, as it was in the late Second Temple period. The main religious movements, and indeed the main non-religious philosophies, all boast substantial numbers of adherents, and none of them can reasonably claim to be the only authentic expression.

The point has been reached, I believe, where it is no longer possible (if it ever was) to describe Judaism in terms of a single ideal model (for example the revealed Torah) and different ways of relating to it (rabbinic Judaism accepts the Torah as interpreted by the rabbis; Karaism accepts the Torah but rejects the rabbis; Reform accepts the Torah and the rabbis but subjects both to historical criticism, and so forth). Rather we are confronted now by different models of Judaism, existing side by side.

A leading Orthodox theoretician of Jewish unity, Jonathan Sacks, has argued that *halakhah*, law, is an indispensable feature of Judaism, and that there is no authentic Judaism that does not recognise the divine authority of *halakhah*.[1] Sacks represents an Orthodox position that strives conscientiously to see the positive aspects of non-Orthodox forms of Judaism and to reach a practical *modus vivendi* with them in the interest of the unity of the Jewish people. The weakness in his model is that it is not, and cannot be, accepted by Reform or secular Jews. For them, the concept of a divinely ordained *halakhah* is an outmoded concept which is incapable of providing the framework for an authentic Jewish life.

---

[1] Jonathan Sacks, *One People? Tradition, Modernity and Jewish Unity* (London, 1993).

Halakhah is not the only issue dividing Jews today; in fact it is itself no more than a symptom, because, despite some often-heard criticisms of this or that law, it is the theology that underpins it that really divides Orthodox Judaism from the progressive movements and the secularists. It is simply not possible for progressive or secularist Jews to accept the idea of the *halakhah* as a law from heaven. Yet if it is interpreted in any other way the *halakhah* is not the *halakhah* of the Orthodox. Many Conservative Jews lead a life outwardly indistinguishable from that of a Modern Orthodox Jew. Yet there is a profound difference between them, namely the doctrine of Torah from Heaven. Reconstructionist and Reform Jews lay great emphasis on observance: Judaism is not merely in the mind and heart but in action too. Many Jewish secularists, too, assert that some observances are necessary if one is not to lose all touch with what it means to be a Jew. But their observance differs from the identical observance practised by an Orthodox Jew, because of this issue of the divine origin and sanction of the *mitsvot*.

This fundamental division is not going to be overcome, any more than the equally profound division between theists and atheists will be overcome. There may be room for some dialogue; there is certainly room for a great deal of co-operation in areas where doctrine is not an issue. But there will never again, at least not in the foreseeable future, be a single version of Judaism which holds sway as widely and for such a long time as rabbinic Judaism did.

Of the three main religious denominations, Orthodoxy, Conservatism and Reform, it is Orthodoxy that is currently facing the greatest challenges. Having undergone a serious eclipse in the West in the late nineteenth and early twentieth centuries it first moved with the current and became more liberal, and then, mainly as a result of immigration from eastern Europe, it put on the brakes and seemed to be discovering a new and more confident identity. As the rift between the Orthodox and the other modernist movements (particularly Conservatism) became more sharply defined, Orthodoxy felt strong pressure to move closer to the traditionalist ('ultra-Orthodox' or Haredi) sector, and this move, while it has pleased some, has left others feeling confused and betrayed. Currently in the United States it is thought that there are about three times as many Modern Orthodox as traditionalists, but the latter exercise a strong influence on the former halakhically, theologically and culturally. Much the same is true in Israel.

Nor have the leaders of Orthodoxy succeeded in solving what are widely acknowledged to be shortcomings with the *halakhah*, mainly concerned with issues of personal status. The most acute of these problems concerns the condition of the *agunah* and the *mamzer*. The *agunah* or 'chained woman' is a woman who is married in law to a man with whom she does not live, and who is therefore unable to remarry. There are various situations that give rise to this regrettable status: the husband may have disappeared without trace (there is no presumption of death in Jewish law), or he may be unwilling or unable to issue a divorce. That the condition of the *agunah* is highly undesirable has been recognised for a long time, but no satisfactory solution has been found, although several have been canvassed, including a pre-nuptial agreement by the husband to issue a divorce in certain circumstances, recourse to the civil courts, and latterly the dissolution of the marriage by a rabbinic court on grounds of nullity.

The *mamzer* is the issue of an adulterous or incestuous union. A *mamzer* is not permitted to marry another Jew. (A *mamzer* may marry another *mamzer* or a proselyte, in which case any child will be a *mamzer*.) The child of an *agunah* by a man other than the one to whom she is halakhically married is considered a *mamzer*, and this fact further aggravates the predicament of the *agunah*.

A third contentious issue is levirate marriage and *halitsah*. If a husband dies childless, the Bible (Deuteronomy 25:5–10) prescribes that his brother should marry her and have a child by her so as to perpetuate his dead brother's name. This is called levirate marriage. If he refuses to marry his brother's widow, the ceremony known as *halitsah* must take place: she removes his shoe, spits in his face, and says, 'Thus shall be done to a man who will not rebuild his brother's house.' Objections have been raised both to levirate marriage and to *halitsah*, on various grounds. In Israel levirate marriage was abolished in 1950, but *halitsah* is still practised. Additional problems may arise if the brother is an infant or minor, if he lives far away or his whereabouts are unknown, if he refuses to undergo *halitsah* or if he is not a Jew or has adopted another religion.

These three areas of *halakhah*, with others that have attracted criticism, mainly affect Orthodox and traditionalist Jews. Reform Judaism has rejected all three. Conservative Judaism does not recognise levirate marriage, and is more flexible than Orthodoxy in dealing with the *agunah* and *mamzer*.

The status of women and their place within Jewish worship and public life is another area which particularly troubles Orthodoxy. Reform and Conservative Judaism have accepted the principle of equality of the sexes, but Orthodoxy has consistently refused to do so and shows no signs of movement in that direction. The rapprochement with traditionalism militates against any such movement. It remains to be seen whether the movement can succeed in maintaining its appeal while espousing a position which seems to be so out of tune with contemporary life.

THEOLOGICAL DEVELOPMENTS

Our discussion of Jewish theology in chapter 7 ended on a rather negative note: there is relatively little interest in theological issues among Jews today, at least under the explicit label of theology. Theological issues are discussed under other headings, such as *halakhah* or Zionism. As was pointed out above, the debate about the authority of *halakhah* is underpinned by various views about the nature of revelation, which is clearly a theological issue.

Theology likewise underlies much of the seemingly political debate about the place of Zion in Jewish life, and related issues such as the legitimacy of trading territory for peace, relations between Jews and Palestinian Arabs or between Israel and its Arab neighbours, or the nature of the Jewish state. The claims of religious settlers in the Occupied Territories are supported by reference to theological sources and arguments, as are those of the religious political parties, and of the anti-Zionist Haredi community. The arguments deployed are generally not very refined or rigorous, theologically speaking, because of a lack of theological education. Traditional Judaism tended to reserve rigorous argument for halakhic issues, and to regard haggadic (including theological) questions as inherently open-ended and therefore to be approached in a less disciplined way. The perpetuation of this traditional approach in some quarters at a time when there is a need for greater theological rigour because the serious disagreements are mainly theological rather than halakhic has resulted in a poor level of argument, particularly in Israel, where all too often even traditional Jews tend to end up shouting slogans at each other, in a most un-Talmudic way.

Secular Judaism has also displayed a lack of subtlety and system in the debate concerning religion, which contrasts with the higher level of argument deployed in political debate. Secular Jewish humanism developed out of the Jewish Enlightenment, with its strong anti-religious impetus, and consequently ignored the developments in naturalistic theology described in chapter 7. Its intellectual leaders still find themselves fighting rather old battles, and have yet to engage with contemporary theology. God tends to be dismissed rather crudely as a character in the Bible and a figment of earlier ages. There is little or no appreciation of the fact that the quest for a Jewish identity and values divorced from supernatural beliefs has already been pursued for several decades by Reconstructionist thinkers, and that common ground can also be found with some Reform theorists. Secular Judaism has been slow to cultivate positive ideas of its own. In confronting religion it has had an easy target in the archaic and monolithic forms of Judaism that have dominated in Israel, and it has not felt called on to engage with subtler forms of Jewish theology, with issues arising from the psychology of religion, or with the quasi-religious elements within the secularist tradition, such as the teaching of A. D. Gordon. These developments lie in the future, and have very rich potential.

Holocaust theology will have to transcend the current theological impasse, and this is one area where religious and secular thinkers might fruitfully meet, not to argue over interpretations of the past but to build frameworks for greater understanding and agreement in the future. The secularists present a challenge to theistic philosophers who are bogged down in the morass of theodicy, and indeed to all students of the Holocaust who feel they must defend classical definitions of God at all costs. Classical theology is among the victims of the Holocaust, and in the effort of creative thinking that is called for, the contribution of sceptics, agnostics and atheists can be as useful as that of believers.

Another area which offers similar challenges and opportunities is that of covenant. Both the Holocaust and the rebirth of Israel compel a re-examination of many of the inherited assumptions concerning this theological topic which is central to the discussion of the historic role and destiny of the Jewish people. Another, related, topic is witness. The Jews have often felt called on to witness to God before the world, a calling which tends to grow stronger in times of persecution. The Holocaust may seem to be a cardinal example of this trend, in that the world really does seem to have paid attention to the Jews in their hour of tribulation. But is it necessary for a witnessing people to suffer so as to witness authentically? If so, what are the implications for Israel, and its desire to witness in the midst of success and prosperity? Or is the whole concept of witness misconceived? These debates are too important for the voice of secularists to be excluded.

Postmodernism as a movement, despite the participation of some very high-profile Jews, particularly in France, has not so far made much contribution to Jewish thought. The outstanding thinker who has had the greatest power to bring religious and non-religious thinkers together, to shake Jewish religious thought out of some of its ruts, and to give a real boost to Jewish ethical reflection, is Emmanuel Levinas (1906–96). Levinas was well known in France, where he regularly addressed meetings of French Jewish intellectuals with his astonishing postmodern readings of the Talmud, but it was only shortly before his death that he began to make an impact in the English-speaking world. A pupil of Husserl and Heidegger, Levinas was a major European thinker who was genuinely in touch with Jewish tradition and profoundly shaped by the experience of the Shoah.

Jewish feminism is pushing theology into facing questions that could not even be phrased before. So far many of the most interesting debates have been confined to rather narrow circles, but they have far-reaching implications and need to percolate out to a wider public. Although the gender-coding of Judaism was first questioned by women, it has serious consequences for men, too; men have been slow to seize the opportunities, with the exception of some gay thinkers operating on the fringes of feminism, but in the future men of all persuasions will no doubt become as angry and passionate and outspoken as women have become in challenging received ideas.[2]

This is an exciting time for Judaism. Jewish life and thought are changing very fast. Old certainties are dissolving and new ones have not yet taken shape. By the same token, for the student Judaism presents a moving target. It is hard to pin it down, or to get answers to quite basic questions. I have tried in this Introduction not to over-simplify, or to provide certainty where none exists. Above all, this is only an introduction, and the last word belongs to the ancient master Hillel, replying to an enquirer who challenged him to teach him the whole of Judaism in a single sentence. Hillel gave him the maxim he was asking for, and then he added this advice: 'Now go and study!'

---

[2] Daniel Boyarin has recently opened up some new avenues with his book *Unheroic Conduct: the Rise of Heterosexuality and the Invention of the Jewish Man* (Berkeley, CA, 1997).

Glossary

Adonai [Hebrew, lit. 'my lords']. Name of God, generally translated 'Lord'.

Adon olam [Hebrew *adon ʿolam*, lit. 'Eternal Lord']. Hymn, generally sung at the end of the additional service.

afikoman [Hebrew *afiqoman*, probably of Greek origin, meaning uncertain]. Piece of *matsah* distributed to participants at the seder and eaten at the conclusion of the meal.

akedah [Hebrew *ʿaqedah*, 'binding']. Biblical story of the trial of Abraham, Genesis 22:1–19, read in synagogue during Rosh Ha-Shanah.

Aleynu [Hebrew *ʿaleinu*, 'It is our duty']. Prayer recited towards the end of the service.

al-het [Hebrew *ʿal-ḥet*, 'for the sin']. Prayer for pardon of sins recited on Yom Kippur.

aliyah [Hebrew *ʿaliyah*, 'ascent']. 1. In Zionist usage, immigration to Israel ('He's made *aliyah*'). 2. Honour of being called to the reading of the Torah in synagogue ('I had an *aliyah* in *shul* today').

almemar [from Arabic *al-minbar*, 'pulpit']. Another name for the *bimah*.

Amidah [Hebrew *ʿamidah*, 'standing']. The main statutory prayer, recited thrice daily in a standing position. Cf. *shmoneh esreh*, *tefillah*.

aron ha-kodesh [Hebrew *aron ha-qodesh*, 'ark of the sanctuary']. Item of synagogue furniture, often resembling a wardrobe, in which the Torah scrolls are kept. Generally referred to in English as 'the ark'.

Ashkenazi [From the biblical Hebrew name Ashkenaz, identified in the Middle Ages with Germany. Pl. Ashkenazim]. Originating in German Jewry or its offshoots, e.g. in Poland.

avel [Hebrew 'mourner']. A mourner

Bar Mitsvah [Am. *bar*, 'son', and Hebrew *miṣvah*, 'command']. Strictly an adult male Jew, who is subject to all the commands of the *halakhah*. In practice often applied in English to the ceremony of coming of age or to the party that accompanies it, the star of the show being termed 'the bar mitzvah boy'.

Bat Mitsvah [Hebrew *bat*, 'daughter' and *misvah*, 'command']. Female equivalent of the preceding.

BCE ['Before the Common Era']. Abbreviation used by Jews in preference to 'BC'. Cf. CE.

berakhah [Hebrew, pl. *berakhot*]. A blessing or benediction.

Bet Din [Hebrew, 'place of judgment' or 'house of justice']. A rabbinic lawcourt.

bimah [Hebrew, borrowed from Greek]. Raised platform in a synagogue, on which the reading desk is situated.

birkat hamazon [Hebrew, 'blessing of food']. Grace recited or sung after a meal.

Bund [Yiddish, 'federation'] Jewish socialist political movement, founded in Russia in 1897.

CE ['Common Era']. Abbreviation used by Jews for years of the Christian reckoning in preference to 'AD', because of the Christian reference of the latter term. Cf. BCE.

Conservative Judaism. Branch of modernist Judaism, especially in the USA, non-fundamentalist but resistant to change.

dati [Hebrew, pl. *datiim*, 'religious']. Term applied in Israel to the traditionalist and militantly religious section of the Jewish population. Cf. *hilloni*.

Days of Awe. *See yamim noraim*.

dayyan [Hebrew, 'judge']. A rabbi who sits as a judge in a Bet Din.

devekut [Hebrew *devequt*, 'clinging']. Devotion in prayer.

Diaspora [Greek 'dispersion']. Collective term for the Jewish communities outside Eretz Israel.

din [Hebrew]. Law.

eikhal. *See heikhal*.

Ein Keloheinu [Hebrew, 'There is no one like our God']. Hymn generally sung towards the end of a morning service (in Ashkenazi synagogues only on Sabbaths and festivals).

El [Hebrew 'god']. Name of God.

el male rahamim [Hebrew *el male raḥamim*, 'God full of compassion']. Prayer for the souls of the dead, sung at funerals and memorial services.

Elohim [Hebrew 'gods' or 'God']. Name of God.

En Sof [Hebrew, 'infinite']. Ultimate, unknowable aspect of the Godhead in the kabbalistic system. Cf. Sefirot.

Eretz Israel [Hebrew *eres yiśrael*]. The land of Israel.

erusin [Hebrew]. Betrothal.

etrog [Hebrew]. Citron, a lemon-like fruit, one of the four species used in the ritual of the festival of Sukkot.

gabbai [Hebrew, 'tax collector', pl. *gabbaim*]. Synagogue warden or treasurer.

galut [Hebrew, 'exile']. A name for the Diaspora. Cf. *golah*.

gaon [Hebrew, 'excellency', pl. *geonim*]. Title of the head of the main Talmudic academies in Iraq, from the middle of the sixth to the middle of the eleventh century (the 'geonic period').

genizah [Hebrew 'concealment']. Disposal of worn-out sacred texts, generally by burial; the place where they are disposed of. (The famous Cairo Genizah was, exceptionally, a chamber on the roof of a synagogue.)

ger [Hebrew]. A proselyte.

get [Hebrew *geṭ*]. A deed of divorce.

golah [Hebrew, 'exile']. A name for the Diaspora. Cf. *galut*.

gomel [Hebrew, 'bountiful']. Benediction pronounced in synagogue on deliverance from danger.

goy [Hebrew, 'nation', pl. *goyim*]. A non-Jew.

Haftarah [Hebrew *hafṭarah*]. Reading from the Prophets following the Torah reading in the synagogue.

hag [Hebrew *ḥag*]. A festival. The greeting on a festival is *hag sameah*, 'happy festival'.

haham [Hebrew *ḥakham*, 'sage']. Title of a Sephardi rabbi.

halakhah [Hebrew]. Jewish law.

halitsah [Hebrew *ḥaliṣah*, 'drawing off']. 'Drawing off of the shoe', ceremony of renouncing levirate marriage.

hallah [Hebrew *ḥallah*]. 1. Ancient dough offering. 2. Loaf of bread for Sabbath and festivals, generally made with a rich dough and plaited.

Hallel [Hebrew, 'praise']. Sequence of psalms (Psalms 113–18) recited on festive days. The term can be applied to Psalm 136 (the 'Great Hallel') and to other sequences of psalms recited liturgically.

hamets [Hebrew *ḥameṣ*]. Leaven, banished from Jewish homes during Passover.

Hanukkah [Hebrew *ḥanukkah*, 'dedication']. Winter festival commemorating the rededication of the Temple in 165 BCE. The term is also applied to the dedication of a home (*ḥanukkat ha-bayit*), especially among Sephardim.

ḥanukkiyah [Hebrew]. Nine-branched candlestick or lamp used at Hanukkah.

ḥaredi [Hebrew *ḥaredi*, 'fearful', pl. *ḥaredim*]. Adherent of traditionalist Judaism.

ḥaroset [Hebrew *ḥaroset*]. A sweet reddish-brown paste eaten during the Passover seder.

Ha-Shem [Hebrew, 'the Name']. Substitute for the name of God.

ḥasid [Hebrew *ḥasid*, 'pious', pl. *ḥasidim*]. An exceptionally pious person. Nowadays the term is applied almost exclusively to a member of the revivalist sect (Hasidism) founded in eighteenth-century Poland by the Baal Shem Tov.

Haskalah [Hebrew 'enlightenment']. Hebrew Enlightenment movement, especially in nineteenth-century eastern Europe.

ḥatimah [Hebrew *ḥatimah*, 'sealing']. Liturgical formula ('Blessed are you, Lord, . . .'), typically employed in the concluding formula of a long benediction. Also, at Yom Kippur, Jews greet each other with the words *ḥatimah tovah*, conveying the message 'may your entry in the heavenly Book of Life be sealed for good for the coming year'.

havdalah [Hebrew, 'differentiation']. Ceremony to distinguish the Sabbath from the working week, or exceptionally from a supervening festival.

havurah [Hebrew *ḥavurah*, 'fellowship']. A group of Jews meeting for prayer and possibly other purposes.

heikhal [Hebrew, 'shrine']. Name of the *aron ha-kodesh* among Sephardim.

heter (or *hattarat*) *horaah* [Hebrew, 'permission to teach']. Rabbinic ordination.

Hevrah Kadisha [Hebrew *ḥevrah* and Aramaic *qadisha*, 'sacred society']. Burial society.

Hibbat Zion [Hebrew *ḥibbat ṣiyyon*, 'love of Zion']. Precursor of the Zionist movement in nineteenth-century eastern Europe.

hiddur mitsvah [Hebrew *hiddur miṣvah*, 'embellishment of a command']. Strictness or zeal in religious observance.

High Holy Days. Rosh Ha-Shanah and Yom Kippur.

hilloni [Hebrew *ḥilloni*, 'secular', pl. *ḥillonim*]. A secularist Jew.

hillul ha-shem [Hebrew *ḥillul ha-shem*, 'profanation of God']. An action bringing the Jewish people (and hence God) into disrepute.

hol ha-moed [Hebrew *ḥol ha-moʿed*, 'weekday of the festival']. Intermediate days of Pesah and Sukkot, on which work is permitted.

hoshana [Hebrew *hoshaʿ na*, 'o save!', pl. *hoshaʿnot*]. Prayer for salvation recited in synagogue during Sukkot. (The term derives from Psalm 118:25.)

Hoshana Rabbah [Hebrew *hoshaʿ na rabbah*, 'great *hoshaʿ na*']. Seventh day of Sukkot.

Hovevei Zion [Hebrew *ḥovevei ṣiyyon*, 'lovers of Zion']. Adherents of the Hibbat Zion movement.

humash [Hebrew *ḥummash*]. A volume containing the five books of the Torah.

huppah [Hebrew *ḥuppah*, 'canopy']. Canopy under which a marriage is solemnised. Hence the term is used for a marriage.

hurban [Hebrew *ḥurban*, 'destruction']. Destruction of the First and Second Temples. The term is sometimes applied to the Nazi destruction of Jewish life in Europe.

Israelite. 1. A Jew. 2. Third class of Jew, ranking after Priests and Levites.

kabbalah [Hebrew *qabbalah*, 'tradition']. Theosophical movement that began in medieval Spain and Provence.

Kaddish [Aramaic *qaddish*, 'sanctification']. Aramaic prayer recited at the close of each section of the service, and also by mourners.

Kadosh Barukh Hu [Hebrew, 'Holy one blessed be he']. Name of God.

kasher – see kosher

kashrut [Hebrew, 'suitability']. The rules regulating what may be eaten by Jews.

kavvanah [Hebrew, 'intention']. Intention or concentration, in respect of performing a *mitsvah* or saying a prayer.

Kedushah [Hebrew *qedushah*, 'sanctification']. Part of the synagogue service evoking the worship of God by the angels, who declare 'holy, holy, holy' (Isaiah 6:3).

kehillah [Hebrew *qehillah*, pl. *qehillot*]. A Jewish community.

Ketuvim [Hebrew, 'writings']. The third section of the Hebrew Bible.

kibbutz [Hebrew *qibbuṣ*, 'gathering', pl. *qibbuṣim*]. A collective agricultural settlement, characteristic of the socialist Zionist settlement of *Eretz Israel*. Most are secularist, but some are religious. A member of a kibbutz is known as a kibbutznik.

kiddush [Hebrew *qiddush*, 'sanctification']. Blessing proclaiming the holiness of the Sabbath or a festival, and hence the ceremony at which it is recited over a goblet of wine, immediately before a meal.

kiddush ha-shem [Hebrew *qiddush ha-shem,*'sanctification of God']. Martyrdom.

kiddushin [Hebrew *qiddushin,* 'sanctifications']. Betrothal, and the name of the Talmudic tractate dealing with the topic.

kinah [Hebrew *qinah,* pl. *qinot*]. Poem of elegy or lamentation.

kippah [Hebrew, 'dome']. A skullcap. Also called, in Yiddish, *yarmulke* or *kappel.*

kittel [Yiddish]. White robe worn by some Ashkenazim on the High Holydays and on some other occasions. It forms part of the clothing in which the dead are buried.

klipot [Hebrew *qelippot,* 'husks']. In Kabbalah, a term for the powers of evil.

kloyz [Yiddish]. Talmudic school. In Hasidic usage, a synagogue.

kohen [Hebrew, pl. *kohanim*]. A hereditary priest.

Kol Nidrei [Aramaic, 'All the vows']. Service on the eve of Yom Kippur, named from its opening prayer.

kosher [Hebrew *kasher*]. Ritually fit (e.g. of food).

Lag Ba-Omer [Hebrew *lag ba-ʿomer*]. Thirty-third day of the *omer*; a joyful day the origins of which are obscure in the extreme.

Lekhah Dodi [Hebrew, 'Come, my beloved']. Kabbalistic hymn welcoming the Sabbath as a bride.

leum [Hebrew]. Nation. *Leumi* means 'national'.

levayah [Hebrew, 'escort']. A funeral.

levi [Hebrew, pl. *leviim*]. A Levite, member of a hereditary class situated in rank between the priests (*kohanim*) and Israelites.

levirate marriage [Latin *levir,* 'brother-in-law']. Biblical requirement that the brother of a man who dies childless marry his widow.

Liberal Judaism. Branch of modernist Judaism. On the continent of Europe Liberalism is generally relatively conservative; in the British Isles (where it is also called 'Progressive Judaism') it is the most radical of the religious movements. With a small 'l' the term is often used interchangeably with 'Reform Judaism'.

lulav [Hebrew]. Palm frond; one of the four species used at Sukkot. The term is also applied to the four species taken together.

Lurianic kabbalah. Kabbalistic system devised by Isaac Luria ('the Lion', 1534–72), which confronted the exile from Spain and gave Kabbalah a collective, redemptive meaning.

magen david [Hebrew, 'shield of David']. A six-pointed star consisting of two superimposed triangles used since the nineteenth century as a symbol of Jewish identity.

mahzor [Hebrew *maḥazor*, 'cycle']. Ashkenazi term for a prayer book for the festivals. Cf. *siddur*.

mamzer [Hebrew]. The offspring of an adulterous or incestuous union.

maror [Hebrew]. Bitter herb used in the seder ritual.

Masorah [Hebrew, 'tradition']. Apparatus accompanying the Hebrew text of the Bible, noting variants and other peculiarities. In a wider sense, the Masorah includes the signs indicating pronunciation and cantillation.

Masorti [Hebrew, 'traditional']. Designation of Conservative Judaism, particularly in Israel and Britain.

matsah [Hebrew *maṣah*, pl. *maṣot*]. Unleavened bread.

megillah [Hebrew]. Any scroll, particularly one containing the book of Esther, read at Purim. Also title of Talmudic tractate dealing with this reading.

mehitsah [Hebrew *meḥiṣah*, 'partition']. A division separating women from men in traditionalist and Orthodox synagogues.

mehutan [Hebrew *meḥutan*, pl. *meḥutanim*]. Anyone related to a particular person by marriage.

menorah [Hebrew]. Seven-branched lampstand or candelabrum, imitating the golden lampstand described in the Bible, and widely used at one time as a symbol of Jewish identity.

mezuzah [Hebrew, 'doorpost']. Parchment scroll inscribed with two paragraphs from the Shma, enclosed in a case and fixed to doorposts of Jewish homes.

mikveh [Hebrew *miqveh*, 'gathering']. A ritual bath.

millah [Hebrew]. Circumcision.

minhag [Hebrew]. Custom.

minyan [Hebrew, 'enumeration']. Quorum of ten male Jews required for public prayer or Torah reading.

misheberakh [Hebrew *mi she-berakh*, 'He who blessed']. Synagogue blessing of those called to the reading of the Torah and their families.

Misnagdim [Yiddish, from Hebrew *mitnagged*, 'opponent']. Opponents of Hasidism.

mitsvah [Hebrew *miṣvah*, 'command', pl. *miṣvot*]. A law or duty understood as a religious command. Also, in popular usage, any meritorious action.

mohel [Hebrew]. A circumciser.

Musaf [Hebrew, 'supplement']. Additional service for Sabbaths and festivals.

Musar [Hebrew, 'ethics']. A movement of ethical renewal originating in nineteenth-century Lithuania.

Neilah [Hebrew *ne'ilah*, 'locking (of gates)']. Last of the five services of Yom Kippur, recited at sunset.

Neolog. Form of Jewish modernism confined to Hungary.

ner tamid [Hebrew]. Perpetual lamp kept burning in synagogues above the *aron ha-kodesh*.

niddah [Hebrew]. A woman in a state of menstrual impurity. Also the name of a Talmudic tractate dealing with this topic.

niggun [Yiddish *nign*, from Hebrew *niggun*, 'tune']. Wordless melody favoured by the Hasidim.

nisuin [Hebrew *niśśuin*]. Betrothal.

olam ha-ba [Hebrew *'olam ha-ba*, 'coming age']. Future age, contrasted with *olam ha-zeh*, the present world.

oleh [Hebrew *'oleh*, 'ascending']. Immigrant to Israel. (Cf. *aliyah*).

omer [Hebrew *'omer*, 'sheaf']. Solemn period of seven weeks between Pesah and Sukkot.

oneg shabbat [Hebrew *'oneg shabbat*, 'Sabbath delight', based on Isaiah 58:13]. Principle of adorning the Sabbath with aesthetic embellishments and physical self-indulgence. The term is also applied to a Friday evening gathering for cultural and/or religious purposes.

onen [Hebrew]. A mourner in the period before the funeral.

Orthodox Judaism. The most conservative strand of Jewish modernism. The term is also applied, confusingly, to traditionalist Judaism, leading to the invention of such expressions as 'neo-Orthodoxy' or 'modern Orthodoxy' to designate the modernist version.

parashah [Hebrew, 'division']. In Sephardi usage, the weekly reading of the Torah. In Ashkenazi usage, a sub-division of the weekly reading (*see sidrah*).

parokhet [Hebrew, 'curtain']. In Ashkenazi synagogues, the curtain that hangs in front of the *aron ha-kodesh*.

partsuf [Hebrew *parṣuf*, from Greek *prosōpon*, 'face', pl. *parṣufim*]. In Kabbalah, a configuration of Sefirot.

Pesah [Hebrew *pesaḥ*]. Passover, the spring festival commemorating the Exodus from Egypt. In the Bible, the term designates the lamb which was sacrificed on the eve of the festival in ancient times. *See* seder.

pidyon ha-ben [Hebrew]. Redemption of the first-born.

piyyut [Hebrew *piyyut*, derived from Greek, 'poem']. A liturgical poem or hymn.

porging. Removal of forbidden fats and sinews from meat. Porging (in

Hebrew *niqqur*) is a highly skilled operation performed by a specialist known as a *menaqqer*.

Progressive Judaism. *See* Liberal Judaism.

Purim [Hebrew, 'ballots']. Early spring festival, commemorating the saving of the Persian Jews from genocide, as recounted in the book of Esther. Cf. *megillah*.

rav [Hebrew, 'great']. A rabbi.

rebbe [Yiddish]. A Hasidic leader. Cf. Tsaddik.

Reconstructionism. American branch of modernism, founded in the 1920s to inculcate western democratic values and social science into Judaism.

Reform Judaism. Generic term for the more liberal strands of modernism, and the specific designation of two organised movements, one in the United States and one in Britain. British Reform is markedly less radical than its American homonym.

Rosh Ha-Shanah [Hebrew]. Autumn New Year festival, a time of self-searching and penitence.

rosh yeshivah [Hebrew]. Head of a yeshivah.

sandek [Hebrew *sandaq*, from Greek]. The person given the honour of holding the child on his knees during the circumcision ceremony.

seder [Hebrew, 'order']. Home service for the eve of Pesah, conducted around the dinner table.

Sefirot [Hebrew pl., from Greek]. In Kabbalah, manifestations of the Godhead emanating ultimately from the En Sof.

selihot [Hebrew *selihot*, from *selihah*, 'pardon']. Penitential prayers recited during the *yamim noraim* and the preceding period.

semikhah [Hebrew, 'laying on [of hands]']. Rabbinic ordination.

Sephardi (also written Sefardi) [From the biblical Hebrew name Sepharad, identified in the Middle Ages with Spain. Pl. Sephardim]. Originating in Spanish Jewry or its offshoots, e.g. in the former Ottoman Empire.

seudah shlishit [Hebrew *se'udah shelishit*, 'third meal']. Meal eaten towards the close of the Sabbath, particularly by kabbalists and Hasidim, and accompanied by hymns and religious discussions.

shabbat [Hebrew]. Sabbath.

Shaddai [Hebrew]. A name of God.

shaliah tsibbur [Hebrew *sheliah sibbur*, 'representative of the congregation']. Person who leads the congregation in prayer.

Shavuot [Hebrew, 'weeks']. Summer festival also known as Pentecost, commemorating the giving of the Torah at Mount Sinai.

shehitah [Hebrew *shehitah*]. Slaughter of animals according to the rules of *kashrut*.

sheitl [Yiddish]. Wig worn by married women in traditionalist Judaism.

Shekhinah [Hebrew]. The immanent presence of God.

shema – *see* Shma.

Shivah [Hebrew *shiv'ah*, 'seven [days]']. Period of mourning following the death of a close relation.

Shloshim [Hebrew, 'thirty [days]']. Period of mourning following the death of a close relative.

Shma [Hebrew *shema'*, 'hear']. Passages from the Torah prescribed to be recited twice daily, and named from the opening words, 'Hear, Israel'.

shmoneh esreh [Hebrew *shemoneh 'esreh*, 'eighteen']. 'Eighteen Benedictions': the statutory daily prayer (also known as Amidah).

Shoah [Hebrew, 'devastation']. A name for the Nazi destruction of Jewish life in Europe.

shofar [Hebrew]. A ram's horn, blown on Rosh Ha-Shanah and at the end of Yom Kippur.

shohet [Hebrew *shohet*, 'slaughterer']. A properly qualified slaughterer. Cf. *shehitah*.

shomer [Yiddish and Hebrew, 'watcher', pl. *shomrim*]. 1. A *kashrut* supervisor, appointed to oversee the preparation of food. 2. One who watches over a dead body. The word is also used in such phrases as *shomer mitsvot* or *shomer shabbat* for someone who is scrupulous in observing the commandments.

shool or *shul* [Yiddish]. In Ashkenazi usage, a synagogue.

shtetl [Yiddish, 'little town']. A term that now designates the whole lost world of eastern European Jewry.

shtibl [Yiddish, 'little room']. A room used for prayer, particularly among Hasidim.

siddur [Hebrew, 'arrangement']. A prayer book.

sidrah [Hebrew, 'arrangement']. Weekly reading of the Torah. Cf. *parashah*.

Sukkot [Hebrew, 'booths']. The feast of Tabernacles.

taharah [Hebrew *tohorah*, 'purification']. Preparation of a corpse for burial.

takhrikhim [Hebrew]. Shrouds, garments in which a corpse is buried.

takkanah [Hebrew *taqqanah*]. Regulation or ordinance issued by a recognised legal authority or by a community for the public good or to strengthen religious life.

tallit [Hebrew *ṭallit*]. A striped shawl with tassels at the four corners, worn during prayer.

tashlikh [Hebrew]. Private penitential ceremony performed near water (generally by a river or at the seashore) on the afternoon of Rosh Ha-Shanah.

tebah [Hebrew *tevah*, 'chest']. In Sephardi usage, the raised platform in the synagogue. Cf. *bimah*.

tefillah [Hebrew, 'prayer']. 1. Technical name of the *amidah* or *shmoneh esreh*. 2. In Sephardi usage, a prayer book.

tefillin [Hebrew]. Phylacteries: black leather boxes containing parchment texts, and attached with straps to the forehead and upper arm during prayer.

terefah [Hebrew]. Non-kosher food. Also *tref* (among Ashkenazim) or *taref* (among Sephardim).

teruʿah [Hebrew]. A blast on the *shofar*. Hence Rosh Ha-Shanah is also termed yom *teruʿah*, 'day of blowing the *shofar*'.

teshuvah [Hebrew]. Repentance. A *baʿal teshuvah* is a person who repents of not observing a *mitsvah*. Nowadays the term often designates a formerly non-religious Jew who has adopted traditional Judaism.

tevilah [Hebrew]. Immersion in a *mikveh* or in running water.

tikkun [Hebrew *tiqqun*, 'reparation', 'regulation']. 1. Night vigil observed on various occasions, particularly but not exclusively among kabbalists. 2. *tikkun olam* [Hebrew *tiqqun ʿolam*, 'setting the world to rights']. In Lurianic Kabbalah, the process of repairing the cosmos; nowadays the term is given a variety of non-kabbalistic interpretations.

Torah [Hebrew, 'instruction']. 1. The Five Books of Moses, or by extension the whole sacred scripture. 2. The whole religious teaching of Judaism.

Tsaddik [Hebrew *saddiq*, 'righteous']. 1. An exceptionally righteous person. 2. In Hasidism, a charismatic teacher and spiritual leader. *See* rebbe.

tsedakah [Hebrew *ṣedaqah*, 'righteousness']. Charity, almsgiving.

tseniut [Hebrew *ṣeniʿut*, 'modesty']. Scrupulously seemly behaviour and dress, especially as required in traditional Judaism from women.

tsitsit [Hebrew *ṣiṣit*]. 1. tassel or fringe, as on the *tallit*, worn as a reminder of the commands of the Torah. 2. A fringed garment, generally worn under the clothes, also known as *tallit katan* (*ṭallit qatan*).

viddui [Hebrew]. Confession of sins, pronounced on Yom Kippur or on one's deathbed.

yahrzeit or *yortsait* [Yiddish]. Among Ashkenazim, anniversary of a death.

yamim noraim [Hebrew, 'awesome days']. The ten penitential days at the beginning of the year, from Rosh Ha-Shanah to Yom Kippur.

yeridah [Hebrew, 'descent']. In Zionist usage, emigration from Israel. One who 'descends' is termed a *yored*. Cf. *aliyah, oleh*.

yeshivah [Hebrew, 'sitting']. A traditional Talmudic academy.

yetser [Hebrew *yeṣer*, impulse']. Human inclination, as used in the two contrasting terms *yetser ha-ra* (*yeṣer ha-raʿ*), impulse to evil, and *yetser ha-tov* (*yeṣer ha-tov*), impulse to good.

yibbum [Hebrew]. Levirate marriage.

Yigdal [Hebrew, 'May [God] be magnified']. Hymn, based on Maimonides' Thirteen Principles, sung at the end of Sabbath and festival evening services.

yihud [Hebrew *yiḥud*, 'unity']. 1. Declaration of God's unity. 2. Seclusion of a man and a woman together, forbidden if they are not husband and wife, and required of the bride and bridegroom on the occasion of marriage.

Yom Kippur [Hebrew]. Day of Atonement, the solemn autumn fast day.

Zemirot [Hebrew, pl. of *zemirah*]. Table songs that enliven the Sabbath meals.

Further Reading

REFERENCE

Encyclopaedia Judaica (16 vols). Jerusalem, 1971–4.

Abramson, Glenda, ed., *The Blackwell Companion to Jewish Culture: From the Eighteenth Century to the Present*. Oxford, 1989.

Bacon, Josephine, *The Illustrated Atlas of Jewish Civilization*. London, 1990.

Barnavi, Eli, *et al.*, eds., *A Historical Atlas of the Jewish People: From the Time of the Patriarchs to the Present*. London, 1992.

de Lange, Nicholas, *Atlas of the Jewish World*. Oxford/New York, 1984.

Friesel, Evyatar *Atlas of Modern Jewish History*. New York/Oxford, 1990.

Jacobs, Louis *The Jewish Religion. A Companion*. Oxford, 1995.

Werblowsky, R. J. Zwi, and Geoffrey Wigoder, eds., *The Oxford Dictionary of the Jewish Religion*. New York/Oxford, 1997.

CHAPTER 1 THE JEWS IN THE WORLD

Bach, Hans I., *The German Jew: A Synthesis of Judaism and Western Civilization, 1730–1930*. Oxford, 1984.

Bauer, Yehuda, *Out of the Ashes: The Impact of American Jews on Post-Holocaust European Jewry*. Oxford, 1989.

Gerber, Jane S., *The Jews of Spain: A History of the Sephardic Experience*. New York/London, 1992.

Glazer, Nathan, *American Judaism*. 2nd edn. Chicago, 1972.

Heilman, Samuel C., *Portrait of American Jews: The Last Half of the 20th Century*. Seattle, 1995.

Hoffman, Charles, *Gray Dawn: The Jews of Eastern Europe in the Post-Communist Era*. New York, 1992.

Karp, Abraham J., *Haven and Home: A History of the Jews in America*. New York, 1985.

Laskier, Michael M., *North African Jewry in the Twentieth Century: the Jews of Morocco, Tunisia, and Algeria*. New York, 1994.

Litvinoff, Barnett, *A Peculiar People: Inside the Jewish World Today*. London, 1969.

Lucas, Noah, *The Modern History of Israel*. London/New York, 1974.

Marcus, Jacob Rader, *The Jew in the American World: A Source Book*. Detroit, 1996.

Pinkus, Benjamin, *The Jews of the Soviet Union: The History of a National Minority*. Cambridge, 1988.

Ro'i, Yaacov, ed., *Jews and Jewish life in Russia and the Soviet Union*. Ilford, 1995.
Sachar, Howard M., *A History of the Jews in America*. New York, 1992.
A History of Israel from the Rise of Zionism to Our Time. 2nd edn. New York, 1996.
Sarna, Jonathan, *The American Jewish Experience*. New York, 1986.
Schnapper, Dominique, *Jewish Identities in France. An Analysis of Contemporary French Jewry*, tr. Arthur Goldhammer. Chicago/London, 1983.
Wasserstein, Bernard, *Vanishing Diaspora: the Jews in Europe since 1945*. London, 1996.
Wigoder, Geoffrey, *Jewish-Christian Relations since the Second World War*. Manchester, 1988.
Woocher, Jonathan S., *Sacred Survival: the Civil Religion of American Jews*. Bloomington, IN, 1986.

CHAPTER 2 THE JEWISH PEOPLE AND ITS PAST

Avineri, Shlomo, *The Makings of Modern Zionism: The Intellectual Origins of the Jewish State*. London, 1981.
Bauer, Yehuda, *The Holocaust in Historical Perspective*. Seattle, 1978.
Bauman, Zygmunt, *Modernity and the Holocaust*. Ithaca, NY, 1989.
Beller, Steven, *Herzl*. London, 1991.
Ben-Yehuda, Nachman, *The Masada Myth: Collective Memory and Mythmaking in Israel*. Madison, Wisconsin, 1995.
Biale, David, *Power and Powerlessness in Jewish History*. New York, 1986.
Birnbaum, Pierre, and Ira Katznelson, eds., *Paths of Emancipation: Jews, States, and Citizenship*. Princeton, NJ, 1995.
Cohen, Mark R., *Under Crescent and Cross: The Jews in the Middle Ages*. Princeton, NJ/Chichester, 1994.
Forster, Brenda, and Joseph Tabachnik, *Jews by Choice: a Study of Converts to Reform and Conservative Judaism*. Hoboken, NJ, 1991.
Frankel, Jonathan, *Prophecy and Politics: Socialism, Nationalism and the Russian Jews, 1862–1917*. Cambridge, 1981.
Frankel, Jonathan, and Steven J. Zipperstein, eds., *Assimilation and Community: The Jews in Nineteenth-Century Europe*. Cambridge, 1992.
Friedlander, Saul, *Memory, History, and the Extermination of the Jews of Europe*. Bloomington, IN, 1993.
Gilbert, Martin, *The Holocaust. A History of the Jews of Europe during the Second World War*. New York, 1985.
Haberer, Erich, *Jews and Revolution in Nineteenth-Century Russia*. Cambridge, 1995.
Halpern, Ben, *The Idea of the Jewish State*. 2nd edn. Cambridge, MA, 1969.
Hertzberg, Arthur, *The Zionist Idea*, Westport, CT, 1959.
Hilberg, Raul, *The Destruction of the European Jews*. Rev. edn, 3 vols. New York, 1985.
Katz, Jacob, *Tradition and Crisis; Jewish Society at the End of the Middle Ages*. New York, 1971.

Out of the Ghetto: the Social Background of Jewish Emancipation, 1770–1870. Cambridge, 1973.

Kochan, Lionel, *The Jew and his History.* London, 1977

Jews, *Idols and Messiahs: The Challenge from History.* Oxford, 1990.

Kochan, Lionel, ed., *The Jews in Soviet Russia since 1917.* 3rd edn, London, 1978.

de Lange, Nicholas ed., *The Illustrated History of the Jewish People.* Toronto/New York/London 1997.

Laqueur, Walter, *A History of Zionism.* London, 1972.

Lipstadt, Deborah, *Denying the Holocaust: the Growing Assault on Truth and Memory.* New York, 1993.

Mendes-Flohr, P. R., and J. Reinharz, *The Jew in the Modern World: A Documentary History.* New York/Oxford, 1980. 2nd edn. 1995.

Myers, David N., *Re-Inventing the Jewish Past: European Jewish Intellectuals and the Zionist Return to History.* Oxford/New York, 1995.

Novak, David, *The Election of Israel: the Idea of the Chosen People.* Cambridge, 1995.

Ravitzky, Aviezer, *Messianism, Zionism and Jewish Religious Radicalism.* Chicago, 1996.

Reinharz, Jehuda, ed., *Living with Antisemitism: Modern Jewish Responses.* Hanover, NH, 1987.

Reinharz, Jehuda, and Walter Schatzberg, eds., *The Jewish Response to German Culture: from the Enlightenment to the Second World War.* Hanover, 1985.

Reinharz, Jehuda, and Anitas Shapira, eds., *Essential Papers on Zionism.* London, 1996.

Schorsch, Ismar, *Jewish Reactions to German Anti-Semitism, 1870–1914.* New York, 1972.

From Text to Context: The Turn to History in Modern Judaism. Hanover, NB, 1994.

Schwarzfuchs, Simon, *Napoleon, the Jews and the Sanhedrin.* London, 1979.

Sorkin, David, *The Transformation of German Jewry, 1780–1840.* New York/Oxford, 1987.

Talmon, J. L., *Israel among the Nations.* London, 1970.

Tobias, Henry J., *The Jewish Bund in Russia, from its Origins to 1905.* Stanford, CA, 1972.

Vital, David, *The Origins of Zionism.* Oxford, 1975.

Yahil, Leni, *Holocaust: The Fate of European Jewry, 1932–1945.* New York, 1990.

Young, James, *The Texture of Memory: Holocaust Memorials and Meaning.* New Haven, CT, 1993.

Zerubavel, Yael, *Recovered Roots: Collective Memory and the Making of Israeli National Tradition.* Chicago, 1995.

Zweig, Stefan, *The World of Yesterday.* New York/London, 1943.

CHAPTER 3 JEWISH BOOKS

Appel, Gersion, *The Concise code of Jewish Law: Compiled from Kitzur Shulhan Aruch and Traditional Sources: A New Translation with Introduction and Halachic Annotations Based on Contemporary Responsa.* New York, 1989– .

The Authorised Daily Prayer Book of the United Hebrew Congregations of the Commonwealth, based on the original translation of S. Singer . . . 3rd rev. edn. Cambridge/London, 1990.

Blumenthal, David, *Understanding Jewish Mysticism: A Source Reader.* 2 vols. New York, 1978–82.

Cohen, Boaz, *The Shulhan Aruk as a Guide for Religious Practice Today.* New York, 1983.

Donin, Hayim Halevy, *To Be a Jew: a Guide to Jewish Observance in Contemporary Life: Selected and Compiled from the Shulhan Arukh and Responsa Literature, and Providing a Rationale for the Laws and the Traditions.* New York, 1972.

Finkelman, Shimon, *The Chazon Ish: The Life and Ideals of Rabbi Yeshayah Karelitz.* New York, 1989.

Fishbane, Simcha, *The Method and Meaning of the Mishnah Berurah.* Hoboken, NJ, 1991.

Forms of Prayer for Jewish Worship, Edited by the Assembly of Rabbis of the Reform Synagogues of Great Britain, I. Daily, Sabbath, and Occasional Prayers. 7th edn. [London], 1977.

Guttmann, Julius, *Philosophies of Judaism.* New York, 1973.

Hertz, J. H. ed., *Pentateuch and Haftorahs. Hebrew Text, English Translation and Commentary.* 5 vols. Oxford/London, 1929–36; 1 vol. edn, London, 1938; 2nd edn, 1 vol., London, 1978.

The Holy Scriptures: the New JPS Translation. Philadelphia, 1985.

Kellner, Menachem, *Dogma in Medieval Jewish Thought, from Maimonides to Abravanel.* Oxford, 1986.

Leaman, Oliver, *Moses Maimonides.* London, 1989.

Loewe, Raphael, *Ibn Gabirol.* London, 1989.

Maimonides, Moses, *The Guide of the Perplexed*, tr. Shlomo Pines. Chicago/London, 1963.

Scherman, Nosson, ed., *Tanach: The Torah, Prophets, Writings* (ArtScroll series). Brooklyn, 1996.

Silman, Yochanan, *Philosopher and Prophet: Judah Halevi, the Kuzari, and the Evolution of his Thought*, tr. Lenn F. Shramm. Albany, NY, 1995.

Sirat, Colette, *A History of Jewish Philosophy in the Middle Ages*, tr. M. Reich. Cambridge/Paris, 1985.

Twersky, Isadore, ed., *A Maimonides Reader.* New York, 1972.

The Wisdom of the Zohar. An Anthology of Texts, arranged by Fischel Lachower and Isaiah Tishby, tr. David Goldstein. 3 vols. Oxford, 1989.

Yashar, Mosheh M., *Saint and Sage: Hafetz Hayim.* New York, 1937.

CHAPTER 4 THE JEWISH RELIGION

Borowitz, Eugene B., *Liberal Judaism.* New York, 1984.

Borowitz, Eugene B., ed., *Reform Jewish Ethics and the Halakhah: An Experiment in Decision Making.* W. Orange, NJ, 1994.

Bulka, R. P., ed., *Dimensions of Orthodox Judaism.* New York, 1983.

Gordis, R., *Understanding Conservative Judaism*. New York, 1978.
Grunfeld, I, ed. and tr., *Judaism Eternal: Selected Essays from the writings of Rabbi S. R. Hirsch*. London, 1956.
Gunther Plaut, W., *The Growth of Reform Judaism*. New York, 1969.
Helmreich, W. R., *The World of the Yeshiva: An Intimate Portrait of Orthodox Jewry*. New Haven/London, 1986.
Kogel and Katz, *Judaism in a Secular Age: An Anthology of Secular Humanistic Thought*. Hoboken, NJ, 1995.
Lilker, Shalom, *Kibbutz Judaism: A New Tradition in the Making*. New Brunswick, NH, 1986.
Meyer, Michael A., *Response to Modernity. A History of the Reform Movement in Judaism*. New York/Oxford, 1988.
Prell, Riv-Ellen, *Prayer and Community: The Havurah in American Judaism*. Detroit, 1989.
Raphael, M. L., *Profiles in American Judaism: The Reform, Conservative, Orthodox, and Reconstructionist Traditions in Historical Perspective*. San Francisco, 1984.
Rosman, Moshe, *Founder of Hasidism: A Quest for the Historical Ba'al Shem Tov*. Berkeley, CA, 1996.
Wine, Sherwin, *Judaism Beyond God*. Hoboken, NJ, 1995.

CHAPTER 5 THE FAMILY

Biale, David, *Eros and the Jews: From Biblical Israel to Contemporary America*. New York, 1992.
Biale, Rachel, ed., *Women and Jewish Law: The Essential Texts, their History, and their Relevance for Today*. New York, 1995.
Cooper, John, *Eat and Be Satisfied. A Social History of Jewish Food*. London, 1998.
Feldman, David M., *Marital Relations, Birth Control, and Abortion in Jewish Law*. New York, 1968.
Heschel, A. J., *The Sabbath: Its Meaning for Modern Man*. New York, 1983.
Jacobs, Louis, *Religion and the Individual. A Jewish Perspective*. Cambridge, 1992.
Kaufman, Michael, *Love, Marriage, and Family in Jewish Law and Tradition*. Northvale, NJ, 1992.
Klein, Isaac, *A Guide to Jewish Religious Practice*. New York, 1979.
Lamm, Maurice, *The Jewish Way in Death and Mourning*. New York, 1966.
Magonet, Jonathan, ed., *Jewish Explorations of Sexuality*. Providence, RI/Oxford, 1995.
Maybaum, Ignaz, *The Jewish Home*. London, [1945].
Rabinowicz, H., *A Guide to Life*. London, 1964.
Roden, Claudia, *The Book of Jewish Food: An Odyssey from Samarkand and Vilna to the Present Day*. London, 1997.
Talmon, Y., *Family and Community in the Kibbutz*. Cambridge, MA, 1972.
Weidman Schneider, Susan, *Jewish and Female: Choices and Changes in Our Lives Today*. New York, 1984.

CHAPTER 6 THE COMMUNITY

Black, Naomi, ed., *Celebration: The Book of Jewish Festivals*. London, 1987.
de Breffny, Brian, *The Synagogue*. New York, 1978.
Donin, Hayim Halevy, *To Pray as a Jew: Guide to the Prayer Book and the Synagogue*. New York, 1980.
Elbogen, Ismar, *Jewish Liturgy*, tr. Raymond P. Scheindlin. Philadelphia etc., 1993.
Heilman, S. C., *Synagogue Life: Study in Symbolic Interaction*. Chicago, 1976.
Jacobs, Louis, *Hasidic Prayer*. London, 1972.
Meek, Harold A., *The Synagogue*. London, 1995.
Millgram, Abraham, *Jewish Worship*. Philadelphia, 1971.
Petuchowsky, Jakob J., *Theology and Poetry*. London, 1978.
Schwarzfuchs, Simon, *A Concise History of the Rabbinate*. Oxford/Cambridge, MA, 1993.
Weinberger, Leon J., *Jewish Hymnography. A Literary History*. London/Portland, OR, 1998.
Wertheimer, J., ed., *The American Synagogue: A Sanctuary Transformed*. Cambridge, 1987.

CHAPTER 7 GOD AND THE JEWISH PEOPLE

Altmann, Alexander, *Moses Mendelssohn: a Biographical Study*. London, 1973.
Baeck, Leo, *The Essence of Judaism*, tr. V. Grubwieser and L. Pearl. London, 1936.
Borowitz, Eugene B., *A New Jewish Theology in the Making*. Philadelphia, 1968.
Buber, Martin, *I and Thou*, tr. W. Kaufmann. 3rd edn. Edinburgh, 1971.
Cohen, Arthur A., *The Natural and Supernatural Jew*. London, 1967.
Cohen, Hermann, *Religion of Reason Out of the Sources of Judaism*, translated by Simon Kaplan. New York, 1972.
Eisenstein, Ira, ed., *Varieties of Jewish Belief*. New York, 1966.
Frank, Daniel H., and Oliver Leaman, eds., *History of Jewish Philosophy*. London, 1997.
Heschel, A. J., *God in Search of Man: Philosophy of Judaism*. London, 1956.
Jacobs, Louis, *A Jewish Theology*. London/New York, 1973.
Rosenzweig, Franz, *The Star of Redemption*, tr. by William W. Hallo. London/New York, 1971.
Sorkin, David, *Moses Mendelssohn and the Religious Enlightenment*. London, 1996.
Steinberg, Milton, *Anatomy of Faith*, ed. A. A. Cohen. New York, 1960.
Wolf, Arnold J., ed., *Rediscovering Judaism. Reflections on a New Jewish Theology*. Chicago, 1965.

CHAPTER 8 OBJECTIVES

Fackenheim, E., *To Mend the World: Foundations of Post-Holocaust Jewish Thought*. 2nd edn. Bloomington, IN/Indianapolis, IN, 1994.

Frankel, Jonathan, ed., *Jews and Messianism in the Modern Era: Metaphor and Meaning*. New York, 1991.

Freehof, Solomon B., *Current Reform Responsa*. Cinncinati, OH, 1969.

Modern Reform Responsa. Cinncinati, OH, 1971.

Reform Responsa and Recent Reform Responsa. New York, 1973.

Jacobs, Louis, *Faith*. London, 1968.

Leibowitz, Yeshayahu, *Judaism, Human Values and the Jewish State*, ed. E. Goldman. Cambridge, MA, 1992.

Scholem, Gershom, *Sabbatai Sevi, The Mystical Messiah*, tr. R. J. Zwi Werblowsky. Princeton, NJ/London, 1973.

Soloveitchik, J. B., *Halakhic Man*, tr. Lawrence Kaplan. Philadelphia, 1983.

The Halakhic Mind: an Essay on Jewish Tradition and Modern Thought. New York, 1986.

The Lonely Man of Faith. New York, 1992.

Vermes, Pamela, *Buber on God and the Perfect Man*. London, 1994.

CHAPTER 9 JUDAISM AND THE FUTURE

Borowitz, Eugene B., *Exploring Jewish Ethics: Papers on Covenant Responsibility*. Detroit, 1990.

Renewing the Covenant: a Theology for the Postmodern Jew. Philadelphia, 1991.

Boyarin, Daniel, *Unheroic Conduct: the Rise of Heterosexuality and the Invention of the Jewish Man*. Berkeley, CA, 1997.

Cohen, Richard, *Elevations: the Height of the Good in Rosenzweig and Levinas*. Chicago, 1994.

Gibbs, Robert, *Correlations in Rosenzweig and Levinas*. Princeton, NJ, 1992.

Goldberg, Michael, *Why Should Jews Survive?: Looking Past the Holocaust Toward a Jewish Future*. New York/Oxford, 1995.

Hand, Seán, ed., *The Levinas Reader*. Oxford, 1989.

Jacobs, Louis, *A Tree of Life: Diversity, Flexibility, and Creativity in Jewish Law*. Oxford, 1984.

Marmur, Dow, *Beyond Survival: Reflections on the Future of Judaism*. London, 1982.

Novak, David, *Jewish-Christian Dialogue: a Jewish Justification*. New York, 1989.

Jewish Social Ethics. New York/Oxford, 1992.

Plaskow, Judith, *Standing again at Sinai: Judaism from a Feminist Perspective*. San Francisco, 1991.

Sacks, Jonathan, ed., *Orthodoxy Confronts Modernity*. Hoboken, NJ/London, 1991.

One People?: Tradition, Modernity, and Jewish Unity. London, 1993.

Webber, Jonathan, ed., *Jewish Identities in the New Europe*. London/Washington, 1994.

Wyschogrod, Edith, *Saints and Postmodernism: Revisioning Moral Philosophy*. Chicago/London, 1990.

Index